THE MUSKEGON

THE MUSKEGON

The Majesty and Tragedy of Michigan's Rarest River

Jeff Alexander

Michigan State University Press • *East Lansing*

♾ The paper used in this publication meets the minimum requirements of ANSI/NISO Z39.48-1992 (R 1997) (Permanence of Paper).

Michigan State University Press
East Lansing, Michigan 48823-5245
www.msupress.msu.edu

Printed and bound in the United States of America.

12 11 10 09 08 07 06 1 2 3 4 5 6 7 8 9 10

LIBRARY OF CONGRESS CATALOGING-IN-PUBLICATION DATA
Alexander, Jeff, 1962–
The Muskegon : the majesty and tragedy of Michigan's rarest river / Jeff Alexander.
p. cm.
Includes bibliographical references and index.
ISBN-13: 978-0-87013-786-0 (pbk. : alk. paper)
ISBN-10: 0-87013-786-7 (pbk. : alk. paper)
1. Muskegon River (Mich.)—History. 2. Natural history—Michigan—Muskegon River. 3. Muskegon River (Mich.)—Description and travel. 4. Muskegon River (Mich.)—Environmental conditions. 5. Stream conservation—Michigan—Muskegon River. I. Title.
F572.M93A44 2006
977.4'5—dc22
2006021613

The Dave Dempsey Environmental Series

Cover design by Heather Truelove Aiston
Book design by Sharp Des!gns, Inc., Lansing, Michigan

Cover photo: An aerial view of Croton Dam, which divides the lower Muskegon River from the upper 172 miles of the river and its major tributary, the Little Muskegon River (upper right). (Photo by Marge Beaver, photography-plus.com.)

green press INITIATIVE Michigan State University Press is a member of the Green Press Initiative and is committed to developing and encouraging ecologically responsible publishing practices. For more information about the Green Press Initiative and the use of recycled paper in book publishing, please visit *www.greenpressinitiative.org*.

Please visit the Michigan State University Press on the World Wide Web at *www.msupress.msu.edu*.

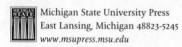

To Jessica, Kelsey, and Eric
for making our river journeys memorable.

CONTENTS

ACKNOWLEDGMENTS

I COULD NOT HAVE WRITTEN THIS BOOK WITHOUT THE MANY PEOPLE who share my passion for the Muskegon River or who helped me overcome the personal challenges associated with writing a manuscript of this length. Words do not fully reflect my appreciation for the support I received from the Wege Foundation and the Great Lakes Fishery Trust. Specifically, Peter Wege and Jack Bails have earned my lasting gratitude and respect for their ambitious and incredibly generous support for efforts to restore and preserve the Muskegon. Peter Wege's assistant, Terri McCarthy, provided valuable counsel when I questioned my ability to complete this book. Gale Nobes spent countless hours of his free time over the past few years showing me various aspects of the Muskegon River system and explaining the finer points of river ecology. I am indebted to countless others who provided me with information about the river and helped me understand how human activities have affected this ecological gem. When it came to writing the manuscript and getting it published, Dave Dempsey served as a mentor. Susan Harrison Wolffis, a colleague and writer whose work I've long admired, read the manuscript and was always a source of encouragement. Most importantly, I must acknowledge the patience and loving support of my wife, Martha, who has stood by me in good times and bad. She is my rock.

TIMELINE OF MUSKEGON RIVER HISTORY

18,000 B.C.E.	The glaciers slowly began to melt.
8,000–6,000 B.C.E.	The last ice sheets over the Great Lakes melted. Native Americans migrated to the region from Asia. The Muskegon River began to take shape as the glaciers receded.
1634	French explorer Jean Nicolet visited the mouth of the Muskegon River. He was believed to be the first non-Indian to visit the area.
1734	Odawa Indians established their first village along the Muskegon River, near where the river flows into Lake Michigan.
1812	Frenchman Jean Baptiste Recollet opened a fur trading post on Muskegon Lake. Fur trading dominated the Great Lakes economy until the 1830s, when the beaver populations were depleted.
1836	The Treaty of Washington, in which Native American tribes sold millions of acres of Michigan land to the

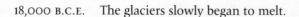

federal government for pennies per acre, sparked a land rush in West Michigan.

1837 The first lumber mill on the Muskegon River, the Penoyer Mill, began operating in Newaygo.

1838 The first lumber mill on Muskegon Lake opened and the first of seventy-three annual log runs took place on the Muskegon River.

1854 The first dam built across the Muskegon River was completed in Newaygo. The dam powered the Big Red Mill, the largest sawmill in Michigan at the time.

1855 The arctic grayling, considered Michigan's most spectacular game fish, was discovered in the Hersey River, a tributary of the Muskegon River. By 1905, the grayling was eliminated from the Muskegon River system, the victim of excessive fishing, logging and the construction of dams.

1887 Logging peaked in the lower Muskegon River basin. Lumber mills on Muskegon Lake cut 661 million board feet of lumber and 520 million shingles in one year.

1905 The last major log run on the Muskegon River.

1906 Rogers Dam was built near Big Rapids.

1907 Croton Dam was built near Newaygo.

1910 The last lumber mill on Muskegon Lake closed.

1931 Hardy Dam was built between Croton and Rogers dams.

1964 The U.S. 31 bridge over the Muskegon River marsh near Muskegon opened to vehicles. The bridge was built atop a levee that dammed much of the marsh.

1967 Chinook salmon were planted in Lake Michigan to reduce alewife population. The Muskegon River eventually became Michigan's most productive salmon stream.

1969 The Newaygo Dam was removed.

1973 The Muskegon County Wastewater Management System was completed, cleaning up the water in Muskegon Lake.

1975 Muskegon residents rallied against a proposed North Star Steel plant, and the firm decided to build elsewhere.

1986 The Muskegon River's worst flood in recorded history nearly burst the Hardy and Croton dams. The flood increased the flow of the river to ten times the normal rate and deposited a thick layer of sand in the Muskegon River marsh near Muskegon.

1994 Federal operating licenses were renewed through 2034 for the Croton, Hardy, and Rogers hydroelectric dams. The license required Consumers Energy to mimic the river's natural flow downstream of Croton Dam, a change that contributed to the creation of a nationally recognized trout fishery in the lower river.

1997 A state study of the Muskegon River concluded that it had been fundamentally altered and harmed by human activities over the past 160 years but was capable of a dramatic recovery.

1998 Muskegon River Watershed Assembly formed to preserve, protect, and restore the Muskegon River system.

2000 The Muskegon River Watershed Partnership formed and launched scientific studies aimed at restoring and preserving the river in the face of increasing land development. The Great Lakes Fishery Trust contributed $5.5 million to the river restoration effort; the Wege Foundation contributed another $2 million.

2001 The remnants of the Big Rapids dam were removed.

2001 The state of Michigan approved Nestlé North America's $150 million water bottling plant in Mecosta County. The company was permitted to pump 210 million gallons of groundwater out of the Muskegon River watershed annually and sell it as Ice Mountain Natural Spring Water.

2003 Scientists warned that lake sturgeon, the largest fish in the Great Lakes, was on the verge of being eliminated from the Muskegon River.

2003 After opponents of the Nestlé project filed a lawsuit claiming that the Ice Mountain facility would harm nearby lakes, streams, Judge Lawrence Root ordered Nestlé to turn off its spring water wells. Nestlé appealed the ruling and was allowed to continue pumping groundwater at 50 percent of the plant's capacity until the case is settled.

2004 Scientists studying the Muskegon conclude it is one of Michigan's most biologically productive rivers. They warned that poorly managed land development, which contributed to urban sprawl, posed the greatest threat to the river's fragile ecosystem.

PROLOGUE

FATAL ATTRACTON

> My old friend, the Michigan grayling: I shall never again see you or your equal.
>
> —George Alexander, sportsman, circa 1930

Dusk was rapidly descending in the Muskegon River valley as two fishermen raced upstream in a jet-powered boat, desperate to make a few more casts before it was too dark to distinguish between the river and the coal-colored sky. The high-pitched whine of the motor could be heard long before the boat came into view. A half mile upstream, Paul Vecsei feared the worst. The University of Georgia fish biologist with the Hungarian accent knew that the noisy boat would likely dash any chance of seeing a lake sturgeon—an ancient fish that could grow to eight feet long, weigh as much as two hundred pounds, and looked like a cross between a shark and a catfish. A native, sentinel species that lived for thousands of years in the Great Lakes and the rivers that flow into these inland seas, the sturgeon symbolized the Muskegon River's majesty and tragedy.

On a cool spring evening in May, Vecsei patrolled one of the most popular and healthiest stretches of the river, a fourteen-mile section below historic Croton Dam. With the aid of electronic telemetry, Vecsei was trying to find one of the sturgeon he fitted months earlier with a tracking device. He guided his pale green fishing boat down the river's tea-colored water, heading for a pool in the river that served as a sturgeon love shack. Passing over sunken pine logs—remnants of a nineteenth-century logging frenzy that laid waste to Michigan's forests and turned rivers into conveyor belts for pine logs—Vecsei frequently interrupted his impromptu science lesson with vitriolic tirades about fast, noisy jet boats that he believed could drive the last few sturgeon from the Muskegon River.

Rounding a bend, Vecsei spotted Boathouse Riffle, a stretch of clear water in an area of the river too wide to throw a stone across. Suddenly, a low-pitched beep burst from the electronic tracking equipment. "Did you hear that?" Vecsei asked his passenger. Then another beep, followed by a third. He quickly wheeled the boat around, heading back upstream to the spot where he heard the first indication that a sturgeon was nearby. He headed toward a deep spot along the bank, a place where these massive fish hid in the opaque water. By then the tracking equipment was chattering like a treed squirrel taunting a dog. It told Vecsei that one of the sturgeon he tagged earlier in the year—Fish 744, a large male lake sturgeon, *Acipenser fulvescens,* about twenty-five years old and weighing thirty-one pounds—was lurking beneath the boat. "There's a sturgeon down there. He's hiding. These fish aren't stupid," Vecsei said. Indeed. The fish stayed out of sight.

Knowing that the fish would not surface with a boat nearby, Vecsei headed back downstream to Boathouse Riffle, an area where sturgeon often spawn in the spring, before the water temperature was too warm to nourish their eggs. Nearing the rippling waters of Boathouse Riffle, Vecsei cut the motor, and the boat drifted with the current. He studied the water like a dog on point, examining areas where spawning sturgeon deposited hundreds of thousands of sticky eggs in a blanket of gravel on the bottom. Just then, the jet boat heading upstream roared around the bend, leaving a trail of noxious fumes and a wake large enough to dislodge incubating sturgeon eggs and send adult fish fleeing for cover. Vecsei was livid. "Damn jet boat," he yelled, shaking his fist above his head. He would see no sturgeon that day. The fishermen were oblivious to Vecsei's rage; they respond to his raised fist with a friendly wave.[1]

Prior to 1835, when tens of thousands of European immigrants began streaming into Michigan to settle what was then wilderness occupied by small bands of Indians, sturgeon ruled the Great Lakes and large rivers that empty into these freshwater seas. Scientists estimated that 11 million sturgeon lived in Lake Michigan alone in the 1800s. At that time, thousands of sturgeon—possibly 10,000 or more—likely migrated up the Muskegon River each spring to spawn before returning to Lake Michigan.[2] That was before logging transformed the Muskegon into a working river used to transport millions of logs, and dams built to power sawmills and generate electricity, obliterated fish spawning beds and restricted their upstream migration.

According to a 1991 Ferris State University study, "Human activities over the years have greatly influenced the characteristics of the river. Construction of dams, logging, industrial practices, agricultural practices and recreational activities all have combined to alter the river's natural characteristics."[3] For more than a century, sturgeon that migrated up the Muskegon River to spawn have been limited to the lower 47 miles of the river; since the 1850s, dams built in and near Newaygo have blocked sturgeon from reaching 172 miles of river upstream of the dams.

In the mid-1800s, European immigrants slaughtered sturgeon because the huge fish, which are covered with bony plates, tore fishing nets when hauled in from Lake Michigan with the more desirable whitefish and lake trout. In the late 1800s, smoked lake sturgeon and caviar became a delicacy, and the fish, which have inhabited the world's oceans, lakes, and rivers for 135 million years, since long before the dinosaurs vanished, were driven to the brink of extinction in the Great Lakes basin.

There were between one thousand and three thousand sturgeon in Lake Michigan in 2000, and between thirty and one hundred adult sturgeon in the "Muskegon stock," fish that spawned exclusively in this river.[4] Biologists said that a minimum of five hundred sturgeon must remain in the Muskegon River stock to maintain a viable population. Without human intervention in the form of a fish rearing and stocking program, the Muskegon's sturgeon population appeared destined for extinction, much like the majestic Arctic grayling that once inhabited parts of this magnificent, manipulated river.

COLD, CLEAR WATER FLOWED UNDER THE LOG WHERE THE NATIVE AMERican man lay still, his face close to the creek, fish spear at the ready. His prey would soon come into view: a silver fish eighteen inches long with a purple streak and a freakishly large dorsal fin; it moved gracefully through the shallow stream that spilled into the Muskegon River's midsection, making easy pickings for the skilled fisherman.

Before long, the Indian and his fellow anglers speared thirty of the fish, much to the delight of John T. Elliott. A businessman by trade, Elliott had ventured into what was then wilderness near Big Rapids with a group of Indian men to capture and identify a spectacular fish that was causing a stir among Michigan anglers.[5] It was 1861 and the brutal U.S. Civil War had just begun. But in the wilderness of northern Michigan, much of the talk was about a beautiful, delectable fish found in huge quantities in northern Michigan rivers, including the Muskegon.

Elliott had gone searching for the fish at the urging of J. C. Parker, a fellow Grand Rapids businessman who later served on the Board of Michigan Fish Commissioners. The fish Elliott secured in June 1861 would later be identified as Arctic grayling, *Thymallus articus*. The Arctic grayling was special because it was native to Michigan. A glacial relic that settled in Michigan as the last Ice Age ended, the Arctic grayling captured the attention of anglers and naturalists in the last half of the nineteenth century. And why not? The mere existence of grayling in Michigan was nothing short of miraculous.

Like the sturgeon, grayling migrated to Michigan as the glaciers that created the Great Lakes completed their retreat about eight thousand years ago. As the glaciers melted, schools of Arctic grayling moved into Michigan's coldest streams; the fish flourished for centuries in northern Michigan rivers, which were pristine, cold and had gravel beds ideal for spawning. That was before European immigrants began arriving in Michigan in large numbers in the mid-1800s.

The settlement of Michigan would bring about several ecological disasters, one of which involved the grayling. Within eighty years of its discovery, the grayling was eliminated from all Michigan waters. It was the victim of human-induced changes to the landscape, and a frontier mentality that held that natural resources were inexhaustible.

Michigan's love affair with the grayling was intense and short-lived—a veritable one-night stand on the geologic clock. By 1905, fifty years after it was first documented in the Hersey River, the Arctic grayling was eliminated from the Muskegon River system. In 1936, the state declared Arctic grayling absent from all Michigan lakes and streams. Many factors—

logging, the construction of dams, and the introduction of brook trout (now Michigan's state fish), an exotic species that competed with the grayling for food and habitat—contributed to its demise.

Soon after it was discovered, the grayling became the most coveted sport fish in Michigan. Anglers flocked to tributaries of the upper Muskegon and other cold-water rivers in northern Michigan to catch a fish that was colorful, graceful, and tasty. Michigan's fascination with the grayling was documented in 1880 by Grand Rapids writer Martin Metcalf, who noted that reports had begun to circulate in 1855 of a "new and peculiar kind of brook trout that was being caught in certain tributaries of the Muskegon River."[6]

In an 1889 essay, J. C. Parker told of anglers catching "vast numbers" of grayling in Hersey Creek, a cold-water stream that flows into the Muskegon a few miles north of the city of Big Rapids. "These fishes were slaughtered by the thousand, and no less than a half-dozen wagon loads were hauled away."[7] Similar reports came out of the Au Sable and other northern Michigan rivers, where grayling catches were so numerous that piles of fish were sometimes left to rot on river banks.

For all its beauty, the grayling had a fatal flaw: Because grayling were surface feeders that were easy to spot, the species was annihilated by anglers before the advent of catch limits. By the 1880s, the grayling had come under siege by scores of anglers eager to sample the unusual fish. At the same time, logging in the Muskegon River basin was approaching its peak. Hundreds of thousands of giant pine logs were rolled into the river each spring and floated downstream to sawmills in Big Rapids, Newaygo, and Muskegon; these runs took place at the same time grayling were attempting to spawn in gravel beds on the river bottom. These fragile fish were no match for the ravages of logging: during the spring run, when it was possible to walk across the Muskegon, huge logs clogged the river and scoured its bottom, wiping away fish spawning beds. Spawning areas that were not decimated by massive logjams often were suffocated by tons of sand that washed into the river from eroded stream banks laid bare when logs were rolled into the river.

Metcalf was one of a handful of Michigan conservationists who began to warn in the late 1800s of the grayling's demise. He concluded that grayling could not compete with increasing numbers of brook trout or cope with the harm logging caused to rivers:

> The grayling is fast disappearing from Michigan waters and will, together with his gamy and beautiful kinsman, at no very distant day be remembered with the things that were and are not, unless some effectual bar shall be erected [to prevent] against the indiscriminate slaughter of the innocent and universal use of our most superb fish breeding grounds as deposits for the dust of sawmills and sewers for everything that is vile under the sun.[8]

Many factors contributed to the annihilation of grayling in Michigan waters, all of them caused by human hands. A small number of the fish survived until the 1930s—after logging had ceased and despite the presence of other species of trout—in the Otter River in the Upper Peninsula. That anomaly led Wayne Creaser, a Wayne State University scientist, to suggest that rising water temperatures as a result of the clearing of forests that increased exposure to sunlight and sediment that washed into rivers during logging operations could have played a role in the elimination of grayling. Grayling are more temperature sensitive than most species of fish, including brook trout.[9]

The popularity of grayling prompted efforts to expand its range long before the fish was thought to be in danger of becoming extinct in Michigan. In 1877, adult grayling were transferred from the Manistee River to one lake and three streams in southern Michigan. Similar stocking efforts took place in 1880 and again in 1925. All failed.[10]

As it became clear that grayling were disappearing from many rivers, the state of Michigan stepped up its fish stocking program. Between 1900 and 1930, more than 3.3 million grayling taken from Montana waters were released in Michigan rivers and lakes, most of which were located in areas where grayling were abundant in the 1870s. The Michigan Department of Natural Resources continued its efforts to reestablish grayling in Michigan waters until 1991, to no avail. Many grayling planted in Michigan rivers were eaten by other fish; some died of disease in hatcheries. The bottom line: Arctic grayling have been unable to survive and reproduce in Michigan waters since 1936. "It's a pretty sad story,'" said Andrew Nuhfer, a research biologist with the Michigan DNR.

Although Michigan's rivers were no longer used to transport logs, Nuhfer's 1991 study of the Arctic grayling concluded that the proliferation of dams in Michigan rivers during the early 1900s created a new set of environmental conditions that grayling could not overcome. "Arctic grayling are unlikely to either survive well or reproduce in contemporary Michigan rivers," Nuhfer said in a 1999 interview. "They seem to need large, cold, non-fragmented rivers with few competing fish species, particularly salmonids. Perhaps future river restoration efforts, such as dam removal, will provide some large-river habitats that will better support grayling survival and reproduction."[11] The elimination of Arctic grayling from the Muskegon is a cautionary tale in danger of being repeated. It is evidence that human actions can cause permanent, devastating changes to natural systems.

Losing the Muskegon River's dwindling sturgeon population would constitute another blow to a severely altered ecosystem and represent, biologically and symbolically, a huge setback in efforts to restore the sprawling river system. As the river went, so went the sturgeon. If attempts to restore and preserve the Muskegon succeeded, sturgeon could (with human assistance) stage a dramatic comeback. But if increased pollution, more exotic species, and less fish habitat plunged the river into ecological chaos, the dwindling sturgeon population would be one of the first casualties.

With the Arctic grayling a distant memory, the Muskegon River's new indicator species—canaries in the coal mine, if you will—were sturgeon, trout, salmon, and walleye. Fish provided just one measure of ecosystem health, but they represented an important, tangible indicator. Sick, polluted rivers could not support healthy fish populations. If the Muskegon became too polluted or choked by sand and silt washing off the landscape, the few remaining sturgeon would vanish. If the river's cool water became too warm, the nationally recognized trout fishery below Croton Dam would disappear. Such changes could have profound effects on the river ecosystem and the economies of Muskegon and Newaygo, where people who come to fish in the river spent millions of dollars each year on fishing gear, food, and hotel rooms.

The Muskegon River faced myriad serious environmental challenges at the end of the twentieth century. Still, there were reasons to be optimistic about its future. In the late 1990s, nearly a century after grayling were eliminated, efforts by the state to create a trout fishery below Croton Dam began to pay off. As was the case with grayling, the health of the trout fishery was the result of human activities. Removal of the Newaygo Dam in

1969, followed by operational changes at Croton Dam in 1994 that restored the river's natural flow downstream and a government-run trout stocking program, created the nationally recognized trout fishery.

In the mid 1990s, anglers from across the United States and parts of Europe and Asia began to converge on a stretch of river near the small town of Newaygo to fish for steelhead and salmon. The Muskegon River below Croton Dam soon became known as one of the nation's finest trout fisheries downstream of a dam.

History has shown that humans possess the ability to harness, control, and harm this mighty river; we also possess the scientific knowledge and technology to restore some of its greatest natural features. How will future generations know if early-twenty-first-century efforts to restore the Muskegon's tattered ecosystem succeeded? The answers will be swimming in the river.

THE MUSKEGON

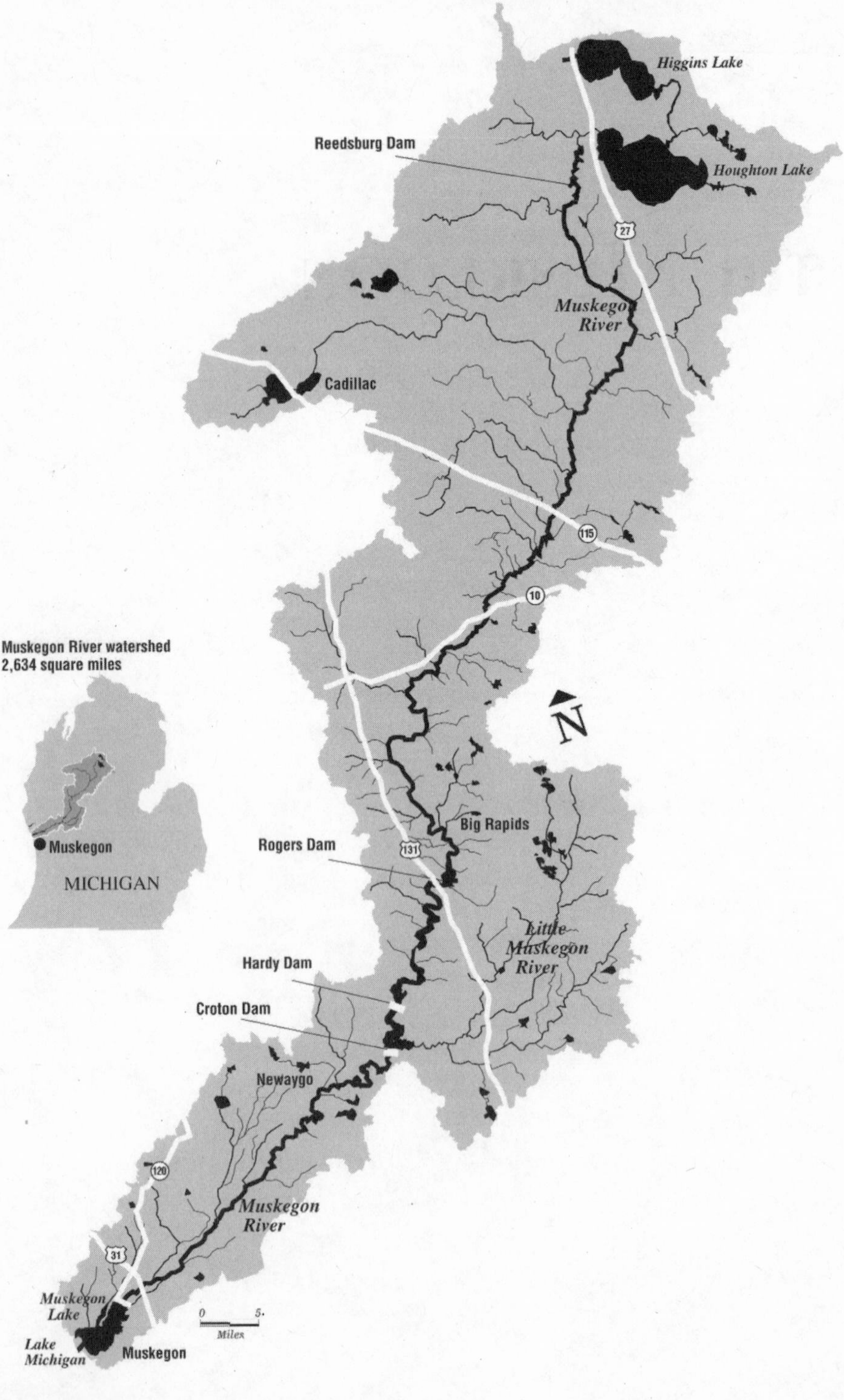
Higgins Lake
Reedsburg Dam
Houghton Lake
27
Muskegon River
Cadillac
115
10
Muskegon River watershed
2,634 square miles
Muskegon
MICHIGAN
N
Big Rapids
Rogers Dam
131
Little Muskegon River
Hardy Dam
Croton Dam
Newaygo
120
Muskegon River
31
Muskegon Lake
0
5
Miles
Lake Michigan
Muskegon

INTRODUCTION

There was a time when the Muskegon River was little more than a visual diversion for me, a momentary break from the monotony of driving along a highway dominated by billboards, chain stores, and fast food joints. It was always a pleasant sight, the dark, mysterious stream that snaked through a huge marsh that marked the river's end on the outskirts of Muskegon. I had crossed over the river by car hundreds of times, but not once did I stop to give this wondrous waterway my complete attention. That changed in the late 1990s.

I was driving across a low-lying bridge that spanned a large wetland in the heart of Michigan's northern Lower Peninsula when it hit me, the enormity and diversity of the Muskegon River system. A small brown sign on the side of the road flipped a switch in my head: "Muskegon River," read the yellow letters carved into the chocolate brown wood. Odd, I thought. The Muskegon River I had come to know was a wide, powerful river that surged through the former logging village of Newaygo and spread out across a mile-wide marsh before spilling into Muskegon Lake. That stretch of river in Newaygo bore a striking resemblance to the Yuba River, a gin-clear Western stream that tumbled down the Sierra Nevada Mountain range and through the California gold mining town of Downieville where I spent summers as a child.

The river I had just driven over was a small, murky stream with ebony water that crawled through a swamp more than one hundred miles northeast of Muskegon. I mistakenly assumed it could not be the same Muskegon River that had carried millions of logs and lumber schooners on its back in the 1800s. Confirmation was needed. A few minutes and an illegal U-turn later, I was headed toward an identical sign on the other side of the highway. There it was, cast in wood: "Muskegon River." Out came the map. Cars hurtled past on the highway as I hunched over in the front seat of my car, my index finger tracing a jagged blue line on the map that flowed out of Houghton Lake, Michigan's largest inland lake, and meandered to Lake Michigan. I had stumbled across the headwaters of Michigan's second-longest river. This was not exactly a discovery—geographers knew in the 1800s that the Muskegon spanned 219 miles, cutting a roughly diagonal path across the northwest portion of Michigan's Lower Peninsula. Still, it was a discovery for me—a life-changing one, no less. For some strange reason, I felt compelled that day to learn and share this river's fascinating story. Questions flooded my mind: What forces created this river? Where was the source of its tremendous volume of water? How had humans affected the river? What lived in this aquatic highway? This is my attempt to answer those questions and, in the process, to ignite in readers the passion I feel for the mighty Muskegon.

There were many ways to relate the story of this river. It could be told from the perspective of nature, focusing exclusively on the glaciers, water, and gravity that etched the Muskegon into the landscape and the creatures that relied on it for sustenance—from microscopic zooplankton to mayflies, clams and crayfish, walleye and sturgeon, kingfishers and bald eagles, white-tailed deer and black bears. Or this river's story could be told from the perspective of humans who have used, abused, ruined, and resurrected parts of the Muskegon. I have chosen the latter approach.

The Muskegon River was a fascinating entity on its own, a vibrant, complex life force ruled by eternal change. Focusing on humans who conquered the Muskegon was not necessary to bestow historical significance on this majestic waterway. The creation and evolution of this river would make a fascinating ecological case study. Still, I have chosen to tell this story through people who have changed the river, for better and worse.

The Muskegon bore little resemblance in 2000 to the river it was in 1800, before it carried millions of pine logs, became strangled by sawmills and hydroelectric dams, and was inundated with storm water runoff from farm fields, parking lots, and roads. Humans have fundamentally altered the Muskegon in a fraction of the time it took the forces of nature to shape this river. Despite those changes, a golden opportunity existed to repair the damage and resurrect some of the river's greatest natural features. To understand how and why the river has been altered and how it could change in coming decades, one must understand the motives of people whose actions transformed the Muskegon from natural wonder to working river and the dreams of those who hoped to restore it. With all due respect to the river, this history of the Muskegon is a people story.

APPRECIATING THE BEAUTY AND BRAWN OF THE MUSKEGON REQUIRES wading in its varied water—dark, opaque and sluggish in some areas, gin-clear, transparent and swift in others—having its current tug at your legs, and watching fish dart beneath your canoe as you float its winding course. My fascination with the Muskegon would be sated over the course of several years. I canoed the length of the river, swam in its cool waters, battled its powerful salmon and chrome-colored steelhead, and observed, from a small airplane, the river's serpentine path through miles-wide marshes, lush forests, deep ravines, farm fields, and small cities. It was impossible to fully understand or appreciate this river from the confines of an automobile while traveling roads that provided fleeting glimpses of this Bunyanesque stream. To know this river required studying its history, spending time in its warm water wetlands and cold water tributaries, and experiencing its evolution from creek to river as it passes through two huge inland lakes, spreads out across the Deadstream Marsh near Houghton Lake, and grows into a wide, Western-style river before eventually losing steam in a large estuary and disappearing into Muskegon Lake and Lake Michigan. Anything less would not do the river justice.

The late Ernest "Jack" Sharpe, a witty Newaygo writer, captured some of the Muskegon River's colorful history in one of his many poems:

Through the county of Newaygo,
Flows the Big Muskegon River;
Once the highway of the red man,
Traveling there with bow and quiver.
Came then, sounds of saws and axes,
Echoing throughout the hills;
Saw-logs floated on its bosom
To the timber barons' mills.
Harnessed now, to serve the white man,
Still it flows through scenes of beauty;
Sheltering shores hide deer and beaver,
As of old, an ancient duty.
Wily pike and bass and rainbows,
Still cavort within its waters,
Now a playground for the sportsmen,
For their sons, their wives and daughters.
Where it flows through old Newaygo,
Gather, yearly, on its shores,
Guides competing from all over,
With the paddles and the oars;
Competing with the bow and arrow,
Like the red man, and as clever,
While the river keeps on flowing,
As it has and will forever.[1]

MICHIGAN IS HOME TO MANY SPECTACULAR RIVERS. THE AU SABLE, Manistee, and Pere Marquette are stunningly scenic cold-water rivers renowned for trout and salmon. The Detroit and Grand rivers spawned the automotive and office furniture industries. And the glorious Two Hearted River in Michigan's Upper Peninsula is a wondrous stream that flows into Lake Superior. Each of these rivers surpasses the Muskegon in some regard.

The Muskegon is not Michigan's longest river—it ranks second to the Grand, which spans 262 miles. But the Grand has lost its grandeur: it is a severely polluted river, a victim of intense urban development, decades of sewage spills, and harmful agricultural runoff in rural areas. The Pere Marquette, Au Sable, and Manistee are cold-water rivers with miles of small rapids, stunning scenery, and nationally known fisheries. The Au Sable River, in northeastern Michigan, is one of America's premier trout streams and features a stretch of water near Grayling that is so magnificent, clean and teeming with fish that it was dubbed the "holy waters." The Detroit River links two of the five Great Lakes, Erie and Huron. And the Two Hearted River captured the imagination of one of America's greatest writers: Ernest Hemingway, who spent part of his youth in northern Michigan, wrote eloquently about fishing the river in "Big Two-Hearted River" (although literary scholars believe that Hemingway was actually referring to the Fox River in this essay):

> Nick looked down into the pool from the bridge. It was a hot day. A kingfisher flew up the stream. It was a long time since Nick had looked into a stream and seen trout. They were very satisfactory. As the shadow of the kingfisher moved up the stream, a big trout shot upstream in a long angle, only his shadow marking the angle, then lost his shadow as he came through the surface of the water, caught the sun, and then, as he went back into the stream under the surface, his shadow seemed to float down the stream with the current, unresisting, to his post under the bridge where he tightened facing up into the current. Nick's heart tightened as the trout moved. He felt all the old feeling. He turned and looked down the stream. It stretched away, pebbly-bottomed with shallows and big boulders and a deep pool as it curved away around the foot of a bluff. Nick walked back up the ties to where his pack lay in the cinders beside the railway track. He was happy."[2]

The Muskegon is a river of many personalities. But it suffers from an identity crisis. It supports a magnificent trout and salmon fishery in the lower forty-seven miles between Croton Dam and Lake Michigan, but it is not a trout stream in the true sense. The Muskegon's trout fishery is sustained by stocking, and more development occurred along the Muskegon than along some of Michigan's other great trout streams. Many anglers and canoers bypass the Muskegon en route to the Manistee or Pere Marquette. Both are spectacular rivers, but neither matches the Muskegon's ecological or biological diversity.

The Muskegon is larger, more ecologically complex, and biologically richer than the Manistee, Pere Marquette, and Au Sable rivers. The Muskegon has the most diverse physical features—lakes, wetlands, and streams—of any Michigan river. It produced more salmon than any river in Michigan by the late 1990s and was home to the state's only genetically pure strain of walleye, providing fish for many other rivers. Its water temperature varies more than most rivers because it straddles a temperature threshold, a natural phenomenon that made it Michigan's largest cool-water river.[3]

The Muskegon flows out of the elevated plains of northern Michigan, the birthplace of many rivers. It follows a southwesterly course toward Muskegon while teetering on the edge of a temperature barrier that divides Michigan's cold- and warm-water rivers. The lower river splits up and spreads out to create one of Michigan's largest and most biologically diverse estuaries, the Muskegon State Game Area. And the mix of warm water from wetlands and cold water from underground springs and dozens of frigid streams created a cool-water river that supports a stunning variety of fish and wildlife that may be unmatched anywhere in the state, if not the entire Great Lakes basin.

In 1929, *Chicago Tribune* outdoor editor Bob Becker chaperoned a group of Boy Scouts on a ten-day canoe trip down the river from Big Rapids to Muskegon. Their trip was one of the last down the mighty Muskegon before Hardy Dam submerged miles of the river's rapids and scenic valley under its massive reservoir. Becker recounted the trip in a newspaper article:

> The scenery of the Muskegon River is superb. The river winds through a wild country for miles without the sign of human habitation. It is an outdoor paradise. I do not want to be disloyal to Illinois, but I must say that the Muskegon valley exceeds anything I have ever seen. No mishap of any kind was encountered on the cruise although the Muskegon, with its swift, treacherous current and long stretches of white water offers a real test for the canoeist.[4]

Mike Wiley, an aquatic ecologist at the University of Michigan and one of the nation's most esteemed river scientists, believed the Muskegon in its natural, presettlement condition was one of the greatest rivers in the Great Lakes basin. His was, to some extent, a subjective assessment: because all rivers are unique, it was difficult to compare one to another. Still, there were ways to objectively assess a river's ecological significance. Wiley has done that for many rivers in the Midwest, and he still comes back to the Muskegon as the most amazing of them all.

> I think you'd be hard-pressed to say, in terms of a Great Lakes ecosystem, that the Muskegon isn't the greatest river. The Muskegon is a very distinctive river. While admitting that the "greatest river" may depend a bit on the eye of the beholder, I think you could make the case that the Muskegon [in its presettlement condition] was the greatest in terms of ecological diversity. [That is] certainly true physiographically, likely true hydrologically, and since it has [had] a tremendous range of thermal variation and also the largest and best-developed estuary system . . . probably biologically, too.[5]

Ecologically speaking, the Muskegon provides a vital link to Lake Michigan. It was home to eighty-nine species of fish, including trout, steelhead, walleye, bass, salmon, red horse suckers, perch, bowfin, freshwater drum, and the mother of all freshwater fish, lake sturgeon.[6] The river has played a starring role in some of this nation's most significant historical developments over the past two centuries. During the nineteenth-century logging boom that leveled Michigan's pine forests, more timber (30 billion board feet) was floated down the Muskegon than any other river in the state. That lumber was used to build much of Chicago and countless other Midwestern towns. In 1930, the world's largest earthen dam—Hardy Dam—was built in the fastest-flowing stretch of the Muskegon. By the late 1990s, the lower Muskegon had become a poster child for river restoration in the Great Lakes basin, supporting phenomenal salmon and steelhead fisheries. And in 2001, the Muskegon River system became the focus of a nationally significant battle over water rights when Nestlé North America (formerly the Perrier Group) built a water bottling facility in the heart of the watershed. Nestlé's Ice Mountain water bottling plant, which was capable of extracting and bottling 210 million gallons of spring water per year from the Muskegon River watershed, sparked a furious debate over whether the operation would cause significant environmental harm or violate rules that restrict the diversion of Great Lakes water out of the basin.

The Muskegon constitutes one of the largest rivers in the Great Lakes basin. Its watershed, which spans 2,725 square miles, accounts for 5 percent of the Lake Michigan drainage basin and spans an area larger than the state of Delaware. The river is a major artery of water and aquatic life in the Great Lakes system, which contains 95 percent of all fresh surface water in the United States, supports a $4 billion sport fishery, provides drinking water for 40 million residents, and is the backbone of the region's economy.

For all its ecological uniqueness, the Muskegon faced many of the same problems at the dawn of the twenty-first century that have tarnished other rivers across the United States: the loss of native species, thermal pollution, flow changes caused by dams, and urbanization that has spread a blanket of impervious surfaces across the landscape and transported more contaminated storm water runoff to the river. Anyone concerned about the Great Lakes would be wise to safeguard the Muskegon and the thousands of other rivers, lakes, and wetlands that make up the world's largest freshwater ecosystem. The fate of the Great Lakes—or Lake Michigan, for that matter—does not hinge on the Muskegon River. However, the river is one of many critical building blocks in the Great Lakes ecosystem. Losing the Muskegon to chemical or biological pollution would strike a blow to the Lake Michigan ecosystem; lose many rivers like the Muskegon, and the environmentally distressed Great Lakes become even more imperiled.

All human activities could affect the river, albeit to varying degrees. Logging in the 1800s tortured the Muskegon; the construction of dams in the 1900s harnessed it; and the strip malls and subdivisions that were beginning to spread like dandelions in 2000 threatened to make it a warmer, polluted river more prone to flooding, unfit for swimming, and less hospitable to fish, insects, and wildlife. By the turn of the twenty-first century, this wondrous river was, quite simply, broken. It no longer functioned the way nature intended. One need only examine the history of human activities in the river basin since 1830 to understand what pushed the Muskegon to the brink of profound, harmful ecological change.

Logging in the 1800s laid waste to the towering pine forests that once shielded the river from the sun's heat. Logging also sent a torrent of sand into the Muskegon, making the river wider, shallower, and warmer. Compounding those lingering problems were the ninety-four remaining dams built in the river and its tributaries from 1850 to 1970. Those structures have altered natural stream flows and divided the river into dozens of shorter, biologically disjointed streams. The four dams that remained in the river's main channel and ninety other dams that choked many of its ninety-four tributaries in 2005 have rendered the Muskegon the ecological equivalent of a dysfunctional family.[7]

Human activities over the past two centuries left the river with a legacy of harmful change: an ecosystem fragmented by dams; thermal pollution (the excessive warming of water temperatures); changes in the river's hydrology (the movement of water in and out of the river); excessive sedimentation, a problem caused by logging, farming, and other activities that cause sand and silt to erode and wash into the river, where it suffocates fish habitat and increases water temperatures; the introduction of alien species, such as the sea lamprey, rusty crayfish and zebra mussel, which threatened native fish, clams, and other aquatic organisms; and water pollution, an isolated but serious problem in parts of the river system where urban development, toxic waste dumps, or sloppy agricultural operations infect the river and its fragile feeder streams.[8]

Despite those problems, the Muskegon has proven remarkably resilient. Portions of the river have made dramatic recoveries since the logging era and now feature transparent water teeming with fish and other aquatic life. The ravages of logging and dams have rendered the Muskegon an ecological paradox: a troubled river where human activities were most intense and a thriving waterway where it was been minimally disturbed or restored. Consider this assessment from Paul Seelbach, one of Michigan's preeminent river experts and a research manager with the Michigan Department of Natural Resources: "The Muskegon River is a shadow of its former self. The river now is only a minimal reflection of what it once was. By today's standards, the Muskegon is a nice river. But it's not functioning like a continuous, 219-mile long river. It's functioning like a series of shorter rivers."[9]

The river was at a crossroads in its history in 2005: Because the Muskegon is a large, durable river, it has the potential to make a dramatic recovery. The flip side was that its relatively good water quality could change for the worse in the coming years. Steady population increases posed new threats to the river. The human population of the Muskegon River watershed is expected to swell to about 508,000 by 2020, nearly double the region's population in 1960.[10] Having more people living in the watershed will increase the volume of treated wastewater discharged into the river. There will be more leaky septic tanks and chemical spills that send harmful pollutants toward the river. And more farmland and forests will be converted into strip malls with parking lots that will drain excessively warm, polluted water into the river, threatening water quality and the tiny amphipods, mayflies, trout, and mink that call the Muskegon home.

As if those threats were not reason enough to be concerned, global climate change could increase water temperatures in the Muskegon, as it may in many of the world's rivers. Yet it might be possible to mitigate some of the effects of global warming by removing dozens of obsolete dams that act as heat sinks in the cold-water streams that help cool the Muskegon's main branch.

Against this backdrop of problems and potential, a group of conservationists, philanthropic organizations, government agencies, and university scientists joined forces in 2000 to keep the Muskegon River from sliding into ecological ruin. Biologists familiar with the Muskegon believed it had all the natural components to be a world-class river: a large volume of water; diverse natural features; relatively good water quality; numerous cold-water tributaries; a large drainage basin with vast areas of second-growth forest and prairies that remain undeveloped; and a direct link to Lake Michigan, the largest lake entirely within U.S. borders.

In 1999, the Great Lakes Fishery Trust declared the Muskegon River a "first priority river" worthy of millions of dollars in grants for research and fisheries improvement projects. The trust, established to replace millions of fish killed by power-generating turbines at the Ludington Pumped Storage Plant on Lake Michigan, aimed to increase the number of naturally reproducing salmon and trout in the Great Lakes by improving fish habitat and water quality in the Muskegon. K. L. Cool, former director of the Michigan Department of Natural Resources and chair of the Great Lakes Fishery Trust in 1999, when the organization chose to spend millions of dollars to restore the Muskegon, reflected on the river's potential: "We think there are real opportunities to work with communities to make the Muskegon a world-class river. It's all there in terms of the mechanics and hydraulics of the system. We consider the Muskegon to be one of the premier river systems we have in Michigan."[11]

The Fishery Trust has provided $5.5 million to scientists, who figured out how future human activities could help or harm the river. Using a series of complex computer models based on extensive monitoring data that gauged the health of the river ecosystem, scientists can now demonstrate cause and effect changes in the river. The river restoration effort has the benefit of science that provides a record of historical change and the ability to predict future changes. The scientific tools and techniques used to understand the Muskegon and to forecast how future human activities could affect the river would be made available for use in other river systems, said Jack Bails, executive director of the Fishery Trust:

> Rivers are pretty critical to the health of the Great Lakes. We want to inform local units of government about the history of the river and the consequences that are likely to occur if they don't do certain things, such as deal with land use. Whether the knowledge we provide to local officials leads to better decision-making remains to be seen. We hope that what the researchers have learned about problem solving in the Muskegon River watershed can be scaled down and used at less cost in other watersheds. The researchers believe this can be a model for watershed management.[12]

Here's the kicker: Restoring the Muskegon's tattered ecosystem has become a race against time. Over the next three decades, human activities will either return the river closer to its natural condition or hasten its descent down a path marked by severe water pollution, increased flooding, and the elimination of more native fish and animal species—problems that could hurt the economies of communities fortunate enough to have the river system in their midst.

This book follows a roughly chronological path, tracing the river's history from creation through devastation at the hands of humans and finally attempts at ecosystem restoration. The first six chapters examine how human activities have damaged the river; the last half of the book explores what has been done to restore the Muskegon and emerging threats to the river. Through a mixture of science and personal histories, this book examines the daunting tasks facing a small band of devotees determined to restore and protect the Muskegon.

Though this book must come to an end at some point, the Muskegon River will be around long after we have perished. Rivers do not die: they merely change in response to natural and human forces. This is the story of how European immigrants, in the name of progress, systematically deconstructed the Muskegon River ecosystem over the course of a century and how a new generation of pioneers plans to resurrect and protect one of Michigan's greatest rivers.

Let the journey begin.

1.

NATURAL WONDER

To stick your hands into the river is to feel the cords that bind the earth together in one piece.

—BARRY HOLSTUN LOPEZ, AUTHOR

VEINS OF INKY BLACK WATER SCATTER ACROSS THE VERDANT MARSH, an infant river headed in no apparent direction through a maze of reeds, cattails, and countless tree stumps. It is a confusing, intimidating scene for anyone attempting to paddle through the sprawling Deadstream Swamp, near Houghton Lake in northern Michigan. This braided stream at the headwaters of the Muskegon River is a distant cousin of the lakes upstream that gave birth to this waterway, and it differs vastly from the stream that settles into its channel below the Reedsburg Dam. It is here that the Muskegon undergoes the first of several transformations.

Downstream of the swamp, the serpentine river creates an entirely different canvas as it grows to a width of thirty feet. It winds slowly through low-lying forests of poplar, maple, and pine as it begins a long, meandering journey from the uplands of northern Michigan until it surrenders to Lake Michigan. By the time water in this river reaches Muskegon, it will have flowed through two lakes, a swamp, and a long, jagged crease in the earth before returning to its roots, crawling through a second sprawling wetland and the last of its three large lakes. In its natural condition, the 219-mile-long river directly linked Michigan's largest inland lake, Houghton Lake, and the largest lake entirely within the U.S. borders, Lake Michigan. This was the Muskegon River the Creator carved into the Earth with glaciers and water, a dynamic artery of life with many faces. Come now, and take a mental journey down this majestic stream.

BORN IN TINY BIG CREEK, A SPRING-FED BROOK, THE RIVER RECEIVES water from one of the world's most scenic lakes (Higgins Lake) and Michigan's largest inland lake (Houghton Lake) before winding its way to Lake Michigan. Before Houghton Lake was surrounded by eight thousand cottages and converted into a playground for powerboats, wild rice covered large areas of the huge but shallow body of water; in 2003, only a few wild rice plants remained in Houghton Lake.[1] This is the first hint of trouble in the river.

Higgins and Houghton Lakes are perched atop a sandy, elevated plateau—575 feet above Lake Michigan and 1,150 feet above sea level—like two bowls carved into the top of a wooden table. Houghton Lake is the low point in this geologic formation shaped by receding glaciers; as such, its outlet gives rise to the Muskegon River. Millions of gallons of water flow out of the Higgins-Houghton uplands every day. Sand and rocky, porous soils in this part of Michigan act like a giant sponge, slowly releasing water for a trinity of large Michigan rivers: the Muskegon, the Manistee, and the Au Sable.

All three of these rivers rank among the nation's finest trout streams and are considered some of Michigan's most spectacular waterways. All support tremendous populations of fish and wildlife; have clear, clean water; and are immensely popular with anglers and canoers. Despite the grandeur of the Au Sable and Manistee—wild and scenic rivers known for spectacular fishing, scenery, and canoeing—the Muskegon stands alone among Michigan rivers.

Huge, biologically rich marshes near the Muskegon's headwaters and its mouth—and dozens of cold-water tributaries in between—feed the river a steady diet of warm, nutrient-rich water coveted by bass and walleye and frigid water favored by trout. The result is Michigan's largest cool-water river, with a complex set of natural features that support what may be the greatest array of fish and wildlife in a state with thirty-six thousand miles of rivers and streams. It is as if the Creator took the best of warm-water rivers in southern Michigan and cold-water rivers in the north and created a hybrid in the heart of Michigan's Lower Peninsula just to see how it would function. The result: a magnificent freak of nature.

The Greek philosopher Heraclitus said, "You cannot step into the same river twice." Rivers come and go and are in a constant state of change. The Muskegon is like a restless child, eager for change. From its headwaters at Higgins and Houghton Lakes, the river spreads out across the forty-five-square-mile Deadstream Swamp before funneling its waters into a navigable stream below the present location of Reedsburg Dam. The river winds for more than one hundred miles through second-growth forests and low, sandy bluffs, slowly expanding to a width of two hundred feet. It gains strength and its water temperature begins to drop near Evart as its major tributaries—the Clam, Middle Branch, Hersey and Little Muskegon rivers—pump huge quantities of cold water into the Muskegon's main branch.

By the river's halfway point, near Evart, the average flow is 493 cubic feet per second (the river is moving 493 cubic feet of water through its channel each second at this locale), or 42 million cubic feet of water per day. The average flow doubles by the time the river reaches Newaygo, where the discharge—fueled by numerous tributaries streams—swells to an average of 1,060 cubic feet per second, a total of 91 million cubic feet daily.[2] The river begins a steeper descent near Evart, winding down sixty miles of moraines, hills created when the glaciers that created the Great Lakes deposited piles of rock across the evolving terrain. The section between Evart and Newaygo features the steepest slope and fastest current before dams tamed most of this unruly stretch river. Nearly half the Muskegon's 575-foot drop in elevation occurs in this section. Most of the Muskegon is a wide, lazy river. The river's average gradient, or slope, over its 219-mile length is just 2.6 feet per mile.[3]

There were relatively steep sections of river, between Big Rapids and Newaygo, where the Muskegon dropped several feet per mile in some places. Rapids in the city of Big Rapids, where the river drops eleven feet in one mile, provide a glimpse of how the heart of the river likely appeared before it was submerged under reservoirs created by the Rogers, Hardy, and Croton hydroelectric dams.

The natural slope of the Muskegon was much like the slope of a slide commonly found on school playgrounds. If you were able to view a profile of the river absent dams, it would bear a striking resemblance to the side view of one of these slides. The river from Houghton Lake to Evart flowed slowly down a sandy channel that drops just one to two feet per mile, much like a person slides slowly down that first small hill at the top of the slide. The section from Evart to Newaygo mirrored the big drop-off on the slide. In its natural condition, this section of river churned with small rapids and swift currents. Below Newaygo, the landscape levels off, and the river loses steam. Here the Muskegon's channel is much like the tail end of a slide, flat and slowing the water in its banks to a crawl.[4]

About nineteen miles below Newaygo, the river splits into several branches and takes on the identity of a shredded rope end as it creeps through a sprawling estuary in the Muskegon State Game Area. On the north side of the marsh, Cedar Creek gives the river a final dose of frigid water before the river flows into Muskegon Lake.

Prior to 1850, part of the Muskegon's south branch split off in the estuary to form the Maple River. The small river surrounded a two-square-mile spit of fertile land that became known as Maple Island. The island lost its distinction in the late 1850s, after logging companies dredged the south branch of the Muskegon so that logs could float more easily down the river. That project cut off the Maple's water supply from the Muskegon, leaving the island and its namesake river with stagnant water, gasping for life. Today, the Maple River is just a trickle, and parts of it dry up in the summer. Its shallow waters and mucky bottom still support stands of native wild rice that grow to a height of more than twelve feet. Mats of duckweed, a single-leaf plant the size of a pea, float slowly past in the barely noticeable current, a sign that the Maple River still has a pulse.

Though lumber companies altered the lower river to accommodate logs, the sprawling marsh in the Muskegon State Game Area remains a foreboding wilderness. It may be the closest thing in Michigan to the swamps of Louisiana. Thick brush, thousands of dead and downed trees, acres of reeds, cattails, mucky soils, unpredictable water levels, and myriad small river channels pose a formidable challenge to anyone who enters the marsh.

Many a hunter has become disoriented in a place so wild it could be mistaken for a jungle river. The rugged terrain of the marsh drove surveyor John

Mullett, the first white man to cross it on foot, in 1838, to exasperation. In his surveyor's notes, which were usually limited to grading the quality of trees for logging and land for farming, Mullett wrote, "This land is good for nothing."[5]

Like all rivers, the Muskegon is a life force capable of self-generated change. When its water level is low, the river cuts down, deepening its channel; when the water is high, the river spreads laterally and cuts into its banks. It is constantly working, changing, evolving. As the glaciers that formed the Great Lakes were receding ten millennia ago, the meltwater that formed the Muskegon often changed course as the stream plowed ahead in search of the path of least resistance to Lake Michigan. Before the last of the glaciers retreated from Lake Michigan, the Muskegon River made a detour above Newaygo and flowed into the Rogue River, which flows into the Grand River near Grand Rapids.[6]

Less dramatic changes continue in the river to this day. In the mid-1990s, for example, high water levels caused another change of course; the river abandoned a large hairpin turn in its channel above Evart and plowed straight through a thick hardwood forest, mowing down trees as it cut a straighter course. The power of the river was evident years later in the dozens of large, dead trees strewn like matchsticks across the new channel, which remained impassable by canoe until a group of volunteers used chainsaws to cut a path. Scenes like this make it clear that the Muskegon remains a forceful river.

THE FIRST HUMANS TO LAY EYES ON THIS RIVER—THE HOPEWELL AND later Odawa Indians—discovered the Muskegon long before the birth of Christ two millennia ago.[7] They pulled giant sturgeon and colorful Arctic grayling from the river. They hunted deer that came to drink its water. Though they used the river in all manner of ways—for transportation, food, and recreation—there is no evidence that the Native Americans caused lasting harm to the Muskegon.

Traces of Native American culture can be found along the Muskegon River in Newaygo County. The Croton-Carrigan Mounds represent the earliest known burial site in Michigan for the Woodland tribes who began moving into the state more than five thousand years ago. The location of those mounds is kept private to prevent collectors from raiding the sites.[8]

The second wave of settlers who arrived in western Michigan ushered in major changes. European immigrants began flooding into the area from the eastern United States in the mid-1800s, hoping to cash in on logging. Ever since, the Muskegon has been used, abused, and manipulated to meet the needs of an increasingly modern society. Today, the river is much like a beautiful woman who has suffered a traumatic injury and no longer recognizes her image in the mirror. The river has been battered, to be sure, but not destroyed. Far from it. Vast areas of the Muskegon River system—the web of water that includes 65,000 acres of lakes and streams and 361,000 acres of wetlands—have made a valiant recovery since the logging era.[9] But powerful human-induced changes, primarily the construction of dams, have prevented a more complete recovery.

The Hopewell and Odawa Indians who arrived in this river valley more than two thousand years ago found a truly pristine river that meandered through thick swamps and reared up miles of rapids that surged through long, sloping valleys. The Muskegon was sheltered by a forest of virgin white pines that measured several feet in diameter at their base and soared as high as two hundred feet above the ground. Massive prehistoric sturgeon migrated up the river each spring from Lake Michigan to spawn and playful rivers otters barked as they bounced along the river's edge. Mountain lions stalked nearby prairies, and Eastern timber wolves broadcast haunting howls through a forest so dense the sun struggled to reach a carpet of needles that blanketed the ground. The natural river and the 1,743,717 acres of land it drained were home to a cornucopia of life: plants, animals, insects and birds. Ninety-seven species of fish, scores of mammals—including moose, lynx and elk—and now-rare birds, including prairie chickens, grouse and passenger pigeons, resided in the Muskegon River Valley home before the onset of logging.[10] Most of the land in the Muskegon's watershed in 1800 was covered with pine or hardwood forest, with white pine being the dominant species.[11]

As the pine forests were cut down and the rivers scoured by logs and plundered by ill-informed anglers, many species of mammals, birds and fish that lived in the Muskegon River's forests, lakes and streams disappeared as well. Twenty species of fish were eliminated from the river, along with the passenger pigeon, lynx, wolf, elk and prairie chicken.[12]

For centuries before they were displaced by white settlers in the late 1800s, Native Americans relied on the Muskegon for food, transportation, clothing, and shelter. Native American men paddled several miles from villages near Lake Michigan to spear sturgeon in the river flats five miles upstream (now known as the Muskegon State Game Area). During the summer and fall, the women grew food crops and the men hunted all variety of animals, including deer, rabbits, and beaver. As summer faded into autumn, the Odawa women would fill handwoven baskets with wild rice from huge stands of the plant that covered acres of the Muskegon Lake shallows. Women stockpiled rice and corn to provide food throughout the brutally cold winters. "The tribes lived along the river because it provided everything they needed," said Joe Genia, an Odawa Indian who lives in Muskegon.[13]

From the 1600s through 1834, French fur traders stopped periodically at the mouth of the Muskegon to exchange knives, tools, and liquor for beaver pelts the Native Americans harvested. One of those Frenchmen, John Baptiste Recollet, stayed briefly; in 1812, he established the first trading post on Muskegon Lake, near the Bear Lake channel.[14] Having decimated the region's population of fur-bearing animals by the early 1800s, the white man's interests turned to a new source of potential wealth: timber.

A few dozen Odawa Indians were living in a village along Muskegon Lake in 1840 when George Ruddiman, an early white settler of Scottish descent, arrived to stake his claim. Birch-bark canoes were parked along the mucky shoreline, boxes of sticky brown sugar the Odawa made were available for trade, and huge sturgeon were stretched out to dry on "temporary scaffolds of brush and small trees near their wigwams," Ruddiman wrote in a letter to the Muskegon Pioneer and Historical Society.[15]

Before the onset of logging in 1837 and completion of the first dam across the river in 1854, fish, animals, and humans could travel the length of the river, from Muskegon to Houghton Lake, without interruption. The only barriers were those created by fallen trees, beaver dams, voracious mosquitoes, and miles of rapids that kept all but the strongest paddlers from traveling upstream of Newaygo.

Though the Native Americans undoubtedly changed the landscape (they were known to burn forests to create prairies where they could grow crops), they had only a limited effect on nature because at most a few hundred Odawa lived in the Muskegon River Valley prior to 1830. An early white settler reported seeing a village occupied by more than one hundred Odawa near the mouth of the river in 1820. With few people working the land, the

Muskegon River valley's wilderness remained largely intact until 1830s, when the U.S. government bought millions of acres of Odawa land and sold it at rock-bottom prices to white settlers whose primary skills were logging and farming.

European immigrants who moved into Michigan in the 1830s encountered a rugged wilderness. Wolves, fleas, and swarms of mosquitoes scared away some early settlers. "As a boy [during the 1840s], I can remember wolves howling out in the middle of [Muskegon] lake at night," recalled William Badeaux Sr., the son of a French fur trader born in Muskegon in 1841. Badeaux traveled all over the lower river as a child and remembered one particularly inhospitable tributary of the Muskegon. "Mosquito Creek deserved its name. When I was a small boy I remembered of an encounter with the mosquitoes in the valley of this creek and they were so numerous and ferocious that they made me cry." Badeaux also noted the beauty of the river saying: "The Muskegon River was a very pretty and deep stream at that time. The banks were covered with fine trees that hung over the water."[16]

Wolves were so plentiful in the Muskegon River Valley that Newaygo County officials in 1855 offered a bounty of eight dollars per animal to reduce their numbers. The bounty unleashed a wolf slaughter. To receive the bounty, hunters had to present a wolf's head to a justice of the peace, who would then burn the animal's ears to prevent its killer from claiming the animal more than once.[17]

Ruddiman, a successful lumberman who was one of the first elected supervisors of Muskegon Township, remembered well the hardships of living along the Muskegon River in the mid-1800s. "Muskegon [in 1840] had many drawbacks, particularly in mosquitoes and fleas. The mosquitoes were bad especially at mealtime, when we could not eat without a smudge [pot] under the table."[18]

Blood-sucking insects and countless other varieties thrived in the lower Muskegon River because of its marshes. The Native Americans called the river Maskigon, a Chippewa term meaning "river with marshes." It was a fitting moniker. The upper and lower parts of the river—in and around Houghton and Muskegon Lakes—were shallow and marshy and supported thousands of acres of wild rice, bulrush, reeds, huge mats of lily pads, and other aquatic plants. In 1840, when logging remained in its infancy, it was possible to navigate the mouth of the river, where it flows into Lake Michigan, by the plants growing in the water. "At one time there was no need of buoys to show the channel, as the rushes grew out to about six feet of water and the wild rice was never found in more than eight feet, so that we knew the depth of the water by the vegetation," Ruddiman said in 1888.[19]

Wild rice was also abundant at the other end of the river, in Houghton Lake, the headwaters of the Muskegon. Now a threatened species in Michigan, the rice that grew in Houghton and Muskegon lakes provided shelter and breeding grounds for fish and abundant food for waterfowl and people. Most of the wild rice is gone now. It thrives only in places such as the Maple River, a ghost stream that branches off from the lower Muskegon.

Though Native Americans relied on wild rice for food, the European immigrants who followed them into the Muskegon River Valley viewed the plant as expendable. The nineteenth century lumber barons who lorded over the river decimated the natural nurseries for wild rice—the huge, shallow marsh at the end of the river and shallow areas along the Muskegon Lake shoreline—to make the river better suited to transporting logs. The single-minded attitude of white settlers—that the value of land was based solely on its ability to produce timber or food—would exact a heavy toll on the Muskegon River ecosystem.

It was true that most of the Muskegon marsh was not suitable for logging or farming, but it did serve an essential purpose. The estuary provided a safe haven, buffet, and breeding ground for countless fish and birds, a place where the river cleansed itself by depositing tons of sediment before forming a deep harbor known as Muskegon Lake.

Less attractive than the river's main channel and inhospitable to humans, the mammoth wetlands that mark the beginning and end of the Muskegon are the building blocks of an incredibly diverse community of life forms—visible and invisible—that make this one of the Great Lakes' most important rivers. This ecological masterpiece was fourteen thousand years in the making; it took humans less than a century to ruin it.

2.

A WORKING RIVER

> There never was such another river and there never will be—pine, pine, pine everywhere!
>
> —JOHN F. GAUWELIER, A MUSKEGON RIVER LUMBERMAN WHO SETTLED IN CROTON IN 1846

MARTIN RYERSON WAS A POOR DUTCH KID FROM NEW JERSEY LOOKing to strike it rich when he headed for the Far West in 1834. For two years, he worked his way to Michigan, a journey that culminated with an arduous fifteen-mile hike through the unbroken wilderness between Michigan's two largest rivers, the Grand and Muskegon. Ryerson arrived on the banks of the Muskegon in 1836 with little more than the clothes on his back. He was eighteen. By age twenty-seven, Ryerson had acquired his first sawmill and was on his way to becoming the first millionaire lumber baron in the Muskegon River valley. He also was one of the early white settlers who would transform the wild and scenic Muskegon into a working river.

Until 1836, the Muskegon River basin was a vast forest of white pine and hardwoods, pristine streams, and untarnished lakes that spanned an area larger than the state of Delaware. There were no roads, no bridges crossing the river, no boat docks, horse and carriage trails, or railroads. The only signs of civilization along the river at that time were an Odawa Indian village near the channel to Lake Michigan and a few fur trading posts, the furthest of which lay fifteen miles upstream at Maple Island.

That began to change after the U.S. Congress in 1836 approved the Treaty of Washington, an agreement that transferred ownership of millions of acres of land in western Michigan from the Odawa Indians to the federal government. The government paid the tribes sixteen cents an acre for millions of acres of land that extended from the Muskegon River north along the Lake Michigan coast to the Straits of Mackinac. That land, blanketed by virgin forests of massive white pines and crisscrossed by several large rivers, was then sold to white settlers for $1.25 an acre. The government's goal: expand the boundaries of a growing nation by relocating Native Americans and encouraging white settlers to establish homesteads and build communities in the wilderness. For many settlers, the Treaty of Washington provided the first chance to own land. Others saw dollar signs in the region's seemingly endless forests of white pines—trees up to two hundred feet tall with trunks up to eight feet in diameter, sometimes larger—that came to be known as "green gold."

Henry Penoyer reached the banks of the Muskegon River the same year as Ryerson. Penoyer, however, was a man of means, a Chicago land speculator who knew that big money could be made logging pine forests that lined the Muskegon and other rivers to the north. Before the Treaty of Washington was finalized, Penoyer and his business partners claimed squatters' rights and built cabins at the mouth of the Muskegon and every other river from the Grand River north to the Manistee. The only other inhabitants of the area at the time were the Odawa Indians who gave Newaygo its name, which may mean "We go no farther."[1]

Within weeks, Penoyer's brother, Augustus, and business partner, Jack McBride, had settled in Newaygo, thirty-five miles upstream of Muskegon. On September 1, 1837, they opened the first Muskegon River sawmill at the mouth of Penoyer Creek; it was the first mill to send cut lumber down the river. Penoyer's cut wood was put on a raft and floated downstream to Muskegon, where it was loaded aboard the schooner *Celeste* and shipped to Chicago. It was a historic occasion. "The beginning of operations of the Penoyer mill was the forerunner of the big pine lumber business that was to continue for more than sixty years and that eventually was to denude the entire Muskegon valley of the dense forests of pine that stretched from Newaygo north to the straits of Mackinaw," wrote historian Harry L. Spooner in his informative book, *Lumbering of Newaygo County*.[2]

Logging dramatically changed the character of the river. Huge pine trees cut down during the winter were rolled down banks and into the river in the spring, when high water and stronger currents could transport the massive logs to sawmills in Newaygo and Muskegon. Clear-cutting of forests wiped away the canopy of trees that helped cool the river and held sandy soils in place. The practice of rolling logs into the river stripped the banks of all vegetation, sending tons of sand and silt into the river, where it buried prime fish habitat. Millions of logs that floated down the river and its tributaries each spring scoured river beds at precisely the time sentinel fish species—sturgeon and grayling—were attempting to spawn on the rocky bottom.

For the next sixty years, the Muskegon River served almost exclusively as an industrial river. Over time, the changes logging inflicted on the Muskegon would make the river wider and shallower. By 1888, virtually all of the trees in the river valley were gone. The landscape was a wasteland, desolate and littered with the stumps of millions of trees. Miles of gravel river bottom where grayling and sturgeon once spawned were buried under sand and silt. Dams built to power sawmills in Newaygo and dozens of smaller streams divided the river and disrupted the natural flow of water in the Muskegon and many of its ninety-four tributaries. This was the environmental legacy of a logging boom that sent 30 billion board feet of timber down the river, enough wood to make about 6 million basketball courts.

Forth to the world went the woodland king,
Rent in a thousand parts,
Born from its home in the northern wood,
On to the busy marts.
Part went to form a laborer's lot,
Part framed a mansion fine,
And many things for the good of man,
Came from the old white pine.[3]

Logging was brutal to Michigan's environment but a financial bonanza for Muskegon and other lumber towns. The industry produced dozens of millionaires in Muskegon alone and by 1890 had produced wood products statewide valued at $3 billion—more than twice the value of gold mined in California during the gold rush.[4]

Pine trees logged from the Muskegon River valley played an important role in the growth of a nation; the lumber and shingles were used to build numerous prairie towns and much of Chicago after the devastating 1871 fire. But the economic benefits of logging came at great expense to the river and to the Native Americans who lived along it and relied on it for sustenance.

Joe Genia, an Odawa Indian whose ancestors lived along the Muskegon, said that the environmental problems caused by logging shocked Native Americans, who for centuries had relied on the river for physical and spiritual nourishment. "The elders say that watching what logging did to the river was like watching someone hurt your life partner and not having the power to stop it," he said.

Some Odawa Indians who trace their ancestry to the Muskegon still fish in the river and hunt in its adjoining forests. Dozens of Odawa gather each spring at the Indian Cemetery in Muskegon, near the banks of Muskegon Lake, to remember their ancestors and pray for the river's recovery. "We pray for Muskegon Lake and the river and our relationship to it," Genia said in a 1999 newspaper interview. "And we ask the Creator to provide us with the wisdom to correct the problems in the river."[5]

More than a century after the lumber barons laid waste to the forests, the Muskegon River has yet to fully recover from the environmental devastation logging left in its wake. Miles of the river bottom still resemble an underwater desert—vast stretches of sand but few signs of life. Sections of the river and its tributaries were straightened and dredged, and hundreds of acres of marsh on the south side of Muskegon Lake were filled with sawdust and wood planks to create building sites for sawmills. Several native species of fish and mammals were eliminated from the river system. Arctic grayling and white bass no longer live in the Muskegon, and the distinctive howls of wolves are no longer heard in the river valley. At the height of logging in the 1880s, the river was an open sewer for all forms of logging waste, human and industrial. Historian Jeremy W. Kilar described the scene on Muskegon Lake in his compelling book, *Michigan's Lumbertowns:*

> The lumbertown waterways took on a different complexion because of industrialization. Muskegon Lake lost its clarity. Fish life changed dramatically

> from what had been present not long ago. The appearance of the waterways also underwent noticeable deterioration. No longer attractive to the hunter or fisherman, they became clogged with logs, strewn with acidic bark, churned by tugs, steamships and ferry boats. The waterways became polluted highways of commerce. The rivers had lost their pristine clarity. Log rafts, bark, sawdust, sedimentation from years of upstream alteration by loggers, and brine runoff had created polluted waterways. Brownish water . . . discolored Muskegon Lake. The sounds of whirling saws and the odor of burning wood confronted the senses day and night."[6]

No environmental laws on the books in the 1800s limited how people used the water, land, or forests. Michigan's first law protecting wildlife took effect in 1859, but it only established when and where turkeys, partridge, and other birds could be hunted. The Michigan Forestry Commission was not established until 1899, after most of the state had been clear-cut, and focused primarily on reforestation.

Environmental laws aimed at protecting forests and surface water would not take effect until the early 1900s, long after the pine forests had been clear-cut and the rivers ruined. Michigan's logging was, by definition, exploitive. According to historian Bruce Catton, the lumber barons who presided over the wholesale destruction of the pine forests were driven by greed, shortsighted, and followed one guiding principle: "Take what there is, take all of it, and take it as fast as you can, and let tomorrow's people handle tomorrow's problems."[7]

William Badeaux Sr. saw Michigan's pine forests vanish during his lifetime. Born in Muskegon in 1841, Badeaux was the son of a French fur trader and spent his adult years working in the logging industry. In a 1903 interview, he fondly recalled growing up along the Muskegon before the forests were felled and the river choked with logs. In 1857, he traveled down the Muskegon River on one of his many jaunts from Newaygo to Muskegon:

> It took about a day and a half to make the trip down the river. Two men navigated the raft, and they were kept pretty busy. Such lumber as fell off was

> appropriated by the settlers and Indian farmers who lived along the banks of the river. The Muskegon River was a very pretty and deep stream at that time. The banks were covered with fine trees which hung over the water, and the water was quite clear. Hornets' nests were sometimes found in the trees and one of the amusements of us boys in rafting days was for the man on the front of the raft to knock the nest loose, compelling the man at the rear oar to get into the water in order to escape the hornets.[8]

Such carefree days on the river became rare after the Civil War, when logging in the Muskegon River Valley escalated at a phenomenal rate. Although the fur trading industry was in steep decline in the late 1830s and Michigan's population grew rapidly after it attained statehood in 1837, the Muskegon River lumbering industry got off to a sluggish start as the economy faltered and sawmills underwent multiple changes of ownership. But in the mid-1840s, a dwindling supply of trees in New York and Maine, coupled with rapid growth in Chicago, fueled increased demand for Michigan pine trees.[9] Lumbermen from the East Coast streamed into western Michigan, eager to exploit the seemingly endless forests.

By then, Ryerson was positioned to make a fortune in logging. Having spent his first five years working for fur traders and taking other odd jobs on the river, he had forged important bonds with the Odawa Indians. His first employer was a fur trader named Joseph Troutier, a half Indian, half French man known as Truckee who was married to a full-blooded Odawa Indian. While working as a cook on one of Truckee's flatboats, Ryerson became enamored of the Indian culture, learning the Odawa language and traditions and marrying a member of the tribe. "By reason of his marriage and due to the friendship of the Indians, Ryerson was able to purchase valuable timber land for very little and those investments yielded him handsome profits," according to Muskegon historian Joe Eyler.[10]

In October 1841, Ryerson and partner S. J. Green signed a deal to operate the Newell and Company sawmill, by then one of several sawmills on Muskegon Lake. Ryerson, who was known to work as much as eighteen hours a day, bought the mill in 1845 and worked tirelessly to ensure its success. He left Muskegon for Chicago in 1851 but kept his businesses on the Muskegon River. When he died in 1887, his fortune was estimated at about $4 million.

Logging fundamentally changed the character of the Muskegon River and many of its tributaries. All of the early sawmills were powered by water, which meant diverting part of the river into a mill raceway, where it could be stored and released when needed to turn a water wheel that powered a giant saw. In 1837, the first dam built in the Muskegon River system was erected across the Little Muskegon River, near Croton. Three years later, a Newaygo mill owned in part by John A. Brooks was the first to float pine logs down the river to sawmills on Muskegon Lake.

Over the next thirty-five years, a series of developments quickened the pace of logging in Michigan. In 1852, the Michigan courts ruled that a river was navigable if it could float a log. The courts also ruled that the public had unrestricted access to navigable waters, a ruling that allowed logging to expand throughout the state.

In 1855, the Michigan Legislature empowered booming companies to "control river traffic by driving, rafting and sorting all logs on a particular river." Booming companies were established to prevent the theft of logs as they entered Muskegon Lake. The companies sorted all the logs according to which lumber mill owned the wood; the mills used metal tools to pound distinctive shapes into the end of each log when they were cut down.

Michigan's first booming company was the Muskegon Lumberman's Association, formed in 1852. It was absorbed in 1864 by a new and ultimately more successful Muskegon Booming Company, which would handle 90 million board feet of lumber in its first year. Booming companies had the legal authority to assess fees on mill owners and used that power to raise money to build docks, dredge channels, and make other improvements necessary to facilitate the movement of logs down rivers.[11]

In 1863, the Muskegon Harbor Company was formed and raised forty thousand dollars to deepen the Muskegon River channel into Lake Michigan. That feat was accomplished by building a fifteen-hundred-foot-long wooden breakwater on the south pier and five-hundred-foot-long breakwater on the north pier. Those piers kept the channel from silting over and stranding lumber schooners. Before the project was undertaken, the channel was rarely more than six feet deep and was often shallow enough to wade across.[12]

A major technological advance in the mid-1870s would open up huge areas of forest that had remained untouched by loggers because they were too far from rivers. In 1877, Winfield Scott Gerrish, a nineteen-year-old Clare

County lumberman, began operating one of the first logging railroads in the United States, the Lake George and Muskegon River Railroad. The railroad enabled loggers to reach more remote areas of forests and haul logs year round to the Muskegon, where they could be floated downstream to sawmills. Prior to the creation of the railroad, most logs were hauled out of the forest only in the winter by teams of horses that pulled sleds on ice-covered paths. In its first year, the Gerrish railroad hauled 11,227 tons of logs along seven miles of track at the rate of five hundred thousand board feet per day. To the dismay of many lumberjacks, who feared that the new technology would put them out of work, other businessmen quickly followed Gerrish's lead. By 1882, Michigan had thirty-two narrow-gauge logging railroads, a number that increased to five hundred by the end of the century.[13]

> Year round cutting opened a new period of the slaughter of the forests. No longer were only the large trees cut on a selective basis. Literally everything went down at the mercy of the saw. Vast areas of untouched timber, five to ten miles or more back from a logging stream were opened up to systematic logging on a take everything basis.[14]

As the industry grew and logging crews pushed deeper into the forest, millions more logs were floated down the Muskegon River each spring. In 1857, the fourteen sawmills located on the Muskegon processed 70 million board feet of timber sent down the river. By 1884, forty-seven sawmills were operating on Muskegon Lake. Production peaked in 1887, when those mills churned out an astounding 661 million board feet of lumber and 520 million shingles.[15] An 1871 visitor to Newaygo commented on the intensity of the logging: "The log running business here, as along the whole river, is being vigorously prosecuted. There is a jam of logs commencing at Newaygo at the present time and extending ten miles up the river nearly to Croton, and the jam is rapidly increasing in length."[16]

The Muskegon was ideal for transporting logs. By Michigan standards it was a large river, with a channel up to three hundred feet wide and up to nine feet deep. It carried a large volume of water and emptied into a deep harbor at Muskegon Lake, where scores of logs could be stockpiled near sawmills. But one section of the river created a bottleneck for logs sent downstream—a wide, shallow marsh near Muskegon that marked the beginning of the river's estuary. Here the river splits, creating several branches that are not as deep or swift as the main channel upstream. As a result, thousands of logs would get snagged in an area early lumbermen called the sand flats. To cure the problem, several sections of shallow river were straightened, deepened, and channeled with walls of logs driven vertically into the soft, mucky soils.

After being elected to the state legislature in 1857, Newaygo lumberman Brooks obtained a fifty-thousand-dollar appropriation to "improve" the sand flats. The following year, levees and a wall of wooden pilings were built along a one-mile section of the river channel, thereby forcing more water into the Muskegon's south branch by cutting off the Maple River tributary.

Coupled with dredging, the pilings and levees created a channel 150 feet wide and 4 feet deep. Subsequent projects extended that channel another eight miles, creating an artificially deep nine-mile channel through the sand flats that was protected on both sides by a row of wood pilings.[17] The Brooks project, which fueled a dramatic increase in logging, was significant enough to draw Michigan Governor Moses Wisner to the Muskegon River marsh in 1859. While touring the site with Wisner, the owner and editor of the *Newaygo Republican,* J. H. Maize, observed,

> It is certainly one of the most forbidding realms on the face of God's earth. It looks like a fit home only for the frog, the snake, the tortoise and, we should think, the alligator. Thousands of acres are covered with cattail flags, marsh shrubbery, and decayed timber. It is through the worst of this repulsive latitude that the improvements are made. No one with less perseverance than John A. Brooks would undertake such a job in such an unhallowed precinct as the Muskegon River sand flats.[18]

The Civil War slowed Michigan's logging industry. Once the bloodshed ended, it was back to the woods for thousands of soldiers who had been lumbermen before taking up arms to put down the Confederate rebellion. An article in the June 9, 1866, edition of the *Big Rapids Pioneer* described the annual log drive, which sent millions of logs down the river each spring:

> Commodore Pingree, of Muskegon, widely known as the oldest navigator of the Muskegon River, has just made an entirely successful experiment in

> getting the "Big Drive'" over the rapids at this place. The logs were piled two or three feet deep for about two miles, and about half a mile on the flat the logs were on dry land, the water having gone down and left them there. The getting them off seemed about an impossibility, but the Commodore got them all afloat by filling the channel below with logs and raising the water over three feet, thus producing slack water for nearly half a mile. The logs are now being floated off rapidly, and new jams are made farther down, as necessity requires.[19]

Over the next two decades, the volume of logs sent down the Muskegon increased at an astonishing rate—as much as 800 million board feet of timber per year—until the supply of trees began to dwindle in 1888 and the industry began its free-fall into oblivion. Skeptics who in the early 1880s questioned how long the blistering pace of logging could continue often were mocked, as was the case in an 1884 pamphlet, *Muskegon and Its Resources:*

> Twenty years ago old croakers said, "Five or ten years more will exhaust the timber supply of Muskegon." They have said the same thing every from that time to this until their prognostications are now considered about as reliable as those of the ordinary weather prophet. . . . The timber prophet of today who lives long enough to see the supply exhausted in the Muskegon valley will be so wrinkled that he can wrap himself in a linen rag and be labeled "a well preserved specimen of the Egyptian mummy" without danger of detection.[20]

Indeed, the 1840–90 period saw unparalleled prosperity in the Muskegon River Valley; the logging era was one of the most financially rewarding and socially colorful eras in Michigan's history. The halcyon days of logging were every bit as freewheeling and bawdy as those of the California gold rush.

Every spring, at the conclusion of the log run, hundreds of lumbermen converged on an area of Muskegon known as Sawdust Flats to drink whiskey, fight, and commiserate with ladies of the night. "Keen-nosed loggers claimed they could smell Muskegon booze as far upriver as Big Rapids, 50 miles away, and said they detected the first erotic whiffs of Sawdust Flats perfume at Newaygo, half as far. Muskegon's Sawdust Flats was a part of the city made by a fill and on it were six solid blocks—long blocks—of what a local divine termed 'unspeakable whoredom.'"[21]

The debauchery was not limited to Muskegon. An area in northeast Newaygo County was known as Whore's Corner. Now a ghost town, the site at the corner of Oak Avenue and Thirteen Mile Road in Home Township was at one time wildly decadent and popular among lumberjacks, according to a display at the Newaygo County Historical Museum: "Because of its location, surrounded by lumber camps, the site was a favorite with logging crews. It ceased to exist when, due to the incapacitating effects of venereal disease, the lumber camp owners drove the women away."

The village of Evart, upstream of Big Rapids, once was a bustling logging village and site of what some consider the greatest fight between lumberjacks in the history of Michigan's logging era. In 1881, a lumberjack named John Driscoll—nicknamed Silver Jack because of his shock of white hair—traded blows with Angus Bronson, the best brawler among lumberjacks on the rival Saginaw River system. Silver Jack Driscoll had earned a reputation as the toughest lumberjack in Michigan in 1880, while working in the Saginaw River valley. The following year, he went to work on the Muskegon, where Bronson tracked him down. The two squared off in an Evart saloon in a makeshift ring created by a circle of rowdy, drunken lumberjacks. Driscoll and Bronson traded bare-knuckle blows for ninety minutes until an exhausted Bronson surrendered with a one-word whisper, "Enough."[22]

The annual brawls between lumberjacks working on the Muskegon and Saginaw Rivers were part of a rivalry between Michigan's two busiest logging streams. Sawmills in Saginaw Bay cut more logs than those in Muskegon, but that was because several large rivers—the Flint, Cass, Tittabawassee, Chippewa, and Rifle—carried logs into Saginaw Bay. The Muskegon River transported far more logs than any other single Michigan river—a total of 30 billion board feet—earning Muskegon the justifiable title of Lumber Queen of the World.

Muskegon's wealthiest and most famous lumber baron, Charles Hackley, got his start in 1856 as a hardworking, hard-drinking laborer in a sawmill. Three years later, after working many different jobs for logging firms and attending business college in Wisconsin, Hackley and his father purchased a bankrupt sawmill. The younger Hackley was twenty-two at the time. Over the next thirty years, he acquired several other sawmills and amassed a fortune while building his logging empire. Unlike many of his peers, Hackley did not leave the Muskegon River valley when the logging industry collapsed in the late 1890s. Instead, he remained active in local politics and economic development efforts. He also donated $6 million to various organizations and established funds to support the Muskegon Public Schools. Today, many Muskegon institutions, including a downtown park, a library, a hospital, and a high school football stadium, bear his name.

Hackley believed that he owed Muskegon a share of the fortune he had earned off the land. In an August 1900 interview with the *American Lumberman,* Hackley shared his view of social responsibility: "After making due allowance for talent, enterprise, and the faculty for improving opportunities, I consider that a rich man to a great extent owes his fortune to the public. To a certain extent I agree with Mr. [Andrew] Carnegie in a remark he recently made to the effect that it is a crime to die rich."[23]

ON A COOL, CLOUDLESS SPRING DAY IN 2004, A CENTURY AFTER THE LAST logs floated down the Muskegon, a mound of water the size of a bushel basket rose above the glimmering river and created a small riffle beyond a mysterious obstruction. From a distance, it was difficult to determine whether the object was a boulder deposited thousands of years ago by a receding glacier or a human-created obstruction that stirred up a slice of the Muskegon River.

As I floated toward the obstruction in my kayak, it became clear that this navigational hazard was not natural—it was a deadhead, a huge pine log rolled into the river during the nineteenth century. Destined for one of more than seventy sawmills that had once lined the river in Big Rapids, Newaygo, and Muskegon, the log sank before reaching its destination. Rising on a mild angle from beneath a blanket of sand that covered the river bottom, the log and sand were remnants of a bygone era.

As my kayak drifted past the log, I looked for a distinctive stamp on the end that would have identified its owner. There was none: time had worn it away. As the river carried me downstream, my mind drifted and I wondered what it was like to paddle up the Muskegon as the Odawa Indians did, fishing for gigantic sturgeon and hunting deer and other game in a virgin forest of towering white pines that cast long shadows over the river. What was it like, I wondered, to be a lumberjack who chopped down giant pines, or a river hog who guided thousands of logs on a treacherous journey down the river? I wondered what the river valley looked like, barren and scarred, before the second-generation forest rose from the ashes of the white pine lumbering era.

Traveling the waters of the Muskegon River was a floating history lesson. In many places, submerged logs measuring more than two feet in diameter and more than ten feet long rose from a blanket of sand that covered the river bottom. Rows of slowly rotting pine logs lined the river's edge in some places, remnants of pilings driven vertically into the riverbed to keep logs moving downstream to sawmills.

Piles of boulders rose periodically from the river, leftovers of the wood-and-rock cribs lumberjacks built to divert logs away from shallow spots in the Muskegon. I looked down the long, wide valley and conjured images of fearless young men—river hogs—who lived along the river in beat camps and joined the log run each spring as it moved downstream. Brave as soldiers and agile as tap dancers, the river hogs guided huge rafts of pine trees down the winding river, thrusting long poles called peaveys into the logs when needed to break up jams.

Shepherding millions of huge logs the length of this sinuous river, from Houghton Lake to Muskegon, was as much an art as a science. And though it caused great harm to the river, the annual log run certainly was a sight to behold. People lined the tops of high banks overlooking the river each spring in communities such as Newaygo and Big Rapids to glimpse the power of a working river. For nearly sixty years, the log run was a spring tradition on the Muskegon, extending further up the river and its tributaries every year until no more trees remained to be cut.

Although logging in the Muskegon River valley declined steadily after 1888, a handful of sawmills continued to operate until the turn of the century, harvesting hundreds of thousands of deadheads that never made it to sawmills on the first pass. The last major log run down the Muskegon took place in 1905. Newaygo historian Robert I. Thompson described the scene in one of his many scrapbooks, "One warm July afternoon in 1905, a number of Newaygoites gathered on the upper bridge to watch the river floats and other belongings of the Muskegon River Boom Co. go over the dam. They took their last long look, for it was the end of the last big drive."[24]

At the end of the nineteenth century, when it became clear that the logging industry was headed toward a self-inflicted death, the businessmen who stayed began dreaming of new ways to profit from the power of the mighty Muskegon. Two years after the final log run, a new industry tightened humans' grip on the river.

3.

THE BERLIN WALL

Water running downhill will make more money than water that's left idle.

—John G. Emery Jr., Muskegon lumber baron and entrepreneur, 1902

A dozen fishermen waded in the river's knee-deep water under gray autumn clouds, each hoping a powerful chinook salmon would be distracted from its spawning run long enough to strike a lure. Over and over, the anglers cast lines into water that changed from translucent to opaque as clouds pass overhead. One large fish after another cruised by, some close enough to poke with a rod. If these fish did not bite the first time, they would almost certainly return for another pass—they had nowhere else to go. The free-flowing Muskegon River ended abruptly around the next bend, where Croton Dam walled off the river to generate electricity for thousands of homes and businesses. Since its completion in 1907, the historic dam that once set the standard for power production has been the ecological equivalent of the Berlin Wall—nothing in the river's lower forty-seven miles gets past this massive concrete barrier.

For the past century, Croton Dam has served as the great divide between the upper and lower sections of the Muskegon. Fish in the lower river, Muskegon Lake, and Lake Michigan cannot reach the upper 172 miles of the river above the dam. Even if fish and other aquatic life could bypass Croton Dam, they could not travel much further up the Muskegon—two other hydroelectric dams, Hardy and Rogers, lie a few miles upstream.[1]

Built without fish ladders, these three dams have parceled off the Muskegon's main branch into three distinct waterways: the upper river, upstream of Rogers Dam, which is biologically detached from the lower river and Lake Michigan and supports a marginal fishery; a thirty-mile section of the river's midsection, which the dams have turned into three human-created lakes; and the lower river, downstream of Croton Dam, which has retained its connection to Lake Michigan and became the healthiest and most popular section of the Muskegon. Built decades before modern environmental laws were written, the Croton, Hardy, and Rogers Dams were the most disruptive and beloved structures in this river.

IT WAS NO MYSTERY WHY HYDROELECTRIC DAMS WERE BUILT IN THE heart of the Muskegon. The river dropped three hundred feet over a span of seventy miles between Hersey and Newaygo, sending water rushing down what is a relatively steep slope for a Michigan river. By constructing a walls at the base of a sloping river, dams choked the river and stored its water in reservoirs. In general, the larger the slope in a river, the larger the dam and the accompanying reservoir.

Dams converted the energy in rivers into electricity by funneling water through turbines. Water flowed through the dam, spinning huge turbines that generated electricity. That electricity was then distributed over power lines to homes and businesses many miles from the dam. The concept was relatively simple—so simple, in fact, that it captured the imagination of a nineteenth-century land prospector who became an accidental visionary in the annals of Muskegon River history.

George Erwin was a Muskegon native and avid fisherman whose childhood adventures and work in the land business had taken him to towns all along the river. In 1884, Erwin's brother, David, led a group of businessmen who formed the Muskegon Lighting Company, the city's first electric utility. The company's power plant in downtown Muskegon, fueled by a steam generator Thomas Edison invented, produced electricity for homes and businesses. By 1892, the company had one hundred miles of transmission lines in its system. Against this backdrop was born one man's dream of building hydroelectric dams on the Muskegon River.

George Erwin was on a fishing trip in 1898 near Big Rapids, one of the steepest and fastest-flowing sections of the Muskegon. At the time, Erwin was aware of a dam being built on the Kalamazoo River near Allegan, one hundred miles south of the Muskegon. The Trowbridge Dam and its state-of-the-art transmission equipment would prove that electricity generated at a hydroelectric dam could be transported via wires to towns more than twenty miles away.

A shrewd businessman, Erwin knew that the mighty Muskegon held tremendous potential for generating hydroelectric power and profits. He would spend the next four years purchasing flowage rights, which gave him permission to flood land along the river. His was a daring business venture that caused the most profound, longest-lasting changes humans ever inflicted on the Muskegon River system. Author George Bush (not either of the presidents) documented Erwin's prowess in *Future Builders: The Story of Michigan's Consumers Power Company:*

> The chubby, kindly faced real estate man from Muskegon, then 42 years old, knew exactly what he was after. The only trouble was that he didn't know how to go about getting it. He wanted to dam up the Muskegon River and sell electricity. Erwin didn't understand the first thing about electricity. . . . But he did know that flowing water somehow manufactures electricity and that the more the river falls, the more electricity can be produced. With the drop of the Muskegon River, which he had experienced often enough in his rowboat, there obviously was a great potential.[2]

Erwin did not know exactly where to build dams on the Muskegon, so he bought land rights—often for as little as five dollars an acre—all along the river between Big Rapids and Newaygo.[3] But he ran out of money before the first spade of dirt was turned over. Broke and lacking blueprints for his dream dam, Erwin was poised to call it quits until he hooked up with Muskegon lumber baron John G. Emery Jr. Emery shared Erwin's belief that damming the Muskegon could create a lucrative source of electricity and income.

At the time, logging in the Muskegon River basin was nearing its demise, and Emery was looking for new business ventures. He reportedly told Erwin, "Water running downhill will make more money than water that's left idle."[4] Another wealthy Muskegon lumber baron, Thomas Hume, later joined Erwin and Emery. In 1904, they formed the Grand Rapids–Muskegon Water Power Electric Company. Still, their dream of damming the river remained just that until, out of desperation, they traveled to Jackson to meet with W. A. Foote.

Foote and his brother, J. B., were brilliant engineers and pioneers in electrical generation and transmission. The Foote brothers launched what would become Consumers Power Company, now Consumers Energy, Michigan's largest electric utility. Erwin and his partners gave W. A. Foote a one-third share in their company and a seat on the board of directors. In return, Foote, who had supervised construction of the Trowbridge Dam on the Kalamazoo River, agreed to shepherd the Muskegon River dam projects.

In 1906, Erwin's dream became reality when Rogers Dam was completed and began generating electricity a few miles south of Big Rapids. Even before the dam was completed, construction began on the Croton Dam, nearly thirty miles downstream. In September 1907, as Croton neared completion, two hundred dignitaries gathered for a party and tour of the dam.

> The mood was that of a celebration, as everyone shared in the immense pride that Michigan was home to this huge enterprise. There was much eating, good fellowship, and singing, including a special song. . . . It was called the "Song of Croton Dam" and was sung to the tune of "Marching through Georgia." Cigars were passed at the conclusion of the splendid New England dinner and then came the call to the baseball grounds."[5]

Rogers was not the first dam or even the first hydroelectric dam to harness the Muskegon River, but it was the first in a trinity of hydroelectric dams that changed the river on a grand scale, transforming forty miles of a fast-flowing river into mammoth ponds.

More than a hundred dams have been built in the Muskegon River and its ninety-four tributaries since European immigrants began settling the region in the early 1800s. Yet none of those other dams was as significant—economically, environmentally, or historically—as the Croton, Hardy, and

Rogers dams. The vast majority of dams built in the river system were small, simple structures compared to the technically sophisticated hydroelectric dams that have towered over the Muskegon for nearly a century. Hardy rises 120 feet above the river, Croton Dam is 60 feet tall, and Rogers is 56 feet high.

The Rogers and Croton dams revolutionized electrical generation and represented technological marvels in the early 1900s. Rogers and its accompanying transformers generated 72,000 volts of electricity, the most by any facility anywhere in the world at the time; Croton was the first dam to generate 110,000 volts of electricity. Hardy Dam was the largest earthen dam in the world when it was completed in 1931. Collectively, the three dams could generate enough electricity for a community of 25,200 people. All three were listed on the National Register of Historic Places.[6]

The dams occupied a special place in the hearts of many residents of western Michigan, who viewed the structures not as destroyers of the Muskegon River but as integral parts of the waterway. Bob Sullivan, director of Newaygo County's Department of Community Development, summed up the mood of many area residents in a 1999 newspaper article: "As far as the natural resources of the county go, and we have a lot, these [three hydroelectric dams] are the greatest."[7] Construction of the huge dams instilled a sense of pride in many residents of the Muskegon River Valley. Newspapers in the early 1900s praised the dams as triumphs of technology over nature.

Still, some locals lamented the changes the dams caused. The construction of Croton Dam at the confluence of the Muskegon and Little Muskegon Rivers created a reservoir that submerged the original village of Croton. The tiny, scenic village once known as the Forks was home to the Stearns Mill, one of the first sawmills on the Muskegon River. In an essay in the *Newaygo Republican,* a longtime resident reflected on changes caused by the dam:

> Many grieved as their homes and businesses were submerged, including the old stage road to Howard City and Grand Rapids, which used the bridges at Croton. As old timers passed on, old Croton became a dear memory and a new town has replaced it. Croton Pond today, as of old, lies in the picturesque valley of the Muskegon River—it is still attractive with its numerous islands, its inlets and bayous, teeming in fish of all kinds. Recreation has taken the place of early lumbering.[8]

The mood in Newaygo County during construction of the mammoth Hardy Dam could only be described as euphoric. After all, the project was initiated during the Great Depression, when millions of Americans were out of work. Built in two years at a cost of $5 million, Hardy spans three thousand feet and forms a reservoir that covers 3,850 acres and holds a whopping 65 billion gallons of water. During the course of construction, an estimated four hundred thousand people came to observe the evolution of a giant earthen berm that filled a superstructure built of logs, with a steel-reinforced concrete retaining wall down its middle. As water rose in the Hardy Dam reservoir, an article in the April 16, 1931, *Newaygo Republican* predicted that the undertaking would become a tourist attraction: "That the big artificial lake behind the new dam will be one of Michigan's most picturesque bodies of water is conceded by all who have visited the project. The beauty of the lake is enhanced by the fact that no trees, stumps, etc., have been left to mar the surface, all obstructions having been carefully removed over the whole expanse of the lake."[9]

Four months later, an article in the *Muskegon Chronicle* noted one of the noneconomic costs of building the Hardy Dam: "The building of the giant dam destroyed one of the outstanding beauty spots on the Muskegon River, the Oxbow. It was at this spot that the Muskegon River flowed between great banks, a spot that attracted hundreds of visitors and was one of the outstanding places of beauty on the autumn color tours."[10]

The second-growth forest that surrounds Hardy Pond has indeed become a popular spot for fall color tours. As the autumn days become shorter and the nights colder, the dying leaves of sugar maples and beech trees paint the hills with splashes of red, orange, and yellow. The only difference from color tours of years past is the absence of the Muskegon cascading down the steep river valley—today, the river channel lies beneath the deep, still waters of ponds created by the Rogers, Hardy, and Croton dams.

Though widely admired in the early 1900s, the three dams are now considered a mixed blessing among scientists, conservationists, and area residents familiar with the problems dams cause in rivers. The Croton, Hardy, and Rogers dams had many benefits. The facilities produced power without polluting the air, as coal-fired plants did, or creating the hazardous wastes associated with nuclear power. Reservoirs created by the dams provided flood control, trapped sand and silt that can be harmful to fish downstream, and were popular playgrounds for boaters. But those benefits came at a huge cost to the river.

Turbines in the dams chewed up tens of thousands of fish each year, and water discharged through the dams during the summer months often violated state standards because it contained too little oxygen, jeopardized fish and other aquatic life downstream.[11] Most significantly, these dams isolated the lower Muskegon from the upper river. As a result, fish and other aquatic life in Lake Michigan and Muskegon Lake are cut off from 80 percent of the river's 219 miles.

A century ago, hydroelectric power constituted one of the main sources of electricity in Michigan. But the power-producing landscape has changed dramatically over the past fifty years. Hydroelectric dams were surpassed in the mid-1900s by coal and nuclear power plants, which generated far more electricity and, some would argue, caused more harm to the environment in the process. In his 1973 history of Consumers Power, Bush concluded, "In Michigan, natural waterpower is a thing of the past."[12] In 2003, the hydroelectric dams on the Muskegon River produced less than 1 percent of all electricity Consumers Energy generates in Michigan. But with the public's demand for electricity increasing and Consumers' hydroelectric dams on the Muskegon River licensed to operate through 2034, those dams are expected to remain in the river for the foreseeable future. Moreover, Consumers officials point out that replacing the electricity generated at the Croton, Hardy, and Rogers Dams would cost the utility an additional $9 million per year.[13]

Built for the sole purpose of generating power for a technologically advancing society, the hydroelectric dams have had unintended benefits. The structures help regulate some human-caused problems in the Muskegon. Where land development increases soil erosion, dam reservoirs helped the river by trapping sand and silt, thereby keeping dirt from filling in prime fish habitat downstream. The flip side was that by removing virtually all sediment from the river, the dams released "hungry water" that could increase soil erosion downstream.

The reservoirs provided flood control, and the Croton Dam prevented sea lamprey and other exotic species in the lower river from expanding their range to the upper 172 miles of the Muskegon, where the voracious, eel-like parasite would be free to feast on fish. Despite those benefits, Rich O'Neal, a Michigan Department of Natural Resources fisheries biologist, claimed that the dams did the river more harm than good. O'Neal and many other biologists contended that the river would be healthier without dams.

> Some dams on the Muskegon River are currently producing some of these benefits for sediment removal and lamprey blockage. It must be pointed out that these dams were not built for these purposes and better alternatives are available to remedy the sediment and lamprey problems. Lamprey can be blocked with low head [dams] or electric barriers that do not have other negative effects of hydroelectric dams. Excessive sediment erosion needs to be dealt with using proper agricultural practices and non–point source control methods. Use of dams for sediment removal is only a temporary solution, because a reservoir will eventually fill with sediment or the dam will be retired from use. When this happens, the volume of stored sediment can be so large there may be no solution to remove it.[14]

Consumers Energy officials countered, correctly, that water discharged from Croton Dam is cooler in the summer than the river's natural water temperatures, a phenomenon that benefited the human-created rainbow trout fishery downstream.

> The fact is that the dams on the Muskegon River serve an extremely useful purpose in providing the cold water necessary to sustain a potential world class cold water fishery downstream of Croton Dam and help maintain optimal temperatures for the growth of cold water fish over a much longer period of time than would ordinarily be possible in a river that the [state] characterizes as having marginal temperatures for cold water species.[15]

Whether the Croton, Hardy, and Rogers dams were, on the whole, good or bad for the Muskegon River has been and will remain a source of intense debate. What could not be debated, however, was the fact that these structures obliterated the river's most vibrant stretch and divided the Muskegon into distinctly different rivers, with the upper 172 miles biologically isolated from the natural receiving water at Lake Michigan.

BRILLIANT GREEN LEAVES UNFURLED ON TREE BRANCHES, TRILLIUM decorated the forest floor, and a huge fish that bore a slight resemblance to a shark swam slowly up the river's clear waters. Spring was here, and the sturgeon arrived to perform their mating ritual. It was a rare treat to see one of these fish in the wild. For a couple of weeks each spring, when the water is clear and hovers around sixty degrees, these prehistoric fish—part of a species that has roamed the world's waters for 200 million years—conduct their mating ritual in the lower Muskegon. Sturgeon have been known to swim more than one hundred miles upstream to spawn, but their territory here is limited to the lower forty-seven miles of the Muskegon. Croton Dam prevents the fish from swimming any further upstream. As a result, these spectacular, endangered fish could not reach more than fifty miles of prime spawning habitat upstream. The construction of dams is one reason the number of sturgeon that spawn in this river plunged from several thousand in the mid-1800s to fewer than a hundred in 2003.[16]

Commercial fishermen who slaughtered sturgeon by the thousands in the late 1800s because the fish damaged nets and later for caviar were the main reason sturgeon struggle to survive in the Great Lakes. But the sturgeon provided an example of how dams have harmed the Muskegon River ecosystem by isolating most of the river from Lake Michigan.

The dams also have contributed to the decline of freshwater mussels, unionids, that once thrived in the Muskegon. Mussels are not nearly as endearing as sturgeon or salmon, but they served two crucial roles in the river. Mussels helped keep the river clean—a single mussel could filter as much as ten gallons of water per day and, in the process, destroy harmful bacteria. Mussels also were considered an indicator species, helping scientists gauge the health of a river. Unfortunately, a study by the Michigan Natural Features Inventory showed that the mussel population in the Muskegon River was spiraling downward: "It appears that mussel populations have significantly declined and that mussel community structures have become dramatically altered. The observed declines in, and losses of, mussel species richness in the Muskegon River watershed are cause for great concern."[17]

Mussels that lived in the Muskegon depended on fish to survive. After ingesting sperm from the male mussel, the female produced offspring called glochidia. The tiny, clam-shaped glochidia, barely the size of a grain of sand, attached to fish, which was how the mussels were distributed through the river system. Dams in the river restricted the movement of fish and, in turn, the distribution of native mussels. This phenomenon occurred in many of the nation's rivers. "Freshwater native clams are the most endangered animal group in North America," according to the U.S. Geological Survey. "A total of 72 percent of our 270 native mussel species are listed as recently extinct, endangered, threatened, or of special concern. By comparison, only 33 percent of all plants and other animals in the United States are considered at risk, according to the Nature Conservancy."[18]

The primary suspects in the decline of the Muskegon River's mussel population: dams, which altered natural water flows and divided the river and its tributaries into smaller sections; increased siltation of the river bottom from logging and ongoing soil erosion; and competition from nonnative zebra mussels. Many of the mussels found in the Muskegon during the 2002 study were dead.[19] The study painted a picture of one small piece of the river ecosystem that has changed dramatically since the early 1900s, when mussels were so abundant in the river that people harvested them for pearls sold to button makers.[20]

EVERY AUTUMN, MARK AND JEANNETTE KNOPH DROVE ABOUT SIXTY miles south from their home in north-central Michigan to fish for salmon making their fall spawning run up the Pere Marquette River. It was a bitter irony for the couple: They lived along the Muskegon River, the most productive salmon river in the Great Lakes, yet they could not fish for salmon near their home. The trouble was, the Knophs' home, part of the Old Log Resort they owned and operated near Marion, was located upstream of the three hydroelectric dams on the Muskegon. As a result, Mark Knoph must be content to fish for northern pike, walleye, and occasionally trout in the remote, sandy stretch of the Muskegon that flows past his campground resort. He could only dream of walking a short distance from his home to cast for salmon. "The fishing isn't great here. I wish it were better. I'd like to be able to fish for salmon, but I don't see how they could ever take those dams out."[21]

Located about sixty miles north of the Muskegon River, the Pere Marquette River is a scenic, cold-water trout stream that flows unobstructed through the steep bluffs and lush forests of the Manistee National Forest. Known affectionately as the PM among anglers, the Pere Marquette flows

138 miles before emptying into Pere Marquette Lake and Lake Michigan. Many anglers considered the PM one of the finest trout streams in the United States. It was not always that way.

Logging ravaged the PM in the late 1800s, just as the industry did the Muskegon and nearly every other river in Michigan. Unlike the Muskegon, the PM has made an extensive recovery from an era when logjams often turned the river into a boardwalk. The state legislature in 1970 designated the Pere Marquette a Michigan Natural River, and the U.S. Congress named it a National Scenic River in 1977. Those designations reflected the river's recovery and were aimed at allowing the blue-ribbon trout stream to function as the Creator intended. "The Pere Marquette River was known throughout the fishing world as one of the finest free-flowing [that is, without dams] trout streams in North America. The continent's first brown trout releases were made here in 1884, and the P.M. has long held a reputation as one of the country's premier brown trout streams," author Tom Huggler wrote in his 1996 book, *Fish Michigan: Fifty More Rivers*.[22]

The PM, like all rivers, had its share of problems. Remnants of nineteenth-century logging practices—mainly excessive amounts of sand that washed into the river from eroding stream banks and filled in gravel beds and deep holes favored by trout and salmon—still plagued the serenely beautiful river in 2005. And the river's popularity created conflict between canoers, anglers, and riverfront property owners. But the PM has recovered from the devastating effects of logging to a much greater extent than the Muskegon for one reason: no dams were ever built in the main branch of the Pere Marquette. As a result, the river was allowed to reclaim its natural form and function after logging ended. Author David N. Cassuto described the condition of the Pere Marquette in the 1930s in his book, *Cold Running River:*

> Thirty years after the end of the logging era, local fishing guides made quite a decent living showing visiting anglers how to catch trout that, thanks to improved habitat and government [fish] stocking programs, once again filled the river. Free flowing, exceptionally clean, and relatively free of development, the Pere Marquette has led a charmed life when compared to, say, the Colorado.[23]

Or the Muskegon.

4.

SMALL WONDERS

> Clearly a lot of the dams in Michigan serve public purposes for recreation and power generation, but many of them could come out.
>
> —Sharon Hanshue, dam specialist, Michigan Department of Natural Resources

A cluster of nature's skyscrapers rose high above the forest floor, reaching toward the heavens for sunlight and water while creating the illusion of dusk far below the dense canopy. Tiny raindrops fell from the sky, but only a fraction passed through the woven brown branches and deep green needles that covered the top half of the mammoth Eastern white pines. These regal giants, *Pinus strobus,* were the few survivors of a nineteenth-century logging era that claimed nearly all of Michigan's virgin pine forests.

One of these majestic trees was particularly striking. As tall as a fifteen-story building and measuring six feet in diameter at its base, the tree appeared to have lost its crown. There were no needles on its branches, and the mottled bark showed signs of an insect infestation. A brochure describing the virgin forest at Hartwick Pines State Park told the story: in 1992, strong winds knocked about 30 or 40 feet off the top of the 155-foot-tall tree, nicknamed Monarch, triggering a chain of events that slowly destroyed it. Without its needle canopy, Monarch lost the ability to photosynthesize—it could no longer feed itself by absorbing carbon dioxide and water into its needles. Lacking food and with insects invading its broken trunk, the tree succumbed over the course of four years. It now waits for the final insult—falling to the ground, where its trunk will slowly dissolve into dirt.[1]

Long before lumber barons exerted their rapacious will on Michigan's virgin forests and pristine rivers, the white pine was the botanical king. The trees, which could live for four centuries and reach a height of 220 feet, were a model of botanical efficiency. Collecting moisture and nutrients in its needles, the *P. strobus* distributed nutrients downward through phloem, a thin layer of porous material inside the tree's bark. Inside the phloem was the xylem, which carried nutrients from the roots to the leaves. On its surface, the white pine displayed little activity, barely swaying when the wind howled through its limbs. Inside the rough bark that encased the tree was an altogether different scene—water and sugars traveled up and down a porous wooden highway, fueling rapid growth and incredible durability.

Natural stands of white pine rarely stagnated, and only a few of the insects and diseases known to attack white pines were capable of causing serious injury or mortality.[2] *P. strobus* was a tree among trees, nurturing wildlife and sheltering rivers that flowed through the shadows it cast across the rolling hills and lowland forests of the northeastern United States.

Glaciers that crushed rock into sandy soils and silt as the mile-thick layers of ice advanced and retreated across the Midwest during the last Ice Age created ideal growing conditions for the white pine: fertile, porous soils flush with water. Over the course of ten thousand years, the northern half of Michigan's landscape evolved from a biological desert into a lush pine forest interspersed with smaller stands of maple, beech, and oak. *P. strobus* ruled the land until nineteenth-century pioneers unleashed a killer wind that laid waste to the forest and the rivers it protected. When the carnage ended, Michigan was again a barren wasteland, and crystal-clear rivers that once teemed with giant sturgeon and colorful grayling were in critical condition.

For thousands of years before logging crews arrived, the Muskegon River system was the aquatic equivalent of *P. strobus*. Sturgeon and other migratory fish in Lake Michigan could swim 219 miles up the river to Higgins Lake, provided they could successfully dodge predators and avoid death by exhaustion. Leaves, insects, and sediment moved down the winding, undulating river channel without interruption. Icy water and nutrients from the river's many tributaries flowed into the trunk, feeding the entire system; conversely, fish and snakes, mink and otter were free to move upstream, just as water flowed up from the roots of a white pine to nourish the tree's core. That was before a second destructive wind blew across the river valley, planting dams in the Muskegon River system like seeds in fertile soil.

The result: The river and its network of tributaries functioned like a pine tree that has been cut into sections and stuck together to resemble its original form. The hacked-up pine may have looked like a tree, but the appearance was entirely misleading. Natural processes that moved water and nutrients up and down the trunk and fed all parts of the tree no longer worked. The tree was broken and headed for an early death. So it was in the Muskegon River system at the beginning of the twentieth century.

A BLUE-RIBBON TROUT STREAM, MUCH LIKE FINE WINE, DEVELOPS OVER a long period of time. Miles before it supported wild trout, the Middle Branch River evolved from the gurgling brook that flowed out of tiny Hicks Lake in northwest lower Michigan. The small river's thirty-three-mile journey from Hicks Lake to the Muskegon River meandered through soybean fields and cow pastures, swamps and small forests before passing through the former logging village of Marion.

Five miles upstream of Marion, the river became large enough to support a resident population of wild trout. Its frigid, crystalline waters, home to a healthy community of insects that trout crave, were shallow enough to wade across but large enough to permit fly casting. This stretch of the Middle Branch earned the designation blue-ribbon trout stream.[3] It was one of just two state-designated blue-ribbon trout streams in the Muskegon River system (the Clam River is the other) and was one of the principal tributaries flowing into the mother river. This section of the Middle Branch was a special place in nature, a river clean and cold enough to support a wild population of brook trout. Here the river snaked around bends and tumbled over rocks for three miles, picking up speed as it fell seven feet per mile before hitting the wall known as the Marion Dam. The old, obsolete dam stopped the Middle Branch dead in its meandering tracks, strangled the wild river and stored its water in a small reservoir. The artificial pond acted like a water heater, increasing the river's temperature before sending it on its way toward the Muskegon. Marion writer Jim Lithen eloquently described the dam's transformation of the river:

> The upper river, unimpeded by man for the better part of its journey, has now felt its first sting of civilization as it moves south under Jones Bridge and prepares to enter the Marion Mill Pond, which it does in a wide, shallow, sandy-bottomed fashion. In the square mile that is the village of Marion, the river falls approximately 16 to 18 feet, with 10 to 12 feet of this being at the Marion Dam. . . . [T]his is the most drastic drop in the entire river's gradient and it is likely a waterfall or whitewater rapids were located here before the damming of the river.[4]

During the summer, when lovers cuddled on a manicured lawn near the dam's spillway and kids splashed in a swimming hole downstream of the structure, water temperatures in the Marion millpond increased as much as thirteen degrees. On average, water temperatures in the pond were between six and eight degrees Fahrenheit warmer than in the free-flowing river upstream. It was a radical warmup for a state-protected trout stream where normal water temperatures were in the sixties just two miles upstream of the dam. The river heated up because water held in the millpond was exposed to more sunlight and heat than the free-flowing stream, much of which was sheltered by a canopy of trees that blotted out the sun. This phenomenon, thermal pollution, was prevalent near many of the ninety small dams that harnessed and heated up water in the Muskegon and its tributaries. It was a serious form of pollution in the river system, one that could transform the Muskegon's main branch into a warm-water river and endanger a trout and salmon fishery downstream of Croton Dam valued at $2 million.[5]

"Thermal pollution has been identified as a major pollutant in the Muskegon River Watershed due to the potential effects to both the cool and cold water stream sections during the warm water months," according to a 2002 Grand Valley State University study. "Some of the major sources of thermal pollution to the Muskegon River Watershed are lake-level control structures, hydroelectric facilities and dams that are located throughout the watershed. Lack of streamside canopy, water inputs from drainage networks, and water withdrawals for irrigation also are known to contribute to thermal pollution, especially in agricultural and urban areas of the watershed. Increases in any of these sources may increase the loading of warm water to a stream, which may adversely affect the cold water fishery, other aquatic organisms and, in extreme cases, the warm water fishery."[6]

Thermal pollution is just half of the two-headed environmental monster that dams unleashed in the Muskegon River system. The other was ecosystem fragmentation—a fancy way of saying that dams have broken the river into a series of shorter, ecologically disjointed streams.

CHRISTOPHER CLARK WAS NOT ON A MISSION TO DESTROY THE MIDDLE Branch River when he arrived in Michigan's dense pine forest in 1875. The Irish-born millwright and his Canadian-born wife, Marion, were typical of thousands of nineteenth-century European immigrants who headed west to carve a better life out of the wilderness. Upon their arrival in northern Michigan, the Clarks set up camp in the pine forest and opened a general store in what would become the village of Marion. They purchased 240 acres of land from Ryerson, Hills, and Company, the firm founded by Muskegon lumber baron Martin Ryerson.

In 1878, Clark built a small dam on the Middle Branch to power his sawmill. The dam created a small pond from which water was drawn to power the saws that transformed huge pine logs into boards, lathe, and shingles. For three decades, Clark's mill and dozens of others like it in the Muskegon River basin churned out the pine siding, shingles, flooring, lathe, and molding used to build homes across the Midwest. Clark's mill burned down in 1909, just as logging in northwestern Michigan was grinding to a halt—few trees remained to be cut.

Although fire destroyed Clark's mill, the dam that powered it remained. Marion Clark donated the dam and millpond it created to the village of Marion in 1911 for use as a park. The original dam was replaced in 1930 with the current structure, which was designated a state historic site in 1999.[7] The dam and millpond were considered community treasures. Local residents protested vehemently in 1998 when fish biologists from the Michigan Department of Natural Resources suggested removing the dam to restore the natural river. "It has a lot of history and there is a very strong community commitment to keeping this dam," Marion Village President Doug Cutler said in an interview. "The people in this community are not real happy about the possibility of losing their dam or mill pond."[8]

A sheet of water slid through the dam's spillway, creating soothing white noise as it spilled over the edge of a concrete ramp and plunged into the lower Middle Branch River. On warm summer days, the hiss of flowing water was periodically drowned out by rambunctious children playfully threatening to push friends into the river. Couples took romantic strolls on a path over the spillway. For more than a century, this small dam has been the centerpiece of Marion, which claimed to be the artesian well capital of Michigan. Motorists traveling through the village routinely parked illegally on a bridge just downstream, got out of their cars, and snapped pictures of the beloved dam and millpond. Few realized they were photographing a structure that has wreaked environmental havoc on a portion of the Middle Branch for more than a century. This was the grim reality at the Marion Dam and other sites where small dams strangle and cause fevers in a network of streams that make up the lifeblood of the Muskegon River.

The multitude of dams scattered about Michigan's rivers were built for a variety of reasons—to power sawmills, maintain artificially high water levels in recreational lakes, and create marshes for waterfowl and irrigation ponds for farmers. Those dams varied greatly in size but had the same general effect on rivers and streams. Dams break a river's vast web of flowing water into smaller, ecologically dysfunctional units.

Building dams was one of the first orders of business for many European immigrants who streamed into Michigan in the mid-1800s to seek their fortune in logging. Dams constituted a simple and efficient way to power sawmills in the decades before scientists harnessed electricity. Settlers from the eastern United States knew that the easiest way to power a sawmill was to build a dam that would use the river's current to create the horsepower needed to move giant saw blades that turned huge pine logs into boards and shingles. Many of those early Michigan residents came from New England, where lumber companies had been using dams to power sawmills since the 1700s.

The first dam in the Muskegon River system, built in 1837, powered the Penoyer sawmill on Penoyer Creek in Newaygo. When it came time to cut logs, water from the dam's reservoir was released into a mill raceway, a narrow channel that often funneled water into a waterwheel, which spun a camshaft that moved a large saw blade up and down, much like a giant jigsaw. As logging spread across the Muskegon River basin, the number of sawmills and dams in the river system multiplied.

In 1854, lumbermen built the first dam across the main branch of the Muskegon River, in Newaygo. A low-lying structure built with logs, the dam powered the Big Red Mill, the largest sawmill in Michigan at the time. At its peak, the mill featured one hundred saws and ten turbine wheels powered by the force of the harnessed river.[9] The Newaygo Dam collapsed twice and was rebuilt both times. It remained in the river until 1969, when the state removed it. In 1866, a second dam was built across the river to power a sawmill in Big Rapids. The Big Rapids dam was converted into the Muskegon River's first hydroelectric dam in 1889. It was rebuilt once and remained in the river until its last remnants were removed in 2001.

Dams also were used in the 1800s to force logs down narrow, shallow creeks during the spring run. On dozens of tiny streams, logging companies built small earth and wooden dams with V-shaped spillways, or flumes, in the middle of the structure. By stacking logs in the flume, lumbermen could raise the water level behind the dam while stockpiling scores of logs in a reservoir behind the structure. When sufficient water pressure had been created behind the dam, the flume was busted open, sending water and the logs crashing downstream. In some cases, several dams and flumes were built on a single stream to move logs downstream in narrow channels until they reached the main branch of the Muskegon. At the time, it was the most efficient way to transport huge logs weighing thousands of pounds from the forest to sawmills in Big Rapids, Newaygo, and Muskegon.[10]

Some small dams washed out when lumber barons abandoned mills when there were no trees to feed into the saws. Dozens remained, however. The fact that many of those small dams no longer served their original purpose and have exceeded the average fifty-year life span of a dam often mattered little in communities where the structures were located.[11]

Dams were an integral part of many small towns across Michigan. In numerous cases, communities have rallied to save dams when government biologists have suggested that removing the structures would benefit rivers or creeks. By and large, people loved dams for reasons usually related to aesthetics and history. Rarely would you hear an informed person argue that dams benefited river ecosystems. Such claims defied logic and ignored the obvious: dams destroyed flowing water.

The beginning of the Muskegon River was disrupted by three dams in the first fifteen miles of its main branch. Two small dams maintained artificially high water levels in Higgins and Houghton Lakes, and the state-owned Reedsburg Dam backed up the river into a 540-acre pond for ducks and other waterfowl. By the time the river was turned loose, it had been deprived of millions of gallons of water, and its channel had been altered by human-created ponds and lakes where water levels were elevated for the benefit of hunters and boaters.

Logging was often blamed for ruining Michigan's rivers. Dams were equally culpable, and most of the ninety-four dams still standing in the Muskegon River system were built after logging ceased in 1905. The first half of the twentieth century represented a period of intense dam construction across the United States, including the nation's most famous dam, the Hoover Dam, near Las Vegas.

At the beginning of the twenty-first century, more than seventy-five thousand dams larger than six feet high existed on rivers in the United States, with tens of thousands of smaller dams. On average, one dam was built every day during the first two hundred years of U.S. history. More than 600,000 miles of rivers in the United States are now impounded behind dams. Only forty-two large rivers more than 125 miles long still flow uninterrupted by dams.[12]

The number of dams in the Muskegon River system soared following completion of Hardy Dam in 1931. Over the next fifty years, nearly eighty small dams were built in the creeks, streams, and small rivers that flowed into the Muskegon. Because most of these dams were small—the average height of the ninety-four state-registered dams in the Muskegon River system was 11.7 feet—many were hard to find, and most appeared to be harmless.

The dam that maintained artificially high lake levels in Cadillac and Mitchell lakes stood just six feet high and held back three feet of water from the Clam River, a blue-ribbon trout stream several miles downstream of the lakes. The dam that controlled water levels on Brooks Lake, in Newaygo County, was just two feet high.

In Mecosta County, a hilly region that marked the geographic middle of the Muskegon River basin, twenty-five dams were built to maintain high water levels for swimmers and boaters and to create ponds for ducks and duck hunters.[13] It was ironic that the Michigan Department of Natural Resources—the government agency that advocated removing all obsolete and dangerous dams in Michigan in the 1990s—owned three times more dams in the Muskegon River system (eighteen) than any other individual or organization. The agency built scores of dams in Michigan, including the Reedsburg Dam near the headwaters of the Muskegon, to create waterfowl habitat. Critics of the department said that the agency's campaign to liberate Michigan rivers from the grip of dams amounts to hypocrisy.

By the time the frenzy of dam construction in the Muskegon River waned in 1980, dams ruled vast areas of the river and its tributaries. Only then were scientists beginning to understand the many ways that dams disrupt rivers. The U.S. Geological Survey, for decades an advocate of dam construction, issued a statement in 1996 that reflected changing attitudes toward dams: "Dams provide many benefits—reducing flood hazards, providing reliable water supplies, producing hydroelectric power and providing places for flat water boating. But with those benefits come environmental consequences—eroding river banks, changes in waterfowl habitat, concerns for safe recreational use and the loss of river sandbars."[14]

For the Muskegon River, that cautionary statement came two decades too late. The damage had been done.

THERMAL POLLUTION COULD CHANGE THE MUSKEGON'S MAIN BRANCH, the largest cool-water river in Michigan, into a warm-water river with a vastly different community of fish.[15] Efforts to maintain the Muskegon's cool-water status may succeed or fail in the dozens of cold-water streams that flow into the river. The abundance of those streams, coupled with the huge amounts of fifty-eight-degree groundwater that continuously seep into the river from underground springs, are the reason the Muskegon is a cool-water river in a geographic region where large, warm-water rivers are the norm. The health of these small streams would play a large role in determining the fate of fish communities in the Muskegon River. "If the tributaries are in bad shape, it's very difficult for the main stem to be in good shape," according to Mike Wiley, a University of Michigan aquatic ecologist studying the Muskegon.[16]

Dams also caused a more fundamental problem—ecosystem fragmentation. Unless equipped with effective fish ladders—few of which existed in the Muskegon River system—dams prevented the natural movement of fish, certain wildlife, insects, sediment, and nutrients up and down the river channel. Their movement was restricted to a section of river between two dams.

Fish and other aquatic life in sixteen miles of the Middle Branch River below Marion Dam, for example, could not reach the upper river. Conversely, sediment from the upper river could not reach its natural destination in the lower river because it gets trapped in the dam's millpond. Brown and brook trout were more abundant in the Middle Branch, above Marion Dam, than below it. Reconnecting the sections of the river by removing the dam and millpond would improve the lower Middle Branch and the Muskegon River, according to a 2002 study conducted by Rich O'Neal, the state fisheries biologist:

> Coldwater streams are a limited resource in lower Michigan, where approximately 25 percent of stream segments are classified as cold water. Restoring habitat conditions in the lower Middle Branch River will contribute, and is essential, to overall protection and restoration of the Muskegon River watershed. The Middle Branch is one of the principal tributaries of this system. The stream has some of the most productive gradient reaches [river slope] for fisheries in the watershed, and especially in the upper portion of the watershed.[17]

Each section of a river bisected by a dam was in many ways a stream unto itself, with little ecological relationship to the water upstream or downstream of the structure. Large dams caused greater change because they submerged longer stretches of river under artificial reservoirs known as impoundments. But it was really just a matter of degree. All dams disrupted the river's natural processes. "The effect of dams is the least reversible of all forms of river degradation. The dam—a discontinuity—creates a break in a line, an obstacle not only to water, but also to plants and animals that evolved to benefit from the river's continuity," according to Thomas F. Waters, a fisheries biologist and author of *Wildstream: A Natural History of the Free Flowing River*.[18]

Dams have broken the Muskegon River system—once a cohesive network of rivers, creeks, lakes, and wetlands—into more than a hundred ecologically isolated sections. Imagine the treelike shape of the Muskegon River system portrayed in a clay sculpture. The main branch would be a thick vein of clay, with the tributaries thinner strands of clay reaching out like the branches of a tree. Drop the sculpture on a cement floor, and it would smash into numerous pieces. This is the current condition of the Muskegon River's ecosystem. "It really comes back to dams; that's probably the thing that is most wrong with the Muskegon River," according to Paul Seelbach, a research manager with the Michigan Department of Natural Resources.[19]

For the better part of two summers, Catherine Riseng led a group of scientists who spent brutally long days wading in creeks and slogging through swamps in the Muskegon River basin. Their mission: document the number of fish living in the small streams that flow into the river's main branch. To their surprise, Riseng's research team found that almost every cold-water stream that flowed into the Muskegon supported healthy populations of trout, an indicator of good water quality. Fish were more sparse near dams and lake level-control structures and near farms where manure drains off fields and livestock were allowed to wallow and defecate in streams. "Most of the creeks are in good shape, depending on what farm they're next to," according to Riseng, a University of Michigan research scientist. "Some creeks, like Brooks Creek, are in bad shape because there is lots of agriculture, especially row crops, in its watershed."[20]

Creeks that emptied into the lower river in the city of Muskegon were severely distressed. Ryerson, Ruddiman, and Bear Creeks, which flowed into Muskegon Lake, supported few fish. No wonder: all were severely polluted by foundries and chemical companies that for decades used the streams around Muskegon Lake as a dumping ground for toxic chemicals and foundry slag.

The ecological benefits of cleaning up the Muskegon's few polluted tributaries and reconnecting dozens of other streams bisected by dams cannot be overstated, according to O'Neal:

> The tributaries are very important to the health of the Muskegon River. The river system is like a human body. You have main arteries and smaller veins. If you lose enough of those veins and arteries, you could lose an arm or a leg,

> and if you keep going, you could lose the whole system. It's the same with the river. It's the cumulative effects. . . . The introduction of exotic species [alewife and sea lamprey] didn't kill the Lake Michigan fishery overnight. It was a long-term series of small changes in the Great Lakes and rivers that brought about those changes. Exotics, dams, land use—all of those things eventually led to huge changes in the fishery.[21]

ONE OF THE MOST POLITICALLY CORRECT TERMS IN MICHIGAN'S LEXICON of resource management is *lake-level control structure*. These structures—which maintain unnaturally high water levels in lakes to promote recreational boating—are dams, plain and simple. They do not produce electricity or power sawmills, but lake-level control structures served the same basic purpose as dams by holding back flowing water. By placing these dams where lakes empty into streams, lake associations and other groups could control water levels in their particular lake, creeks be damned. Hundreds of these structures pumped up Michigan lakes at the expense of rivers and creeks downstream.

In many cases, lake-level control structures deprived creeks of water at their headwaters. The Clam River, which emptied into the upper Muskegon River, offered a prime example of how a lake-level control structure could harm a creek. The Clam flows out of Lake Cadillac, a popular recreational lake in northern Michigan. In addition to starving the creek, the lake-level control structure fed the Clam River an unhealthy diet of warm water from the lake.

The fact that the river reclaimed itself a few miles downstream and is in fact a blue-ribbon trout stream was a minor ecological miracle. The trout stream was short-lived, however; the fifteen-foot-high Falmouth Dam snuffed out the Clam River again, storing and warming water in a twenty-three-acre pond before releasing it downstream. This scenario played out in dozens of creeks and small rivers that flowed into the Muskegon's main branch.

Few lake-level control structures have been as controversial as the one at the outlet of Houghton Lake, the headwaters of the Muskegon River. In 1938, a small log dam was built where Houghton Lake empties into the Deadstream Marsh. Built twelve years after the first dam was constructed and the courts established a "legal lake level," the dam owned by the Roscommon County Road Commission was supposed to maintain consistent water levels in what was a large, deep marsh. By order of the Circuit Court, the legal lake level in Houghton Lake was set at 1,138.1 feet above sea level. For decades, that level seemed reasonable—people cruised the lake in boats, and towering stands of wild rice occupied thousands of acres in the thirty-one-square-mile lake. R. D. Ustipak, a scientist who studied the lake's rice beds in 1995, praised the court's 1926 decision, which was reaffirmed in 1982:

> It is remarkable that a Circuit Court was able to set a level which allowed increased recreational use of the lake yet preserved many of its fishery and wildlife values. We must be aware that with so many people having so many diverse interests in the lake, it is impossible to satisfy everyone. Therefore, management should be focused on doing what is right by the resource. The entire ecology of Houghton Lake is hanging in the balance and must be addressed before it is lost to future generations.[22]

Ustipak warned that increasing water levels any further in Houghton Lake could have disastrous consequences for wild rice beds that included *Zizania aquatica,* a type of rice listed as a threatened species in Michigan. The next year, the Roscommon County Board of Commissioners struck a deal with the Michigan Department of Natural Resources to maintain water levels in Houghton Lake six inches above the legal level. That agreement was reached at the urging of some property owners and local business groups, who complained that weeds were making large parts of the lake impassable for boats. Ustipak's prediction became reality. In a 1998 study, Central Michigan University graduate student Donald J. Bonnette wrote,

> In recent years, the Roscommon County Board of Commissioners who are responsible for lake level management at Houghton Lake . . . have managed summer lake levels far above the legal level in direct violation of the law. The purpose of regulating the lake above legal level was to increase recreational opportunities for the boating public. The decline of wild rice occurred around the same time that Roscommon County began to increase summer lake levels. This does not imply that increased water levels were directly

> responsible for the decline, however, high water levels may have contributed to the decline in some way. Any long term increase in water depth through the growing season will hinder wild rice reestablishment.[23]

Bonnette concluded that efforts to reestablish stands of wild rice in Houghton Lake would be futile unless the water level was lowered to the legal level. That has not happened. As a result, efforts to reestablish wild rice stands in Houghton Lake have failed; in 2005, but a few stalks of this important plant species remained in the lake. The loss of wild rice in Houghton Lake represented just one of many examples of how human wants have superceded the Muskegon River ecosystem's needs.

Houghton Lake's wild rice stands were devastated in 1989, when ice floes ripped acres of rice from the lake bottom and deposited it on the shore. With the rice stands depleted, the lake water became murkier and more suited to exotic plant species, such as Eurasian water milfoil. Boat props also chopped up many wild rice plants. "In the years following 1989, wild rice was essentially eliminated from Houghton Lake," Bonnette wrote in his study.

On a typical summer day, hundreds of boats cruise the vast expanse of Houghton Lake, which spans twenty thousand acres and has few natural obstacles. The greatest challenge may be avoiding other boaters and the ubiquitous Jet Skis. Since 1980, Houghton Lake has come to resemble a very large swimming pool that supports lots of panfish. Much of the lake's natural shoreline, which property owners saw as marshy, wet, and useless, has been filled in so that cottages could be built closer to the water. Cottage owners then built seawalls to keep the lake from spilling onto their manicured lawns; more than 80 percent of Houghton Lake's shoreline now consists of concrete, stone, or steel seawalls.[24] A boaters' paradise, to be sure, but a far cry from the lake European settlers discovered when they arrived in the mid-1800s. Many of the changes can be traced back to the lake-level control structure, a type of small dam that caused big changes in Michigan's largest inland lake.

AUTHOR NORMAN MACLEAN WROTE WHAT MAY NOW BE THE MOST COMMONLY recited line when talk turns to rivers. Maclean in 1976 wrote the novel, *A River Runs through It*, which was popularized by a major motion picture of the same name that featured Brad Pitt. The film turned one of the book's most memorable lines into a cliché. "Eventually, all things merge into one," Maclean wrote, "and a river runs through it."

Taken literally, Maclean's observation did not apply to many rivers, including the Muskegon. This is not a criticism of Maclean. Rather, it is the harsh reality where dams have turned rivers into linear collections of broken water. The small dams on the Muskegon's tributaries starved the main branch of the river, depriving it of cold water, native fish, insects, sediment, and nutrients. As a result, all things in the Muskegon River valley could not merge into one and be carried downstream by the river—dams do not allow it.

5.

ALIEN INVASION

> We're one ballast tank away from a creature which could bring utter devastation to the Great Lakes.
>
> —DENNIS LAVIS, U.S. FISH AND WILDLIFE SERVICE BIOLOGIST, 2003

THE SERENITY OF A SUN-DRENCHED AFTERNOON ON LAKE MICHIGAN was shattered when a large fish struck, bending the fishing pole locked onto the back of the boat into the shape of an inverted U. "Fish on," the charter boat captain yelled. The young angler jumped up from his seat, grabbed the pole, and thrust it into his midsection for leverage. Adrenaline coursed through his body as the fish took off, ripping hundreds of feet of line off the reel. After a valiant struggle the fish grew tired and was reeled into the boat. What should have been be a joyous event was dashed by a ghastly wound on the 20-pound Chinook salmon.

The bloody, quarter-sized scar was the calling card of the sea lamprey, an eel-like fish native to the Atlantic Ocean. Known as Dracula of the Great Lakes, sea lamprey preyed on Great Lakes sport fish coveted by anglers—salmon, trout, and walleye. The sea lamprey has no jaw, but its disklike mouth, sharp teeth, and rasping bite allowed it to bore into the side of a fish and suck its bodily fluids. Fish often died from the wounds or subsequent infection.

The sea lamprey was one of 180 exotic species—nonnative fish, plants, invertebrates, and crustaceans—imported to the Great Lakes over the past two centuries.[1] Most alien species entered the lakes after the St. Lawrence Seaway opened in 1959. The Seaway allowed ocean freighters to reach ports on all five Great Lakes from the Atlantic Ocean. But those ships often carried exotic species in ballast water, which was routinely dumped in the lakes until the mid-1990s. As a result, alien species of fish, plants, and mussels from around the globe have taken up residence in the lakes and turned the Muskegon and other rivers that feed these inland seas into nurseries for nuisance creatures. This complex and costly problem represented an unintended consequence of humanity's determination to control nature.

Before humans altered the Great Lakes to boost the region's economy, these inland seas constituted a model of biological integrity. Covering a surface area of ninety-four thousand square miles and large enough to be seen from outer space, the lakes were a closed system, biologically isolated from the oceans that surrounded North America and large rivers in the continent's interior. Glaciers that formed the Great Lakes left two natural barriers that prevented fish and other organisms living in the world's oceans from reaching the lakes: Niagara Falls and rapids in the St. Lawrence River.

Water from four of the five Great Lakes—Superior, Michigan, Huron, and Erie—spilled over the 180-foot high Niagara Falls near Buffalo, New York. Lake Ontario was the only Great Lake with a direct connection to the Atlantic Ocean, by way of the St. Lawrence River. But the river's fierce current through rapids near Montreal prevented saltwater fish and other aquatic life in the Atlantic from reaching Lake Ontario.

For more than eight thousand years, the St. Lawrence River's rapids and the thunderous Niagara Falls kept saltwater species from entering the Great Lakes. By the late 1800s, the lakes supported what may have been the world's richest freshwater fishery. Anglers annually hauled in millions of pounds of native fish—sturgeon, lake trout, whitefish, chub, perch, and walleye. But there was trouble brewing during those glorious days of Great Lakes sport fishing. Humans built canals in the early 1800s to bypass Niagara Falls, opening the lakes to oceangoing ships and transforming the Great Lakes region into a global economic force. But the canals created a pathway for saltwater species to enter the Great Lakes, a change that would wreak ecological havoc a century later. The U.S. government spent $12 million annually in the 1990s to control one exotic species—the voracious sea lamprey—by poisoning dozens of Great Lakes rivers where they breed. Chemical treatments represented the most efficient way to control the predator, which in the mid-twentieth century nearly eliminated lake trout from the Great Lakes.[2]

On a warm August day, a crew of four scientists gathered along the banks of the Muskegon River to kill thousands of fish. Their target: 2.5 million larval lamprey growing in the silt of streams that flow into the river below Croton Dam. Biologists and technicians from the U.S. Fish and Wildlife Service pumped carefully calculated amounts of a toxic chemical known as TFM into the river. Their goal was to kill as many small lamprey as possible before the slinky pests matured and swam out to Lake Michigan. Adult lamprey that reached the lakes fed for between twelve and twenty months before returning to rivers to spawn before dying; a single lamprey could kill forty pounds of Great Lakes fish before migrating upstream.

On any other occasion, dumping a toxic chemical into these streams would spark public outrage and draw stiff fines from regulatory agencies. But this fish kill was justified. Without the chemical treatment, lamprey populations would explode and cause another Great Lakes fish massacre. The ability of government agencies to reduce the lamprey population by 90 percent and keep it in check constitutes a Great Lakes success story.[3] Unfortunately, there was no similar way to control many other nonnative species of fish, plants, and mussels that have given the Great Lakes and its numerous tributaries an unwanted biological makeover.

SCHEMES TO BUILD CANALS THAT WOULD LINK THE GREAT LAKES WITH the Atlantic Ocean were floated as far back as the late 1600s. Not until the late 1700s, however, did the booming fur trade spark the first effort to build a canal to skirt natural barriers in the Great Lakes system. In 1779, work began on a series of three locks and canals in the St. Lawrence River between Montreal and Lake St. Francis. Just 40 feet long, 7 feet wide, and 2.5 feet deep, these modest locks—the first canals built in North America—were deep enough to allow fur-trading boats to navigate the St. Lawrence River rapids.[4]

The success of that canal sparked more grandiose plans. In 1829, the Welland Canal was built in Ontario to bypass the Canadian side of Niagara Falls. The canal was the first navigable link between Lake Erie and Lake Ontario and was large enough to allow passage of schooners up to one hundred feet long. Before construction began in 1824, the brains behind the Welland Canal—a young Canadian businessman named William Hamilton Merritt—said that the project would join the Great Lakes and the ocean: "We will remove the only natural barrier of importance—the Falls of Niagara."[5] A year before the completion of the Welland Canal, Merritt conceived of a much grander set of locks that would carry oceangoing freighters over rapids in the St. Lawrence River and open all five of the Great Lakes to oceangoing ships. Merritt's critics snickered at the proposal, calling him an "extravagant theorist."[6] But his vision eventually became reality.

Canada enlarged the Welland Canal in 1932, making this first section of the St. Lawrence Seaway large enough to give oceangoing freighters access to the interior of North America. In 1959, after nearly a century of wrangling, the U.S. and Canadian governments opened the last section of locks, completing the St. Lawrence Seaway's massive network of canals, locks, and hydroelectric dams. Completion of the St. Lawrence Seaway was celebrated with great fanfare. President Dwight Eisenhower and Queen Elizabeth met at St. Lambert, across the St. Lawrence River from Montreal, to mark the occasion. After making congratulatory remarks, they boarded the royal yacht, *Britannia,* and headed up the river through the massive St. Lawrence locks. Author Carleton Mabee described the scene and its significance:

> The Great Lakes–St. Lawrence Seaway was open. Man had redesigned the continent. He had given it an interior seacoast with a more productive hinterland than any of its other coasts, on the Atlantic, Pacific, Arctic or Gulf of Mexico. . . . In what may be the Seaway's greatest significance, it will encourage the growth of a world outlook in the one isolated center of North America.[7]

These pioneering engineers had done more than conquer the barriers that had protected the Great Lakes. Their work opened an ecological Pandora's box. The Welland Canal and St. Lawrence Seaway became pipelines for exotic species from all parts of the globe—plants, animals, and microbes that would make the Great Lakes ecosystem the site of one of the world's largest unplanned biological experiments.

Some exotic species were accidentally imported to the Great Lakes from Asia and Europe; others, such as carp, were intentionally introduced. Sea lamprey were first spotted in Lake Erie in 1921, nearly a century after the Welland Canal bypassed Niagara Falls. Within twenty-five years, the bloodsuckers had spread to all the Great Lakes. Lamprey were found in Lake Huron in 1932, in Lake Michigan in 1936, and Lake Superior in 1946. The snakelike fish feasted on lake trout, driving one of the Great Lakes' top predators to the brink of elimination.

Before sea lamprey entered the Great Lakes, commercial fishing operations in the United States and Canada harvested 15 million pounds of lake trout annually from Lakes Superior and Huron. In the early 1960s, that figure plunged to 300,000 pounds.[8] Lamprey also attacked and killed other sport fish, including lake whitefish, herring, chub, and even giant sturgeon. But the lamprey's devastation of lake trout triggered a domino effect that would profoundly change fish communities in the Great Lakes and indirectly affect large rivers such as the Muskegon.

As the number of lake trout plummeted in the Great Lakes, another alien saltwater fish, alewife, enjoyed a population explosion. By the mid-1960s, alewife accounted for 85 percent of fish biomass in Lake Michigan. The small, silver fish competed fiercely for native fish but had a weakness: the alewife struggles to survive in the extremely cold water temperatures that dominate the Great Lakes each winter. With few lake trout to control the alewife population, millions of dead, smelly alewives began washing up on Great Lakes beaches in the 1960s.

Alewife were the reason the Muskegon River and lakes Michigan and Huron supported a salmon fishery. In 1966, officials at the Michigan Department of Natural Resources (DNR) decided that the best way to control the runaway alewife population, which kept people from enjoying beaches, was to introduce a new top predator fish species in the Great Lakes. Instead of propping up the decimated lake trout population, DNR officials began stocking salmon—more voracious predators—in the Muskegon and other rivers that flow into Lake Michigan. This intentional introduction of an exotic species—salmon are native to the Pacific and Atlantic oceans—met with overwhelming success.

Salmon grew quickly by feasting on alewife. By the mid-1980s, salmon were the cornerstone of a Great Lakes sport fishery valued at $4 billion. As with other human activities, the introduction of salmon into Lake Michigan changed the ecosystem of the lake and its tributaries. Howard Tanner, the DNR director who made the decision to battle alewife by importing salmon, never second-guessed his actions. He explained his rationale for stocking salmon in a 1991 interview:

> I think we have a totally altered system and we have to live with what we have. Not only that, it is still changing. People often say, "What have you done to the Great Lakes fishery?" And I say, "All right, which native species do you want. The brook trout is not native. The rainbow or steelhead is not native. The native lake trout of Lake Michigan is gone. Which native species do you want me to manage for? Tell me and I will try. But I don't have a native species. . . ." If it had been a stable, natural system, that is one thing. But we have been disrupting the Great Lakes system and fish population for a hundred years or more.[9]

Three decades after salmon were first stocked in Lake Michigan tributaries, DNR officials declared the Muskegon River the most productive chinook salmon stream in Michigan. Between 100,000 and 300,000 chinook salmon hatch every year in the river below Croton Dam. The state stocked another 150,000 chinook in the same forty-mile section of the river between Croton Dam and Muskegon. Each spring, thousands of salmon and lamprey migrated from the lower Muskegon River into Lake Michigan. One was a prized fish, the other a pariah. Neither species was native to Michigan waters.[10]

BY 1980, GOVERNMENT SCIENTISTS WERE RIDING A WAVE OF CONFIDENCE in the battle against exotic species. They had reason to be proud. The sea lamprey and alewife populations were under control, and biologists had figured out how to keep those exotics from again wreaking havoc on the Great Lakes ecosystem. That was not to say the exotic species problem had been solved. Numerous other nonnative species were causing changes in the lakes and major tributaries.

Carp, which were intentionally imported to North American rivers in the early 1800s, had spread throughout the Great Lakes region by the middle of the twentieth century. A large, bottom-feeding fish that uproots aquatic plants favored by other fish and waterfowl, carp became the dominant species by weight in the Muskegon River.

The rusty crayfish, known as the Terminator, drove its native cousins from the river. Purple loosestrife, a pretty but troublesome plant, squeezed out native plants in many wetlands along the river. And Eurasian water milfoil, which grows in thick mats that disrupt boat traffic, would soon gain entry into the headwaters of the Muskegon River. By 1990, a dozen exotic species were living in the Muskegon River system, making it a microcosm of a much larger problem.[11]

All exotic species affect the Great Lakes ecosystem in some way, but most were child's play compared to a fingernail-sized mollusk imported in the mid-1980s from eastern Europe's Caspian Sea. The zebra mussel was first observed in North American waters in Lake St. Clair, a Great Lakes connecting channel near Detroit, in 1988. By 2000, the prolific mussel had spread to all five Great Lakes and hundreds of inland lakes as well as the Mississippi, Ohio, and Muskegon River systems. By 2005, zebra mussels covered vast areas of lake and river bottoms, clinging to rocks, docks, and almost anything that did not swim. The striped mollusks have clogged municipal and industrial water intakes, causing at least $1 billion in damage and forcing the use of chlorine and mechanical devices to keep the pests at bay.

Because zebra mussels are filter feeders—an adult mussel filters one liter of water per day—the creatures dramatically increased water clarity in inland lakes, which in turn fueled weed growth. A decade after they invaded the Great Lakes, zebra mussels were linked to the disappearance of diporeia from the bottom of Lake Erie and Lake Michigan and blooms of toxic algae that cover parts of numerous inland lakes each summer, including Muskegon Lake. Diporeia are tiny, shrimplike amphipods and a main source of food for fish at the base of the Great Lakes food web. Scientists believed that zebra mussels intercepted microscopic organisms before they settled to the bottom of lakes, where they were usually consumed by diporeia. Tom Nalepa, a biologist at the National Oceanic and Atmospheric Administration in Ann Arbor, Michigan, discovered that diporeia were vanishing from the Great Lakes. He explained the phenomenon in 1997, saying,

> What's happening is energy that used to support amphipod growth is now being turned into zebra mussel tissue. Many species of fish, and particularly young fish, readily eat amphipods, but few species can use zebra mussels for food. There's concern that such a short-circuit in the food chain could lead to declines in a number of fish, including perch, alewives, sculpin, bloater, and smelt, with possible secondary effects on trout and salmon.[12]

Alewives in Lake Michigan started shrinking in 2003, likely because their favorite food—diporeia—was becoming scarce. The problem reached the top of the Lake Michigan food chain in 2004, when scientists discovered that chinook salmon were smaller than in previous years. Chinook feast on alewife; smaller alewife mean smaller salmon. Call it the Caspian Sea diet, triggered by zebra mussels that hitchhiked from Eastern Europe to North America in freighters' ballast water.

Zebra mussels now cover vast areas of the river mouth at Muskegon Lake and have coated rocks and portions of sandy shoreline along the Muskegon River below Croton Dam. They also have invaded Higgins and Houghton lakes, the headwaters of the Muskegon River. Transported from one waterway to another on boat hulls, fishing gear and in live wells, zebra mussels are one of the few exotic species that—thanks to human activities—can bypass the Croton, Hardy, and Rogers dams and spread into the upper reaches of the Muskegon River.

Liz Wade's family has owned a cottage on Higgins Lake for more than forty years. Not until 2002 did Wade first see zebra mussels on boat docks in the scenic, deep lake in northern Michigan. The following year, she found mussels covering every square inch of underwater structures. "They're all over," she said in seeming disbelief.[13]

Zebra mussels have earned a reputation as one of the nation's most notorious and most discussed aquatic invaders. And yet, as troublesome as zebra mussels are, their arrival in the Great Lakes exposed a larger, vexing problem: scores of aquatic species and pathogens are being transported into the Great Lakes in the ballast water of freighters. The oceangoing freighters that were welcomed into the Great Lakes a half century ago when the St.

Lawrence Seaway was completed have become the primary source of a new and costly environmental problem, biological pollution.

In the 1960s and 1970s, chemical pollution from industrial discharges was considered the most serious Great Lakes problem. Toxic chemicals dumped into the lakes by factories and municipalities or spewed into the air and carried to the lakes by the wind poisoned bottom sediments and made some fish unsafe to eat. Chemical contaminants still plague parts of the lakes and taint fish, especially in Muskegon Lake and other harbors where contaminated sediments still linger. But many scientists in 2005 considered biological pollution—zebra mussels and other exotic species that disrupt the food chain, harm water quality, compete with native species of fish, and transform plant communities—the most pressing environmental issue facing the Great Lakes.

Unlike chemical pollution, which could be cleaned up over time, exotic species never leave. Hugh MacIsaac, professor of ecology at Windsor University in Canada, has estimated that 90 percent of the aquatic organisms in Lake Erie have arrived since 1988. "Within one century, we are almost completely revolutionizing the number and types of species found in the Great Lakes," MacIsaac said in 2003. "It's almost entirely human caused."[14]

The U.S. and Canadian governments have tried to address the issue with new shipping regulations. A 1993 federal law required oceangoing ships to exchange ballast water at least two hundred miles offshore before entering the St. Lawrence Seaway. But that law has not stopped the flow of exotics entering the Great Lakes. The law initially was poorly enforced, and technical problems also arose. Ballast tanks could not be completely drained while a ship was at sea, and some species survived in the mud that sloshed around in the bottom of ships.[15]

Studies have predicted that several new invasive species, mostly microscopic organisms, will reach the Great Lakes in coming years; it is just a matter of time. Some scientists believed that sanitizing freighter ballast water was the only way to prevent freighters from bringing more exotic creatures into the lakes. That was a costly proposition and could create new problems if the chemicals used to sterilize ballast water end up polluting Great Lakes waters.

Several prominent scientists believe that banning oceangoing ships from the Great Lakes may be the only sure way to halt the introduction of more exotic species. "Non–Great Lakes boats frankly should be banned from entering the Great Lakes," said Milt Clark, senior health and research adviser with the U.S. Environmental Protection Agency's Chicago office. Some scientists have suggested closing the Great Lakes to transoceanic freighters by closing locks in the St. Lawrence Seaway, in Montreal, or in the Welland Canal near Buffalo, New York.[16] Neither solution is likely to happen.

International shipping is a multibillion-dollar industry for the Great Lakes. Every shipping season, more than two thousand freighters pass through the St. Lawrence Seaway, transporting iron, steel, coal, grain, and wood from the Great Lakes states to overseas ports of call. In 2000, freighters traveling within the Great Lakes system carried 192 million tons of cargo through the St. Lawrence Seaway, part of a $4.3 billion industrial complex that employs 152,000 people in the Great Lakes basin.[17]

However, banning ocean freighters from the lakes would have a nominal economic impact, according to a 2005 Grand Valley State University study. The study concluded that the economic value of ocean freighters moving cargo in and out of the Great Lakes paled in comparison to the costly ecological problems caused by exotic species. Closing the Great Lakes to ocean shipping—and transferring the cargo those ships carry to trucks and trains—would increase the annual cost of shipping steel, grain and other materials in the Great Lakes region by $55 million, or 6 percent. Ocean freighters in 2002 carried just seven percent of all cargo shipped across the Great Lakes and St. Lawrence Seaway; most cargo shipped across the lakes is carried by so-called "lakers," freighters that never leave the freshwater seas. Exotic species, many of which were carried to the Great Lakes in freighters' ballast water, caused damage of between $200 million and $500 million annually.[18]

The study's lead researcher, economist and GVSU business professor John Taylor, said, "There's a general assumption that ocean shipping is a critical part of the (Great Lakes regional) economy, and it's not. We're potentially paying a significant price in harm to the Great Lakes tourism economy and fisheries for the benefit of importing steel." Shipping industry officials criticized Taylor's study as biased, but the study passed muster with a group of independent economists who reviewed the work.[19] Taylor's study did not recommend closing the Great Lakes to ocean freighters. But it ignited an intense, and important, debate about the costs and benefits of allowing transoceanic ships to ply the lakes. Left to deal with exotic species on their own, many companies and communities in the Great Lakes basin spent huge sums of money to protect water quality, native fish and plants, and recreational activities in lakes and streams. One of the more ambitious and controversial efforts to wipe out an exotic species began in 2002 in Houghton Lake, a popular resort community at the headwaters of the Muskegon River.

Donald Bonnette went to Houghton Lake in 1995 to study why native wild rice was disappearing from Michigan's largest inland lake. The Central Michigan University graduate student wanted to figure out what had caused the demise of the wild rice stands that once covered huge areas of the 20,103-acre lake. The near-elimination in the 1980s of wild rice, a threatened species in Michigan, caused a dramatic reduction in the number of ducks and coots stopping at Houghton Lake during the fall migration. In 1972, state biologists counted 18,531 ducks on Houghton Lake between October 12 and November 3. A similar survey performed in 1995 recorded 8,631 ducks, a 53 percent decrease. The number of American coots observed on the lake plummeted from 7,836 in 1972 to 520 in 1995, a 93 percent decrease.[20]

Among the factors that contributed to the loss of wild rice, Bonnette concluded, was Eurasian water milfoil, an exotic weed imported to the United States in the 1940s that resembles a tiny, wispy pine tree and spreads like wildfire in shallow lakes. Milfoil established a stronghold in Houghton Lake sometime after 1989, when ice floes ripped loose in the lake and wiped out hundreds of acres of wild rice. The loss of the wild rice left a biological vacuum, and milfoil quickly filled the void. Bonnette's 1998 master's thesis warned that milfoil would take over the lake and prevent the reestablishment of wild rice beds unless immediate action was taken to control the aquatic weed. But it was already too late.

The following year, thick mats of milfoil covered ten thousand acres of the lake, making half of the popular waterway impassable for boats. Houghton Lake's shallow water—the average depth is nine feet and the maximum is just twenty-two feet—provided optimum growing conditions for milfoil. When storms blew across the lake, waves ripped milfoil from the bottom and deposited piles of dead, rotting vegetation on beaches and lawns. Dick Pastula had vivid memories of the awful conditions: "The smell and the stench would gag you. There were dead fish, dead snails, and dead

A group of lumbermen pictured on a wanigan near Newaygo in the 1880s. (From the collection of the Muskegon County Museum.)

Logs rolled into the river in the 1800s scarred the land and sent tons of sand into the river. (From the collection of the Muskegon County Museum.)

This lake-level control structure maintains artificially high water levels in Houghton Lake, near the headwaters of the Muskegon River. (Photo by the author.)

The Deadstream Swamp downstream of Houghton Lake is the headwaters of the Muskegon River. (Photo by the author.)

A century after the Muskegon River was last used to transport logs, the lower river supports a fantastic trout and salmon fishery that attracts anglers from around the world. (Photo by Dave Carlson, courtesy of the Muskegon Chronicle *© 2000.)*

The Rowe Dam near Newaygo is a defunct hydroelectric dam in Penoyer Creek, near Newaygo. It is one of ninety-four dams in the Muskegon River and its tributaries. (Photo by the author.)

Eroding stream banks, like this one near Newaygo, release enormous amounts of sand into the river. (Photo by the author.)

Anglers fish below Croton Dam in Newaygo, which divides the Muskegon's lower 47 miles from 172 miles of river above the dam. (Photo by Dave Carlson, courtesy of the Muskegon Chronicle, *© 2000.)*

Researcher Paul Vecsei, center, displays a large sturgeon that was struck and killed by a freighter in Muskegon Lake. The ancient fish are struggling to survive in the Muskegon River. (Photo by Dave Carlson, courtesy of the Muskegon Chronicle, *© 2003.)*

Eric Alexander shows off a large Chinook salmon caught near Newaygo while fishing on a foggy day with guide Matt Supinski. (Photo by the author.)

Anglers and people in canoes often compete for space in the most popular stretch of the river between Croton Dam and Newaygo. (Photo by the author.)

This aerial view of the Canadian Lakes development, near Big Rapids, shows how damming a creek, in the foreground, created several lakes that are now surrounded by homes and golf courses. (Photo courtesy of Marge Beaver, photography-plus.com.)

These photos of Cedar Creek near Muskegon, before and after a rain shower, show how paving roads and parking lots and clearing land for farm fields and urban development can send warm, polluted storm water runoff into surface waters. (Photos by Gale Nobes, courtesy of the Muskegon River Watershed Assembly.)

Agricultural drains, like this one near Muskegon, transport excess water off farm fields and into county drains, which empty into streams. The drains provide a conduit for warm, potentially polluted water that can harm the river and its tributaries. (Photo by the author.)

A sign in front of a well-drilling company near Evart shows how some people felt about Perrier's Ice Mountain water bottling plant, which bottles groundwater from the Muskegon River watershed. (Photo by the author.)

ducks entangled in this stuff. Some people were spending a thousand dollars a season to haul milfoil off their beaches."[21]

Boaters who dared to navigate through the milfoil sometimes burned up their motors. The local economy suffered as hotel rooms remained vacant in the peak summer months and fewer people went fishing. Houghton Lake tourism was in crisis. "There was a tremendous amount of backlash from the business community over the problems caused by the weeds," said Pastula, a relative newcomer to the area who was appointed secretary of the Houghton Lake Improvement Board. The solution, chosen after months of study and intense community debate, gave Houghton Lake a new form of notoriety.

In 2001, the lake board decided to attack the problem with a toxic herbicide called fluridone, or Sonar. The following year, the largest chemical-based weed-eradication project ever undertaken in Michigan—covering an area of surface water thirty-three times larger than had ever been treated with chemicals—was carried out on Houghton Lake. On May 15 and again on June 7, 2002, crews from an Indiana company, SePRO, sprayed fluridone across the surface of Houghton Lake. Driving airboats like those used to ferry sightseers through the Florida Everglades, SePRO crews pumped a total of 968 gallons of the chemical into the lake. Some local residents and state fisheries biologists were outraged by the unprecedented use of chemicals to kill nuisance weeds on such a grand scale.[22]

Critics predicted that the chemical treatment, which cost $1.4 million, would cause dead milfoil to pile up on the lake bottom, triggering harmful algae blooms that could kill fish and harm water quality. That did not happen after the first round of treatment. Others wanted to attack the milfoil with weevils that eat the troublesome plants, but weevils do not work as quickly as chemicals, and many locals were growing restless.

Craig Cotterman, a fisherman and duck hunter who has spent much of his life vacationing and living on the shores of Houghton Lake, said that the chemical treatment was done too hastily. He believes that the Houghton Lake Improvement Board was willing to risk the health of the lake to make its shallow waters weedfree and better suited for boating. Cotterman, a blunt man with a temper, has been especially dismayed by the loss of wild rice over the past twenty years, a problem he said would not be corrected by using a toxic chemical to kill milfoil: "Wild rice was an incredible feature to lose in our lake. We had weevils in the lake to reduce milfoil, but then the lake improvement board went ahead with the chemical treatment. It's all because of the boating dollar. They want to squeeze every dollar out of our lake, no matter what."[23]

Carl Geiger, a member of the lake board, said in a promotional video that although he was nervous about spraying a herbicide in the lake, "I thought the problem had gotten to a point where there wasn't any alternative." Members of the lake board hoped that the chemical treatment, which would be repeated if necessary, would allow the return of native aquatic plants, such as wild rice, elodea, and chara. "What we hope is we're going to restore the lake to what it was in past years: a good, sound, healthy lake with a good, diverse weed population, a good fishery and still a place that you can boat in, swim in and enjoy," said James Demaud, president of the lake improvement board.[24]

One year after the first chemical treatment, local residents reported tremendous bluegill and bass fishing and no milfoil in the lake; some of the nuisance weeds were spotted in canals and promptly treated with fluridone. By all accounts, the chemical treatment wiped out milfoil in Houghton Lake, if only temporarily. Still, Cotterman wondered if traces of the chemical would accumulate in the bottom of Houghton Lake, as copper did following years of using copper sulfate to kill a microorganism that causes a rash known as swimmer's itch.

Tests performed by SePro showed that the concentration of fluridone in Houghton Lake's water had dropped to zero by April 2003, nearly a year after the chemical was first applied. Pastula said that the first chemical treatment, part of a five-year, $5 million weed-eradication program funded by a special tax on local property owners, represented an unqualified success. "The lake board is happy, and I think the community is happy. We have maybe four or five critics and about eight thousand property owners who are very happy." Pastula said that longtime Houghton Lake residents such as Cotterman who yearn for an era when duck hunting and fishing in wild rice and bulrush were the primary activities on Houghton Lake must learn to live with the powerboats and Jet Skis that now dominate the lake. Said Pastula, "Things don't remain the same."[25]

Property owners could bet on the lake changing in the future. Richard O'Neal, a fisheries biologist with the Michigan DNR, said that Houghton

Lake property owners determined to keep weeds out of the lake are fighting two powerful forces: the shallow lake was essentially a submerged wetland, the type of waterway favored by aquatic plants; and there has never been a case in Michigan where milfoil has been permanently eliminated from a lake. "The milfoil will come back," O'Neal said. "It always comes back."[26]

The Houghton Lake weed-killing experiment demonstrated that people could undo damage caused by an alien species, at least temporarily. Time will tell whether the chemical solution had staying power. As Houghton Lake property owners were declaring victory over weeds in 2003, scientists were documenting another human-created ecological mess at the other end of the Muskegon River.

6.

BOTTLENECK

> Wetlands have a poor public image. Yet they are among the earth's greatest natural assets . . . mankind's waterlogged wealth.
>
> —Professor Edward Maltby, University of London

MUSKEGON IN 1960 WAS A SMALL TOWN WITH A BIG CITY TRAFFIC problem. Each summer, tourists from across the Midwest flocked to western Michigan to vacation along the sandy beaches of Lake Michigan. Making the trip north along the coast, however, required navigating a crowded two-lane road that crossed the Muskegon River on the northern edge of Muskegon. Old U.S. 31, known among locals as the Causeway, was the only river crossing within ten miles of the Lake Michigan coast. Every vehicle that passed through the north side of Muskegon squeezed onto the Muskegon Causeway, a bottleneck that caused legendary traffic jams and was the site of numerous deadly accidents. City leaders complained the gridlock left a black mark on the region's burgeoning tourism economy. Something had to give.

The solution: Extend U.S. 31, a four-lane highway that paralleled the Causeway three miles to the east but stopped south of the Muskegon River. Extending the highway 14.4 miles to the north would create a four-lane concrete artery that bypassed downtown Muskegon, allowing motorists to zip past the city without having to stop for a single traffic light. But the project faced one very large obstacle: the Muskegon River marsh, a forbidding swamp nearly two miles wide. Engineers figured that the simplest way to cross the marsh and two branches of the river flowing through it was to build a levee through the swamp and lay the road atop it.

On June 29, 1964, dignitaries joined Miss Muskegon, Lucylle Johnson, above the river flats for a ribbon-cutting ceremony for the new road. State Highway Commissioner John C. Mackie said that every effort had been made to preserve natural beauty along the new section of U.S. 31, which stretched from Muskegon to Whitehall. "Although it removes traffic from one of Michigan's most beautiful sections of state highway, it will be a pleasure for motorists to drive, not only as a scenic highway but because it eliminates one of the worst traffic bottlenecks in Western Michigan."[1] As it turned out, the road project solved one problem by creating another. It reduced traffic congestion on the Causeway but caused profound changes in one of the most biologically significant marshes in the Great Lakes.

Some locals suspected that the road would fundamentally alter the river flats. Two years before the project was completed, a headline in the *Muskegon Chronicle* proclaimed, "Giant structures form dam across Muskegon River."[2] W. Ned Fuller, secretary of the Muskegon County Road Commission at the time, told the newspaper that the bridge would act as a huge dam, backing up the river across a vast area of land on the east side of the highway.

Instead of building an elevated bridge on pilings, like the one that allows the ocean to flow freely beneath the highway that connects the Florida Keys to the mainland, U.S. 31 conquered the waters it was built to cross. By funneling the river through two openings in the levee, the new highway created a bottleneck in the river. Slowing the flow of water upstream of the highway would, over time, inundate the sprawling marsh with water, sand, and silt.

Emert Lange saw the lower Muskegon River marsh change seemingly before his eyes. A dentist with a passion for duck hunting, Lange began hunting the sprawling Muskegon River marsh shortly after he moved to Muskegon in 1947. Several times each autumn, Lange would be out of his house by five in the morning to hunt mallards and wood ducks before heading into his dental practice at eight o'clock. "At that time, I had a little aluminum boat. I'd put in at Richards Park and motor up the middle branch of the river and wade into the marsh. At that time, the water was two to three feet deep, shallower in some spots, all the way up to the upper marsh," upstream of the U.S. 31 bridge. Lange hunted ducks in the marsh every autumn for nearly two decades. Ducks loved the place: "I'd go out early in the morning and there would be mallards and teal, and a few wood ducks in the upper marsh where there were woods. I'd get my limit [six ducks] and still make it into the office by 8 A.M."[3] The 1950s and early '60s were the halcyon days of duck hunting in the lower Muskegon River. They were about to end.

FROM THE HIGHWAY, PORTIONS OF THE MUSKEGON RIVER IN THE 1990S marsh looked like Chernobyl, site of the world's worst nuclear disaster. Dead trees rose out of a sprawling swamp, leafless gray branches in stark contrast to the bright green lily pads and cattails that thrived in the labyrinth of inky creeks and slack water that crisscrossed the marsh. From a distance, the marsh appeared still and lifeless, a piece of land cast away to nature's trash heap. It was an entirely misleading image. Through the heart of this morass flowed two main branches of the Muskegon River. This was where the sluggish river deposited tons of sand, silt, and nutrients carried down its channel each year. It was the river's final stage before surrendering to the deep waters of Muskegon Lake and Lake Michigan.

A journey through the marsh—which from the river resembled the bayous of Louisiana but is located just outside the Muskegon city limits—revealed abundant life at every turn. Great blue heron and bald eagles nested in the limbs of dead trees. Turtles, snakes, river otters, and salamanders moved freely between water and mucky soils where cattails, button bush, and alder created impenetrable walls of vegetation. Huge bowfin and bass led a charmed life in the maze of opaque, shallow water that teemed with aquatic plants.

This was the same foreboding marsh that forced John S. Mullett to abandon his survey of the rugged terrain in May 1837. Mullett, who said that the swampy land was "good for nothing," was one of the first white men to hike through the ten-thousand-acre marsh now protected as part of the Muskegon State Game Area. Thick vegetation, deep muck on the river bottom, and variable water levels—three feet in one spot and chest deep a few steps later—forced Mullett to abandon his first survey of the swamp. He took the unusual step of surveying the marsh the following winter, when he could cross on the ice that covered much of the water.

Though the marsh remained as forbidding as ever, human activities over the past two centuries have changed its complexion. The first maps of Muskegon County produced by the U.S. Government Land Office, based on Mullett's survey, showed Muskegon Lake extending nearly two miles east of its present shoreline. In 1837, when Mullett slogged through the marsh, Muskegon Lake stretched from Lake Michigan to where U.S. 31 now crosses the marsh.[4]

During the nineteenth-century logging era, miles of river channel in the marsh were straightened so that logs could be floated downstream to sawmills on Muskegon Lake. The channel into Lake Michigan also was deepened to keep logging schooners from running aground on sandbars. Thousands of tons of fill material dumped into the marsh surrounding the original shoreline of Muskegon Lake—logs and sawdust from sawmills and later foundry slag—shrank the lake and changed the Muskegon River's course through the marsh. The city of Muskegon for years operated a trash dump in the marsh, filling in about sixty-five acres of the wetland. Tons of ash from the coal-burning B. C. Cobb power plant on Muskegon Lake also were dumped into the marsh, eventually filling another sixty-five acres next to the old city dump.

The U.S. 31 extension was not the first road project that changed the river's natural flow through the marsh. The Old U.S. 31 Causeway, built in the late 1800s to link Muskegon and North Muskegon, also constricted the lower river. Several other bridges over the Muskegon and its tributaries altered the natural flow of water and disrupted the natural movement of fish, sediment, and nutrients.[5] Still, no other bridge in the Muskegon River basin caused more harm to the waterway than the stretch of U.S. 31 that spanned the lower river's marsh.

Over the past three decades, sand has filled much of the lower river's middle and south branches. Artificially high water levels trapped behind the levee have drowned thousands of trees and transformed plant communities. It was sadly ironic that the U.S. 31 bridge afforded motorists a stunning, panoramic view of a marsh it was slowly destroying.

The highway's effects on the marsh did not take long to become evident. The first signs of change appeared in 1969, after the state removed the

Newaygo Dam, about thirty miles upstream of U.S. 31, unleashing tons of sand and silt that had accumulated behind the structure over the course of a century. Destination: the Muskegon River marsh.

With the U.S. 31 bridge acting as a tourniquet in the lower river, the huge volume of sediment that washed downstream was a recipe for ecological mayhem. The levee backed up water behind the bridge, forcing the sluggish river to deposit countless tons of sand in the marsh instead of further downstream in the deeper waters of Muskegon Lake. Lange recalled the changes:

> When they put the highway in, the flats began to fill in with sand. Eventually, I stopped hunting in the marsh and went down to the Grand River. In the late '40s there were always a lot of ducks. After the highway went in, there weren't as many ducks flying into the marsh. There was less habitat for the ducks, so just a few hunters could scare away all the ducks.

AS MUCH AS HUMANS DETEST AND FEAR FLOODS, IT IS NATURAL FOR rivers to periodically rise out of their banks. A flood can be a good thing for a river, a cleansing force. High waters help rivers move large amounts of sediment and occasionally carve new channels. Floods have become issues of paramount importance in many river basins as development has crept closer to waterways and increased the speed at which rainwater reaches rivers.

Before the Muskegon River marsh was hemmed in by highways, excess water that flooded the north and south branches spilled into Muskegon Lake over two-mile-wide area. The five miles of roads, levees, and bridges built through and around the marsh boxed in the lower river, creating unnaturally high water levels in the marsh that adjoins Muskegon Lake. Human-created structures rendered the marsh a dump site for sand and silt.

"As the flood water is pooled, it loses energy, and suspended sediments are deposited in channels and wetlands areas. As the river becomes shallower, floods are more frequent and the deposition cycle continues, forcing wider areas of water behind the bridge and road restrictions," according to Richard Rediske, a professor of water resources at Grand Valley State University's Annis Water Resources Institute. "The data . . . support the hypothesis of a shallower and wider Muskegon River that has been severely impacted by siltation. . . . What is certain is that diversity and quality of the Muskegon River watershed have been adversely affected by excessive sedimentation from upstream sources."[6]

Rediske was the first scientist to document the extent to which roads and bridges have changed the lower Muskegon River marsh. An outspoken man held in high regard by his peers, the GVSU researcher documented what many people had suspected: sand from the upstream reaches of the river was filling in the marsh. Each day, the river deposited an astounding 334,000 pounds of sand and silt in the marsh and Muskegon Lake. The trouble was, the sluggish lower river was slowed even more by the U.S. 31 bridge, sapping the waterway of the energy needed to flush dirt through the marsh. "This estimate is significant since large amounts of sediment are destructive to the riverine, wetland and lake habitats present in the area" of the lower river, Rediske said in his study.

Cattails and sedge grass have taken over areas of standing water where willows, elm, and ash trees once thrived in saturated soils. The higher water has drowned acres of trees and bushes, and the torrent of sand overwhelming the marsh has increased water temperatures, creating an underwater haven for less desirable fish species such as carp and catfish. Between 1978 and 1997, excess sediment deposited in the marsh wiped out 240 acres of wetland shrubs downstream of U.S. 31, between the highway built in 1964 and the old Causeway a mile downstream. Those shrubs were replaced by emergents and beds of aquatic plants—cattails, reeds, and rushes—capable of surviving in standing water. Rising water levels also swamped 1,723 acres of wooded wetland forest upstream of the highway, drowning countless trees and creating the appearance of a marsh dominated by death.[7]

MICHIGAN RESIDENTS WERE ACCUSTOMED TO STORMS THAT DUMPED huge amounts of rain or snow in short periods of time. It was not unusual for storms that rolled in across the vast expanse of Lake Michigan to dump precipitation at the rate of one inch or more per hour. But something was different about the storm that moved into western Michigan in September 1986.

For most of the summer of 1986, water levels were low in the Muskegon River and its numerous tributaries. Dry weather had dropped the river to its lowest water level in two years. That quickly changed when a late summer storm crept across western Michigan. Over the course of forty-eight hours, the storm dumped fourteen inches of rain on the sprawling landscape that drains into the Muskegon River. The river and streams that fed it swelled out of their banks; some cottages and trailers built close to rivers were washed away, and many others were flooded with muddy water; raging rivers and streams washed out bridges and roads and paralyzed some riverside communities. But nowhere was the drama more intense than at Hardy Dam, one of the world's largest earthen dams.

The rain began falling during the early morning hours of September 10. By the next day, the deluge had increased the flow of the Muskegon to eleven times its average; twenty-two thousand cubic feet surged down the river *each second*. Workers at Hardy Dam sounded the alarm early on September 11, 1986, warning emergency personnel in the downstream communities of Newaygo and Muskegon that flooding was imminent.

With the downpour sending billions of gallons of excess water into the Hardy Dam reservoir, officials at Consumers Energy feared that one of the utility's most cherished structures would succumb to the rising river. Water levels in the dam's reservoir were rising faster than Consumers workers could release it—even with every turbine in the dam running and every spill gate open, the water continued to rise.

By the second day of the storm, water was washing over the top of the Hardy Dam. Water and sand also were squirting out of seams in the dam's concrete spillway, creating miniature geysers; at times, the mammoth dam shuddered under the immense pressure caused by the rising river. "There was a strong possibility that the emergency spillway at the Hardy Dam would fail [resulting in] an increase in the river's level at that location of 10 to 20 feet," said Charles Smith, supervisor of Consumers' hydroelectric operations.[8]

If Hardy Dam burst, a wall of water would rush down the river and destroy Croton Dam. Some areas of Newaygo would be wiped off the landscape, and "a threat of unparalleled dimensions would be posed to the city of Muskegon," Consumers officials said. Water levels in the Muskegon River downstream of Hardy Dam would have risen as much as fifty-two feet in nine hours, a small community on Maple Island would have been obliterated. and water levels in Muskegon Lake would have soared as much as twenty-two feet over a thirty-five-hour period.[9]

Sam Nesselroad watched anxiously as the river rose behind his Newaygo home during the flood. At one point during the two-day deluge, the river was rising at the phenomenal rate of one foot per hour. Returning home from work on the second day of the flood, Nesselroad discovered that the river had risen seven feet since his departure that morning. His aluminum fishing boat was surrounded by water; Nesselroad could only watch as the raging current ripped the boat from its dock and carried it downstream. By that time, his house too was nearly surrounded by water. Nesselroad recalled the scene: "I had blue heron and ducks in my yard. It was eerie. You have such a feeling of helplessness. It's a scary thing, a flood—the water keeps coming up and up. I saw propane tanks and whole walls of houses washing downstream."[10]

Police soon arrived and ordered Nesselroad and his neighbors to evacuate their homes and head for higher ground. Water continued to wash over the top of Hardy Dam until the afternoon of September 12. Although the rain had subsided, there was still a chance the dam could burst. Crews discovered a sixteen-foot deep cavern under the dam's spillway, a hole created by raging waters eroding sand beneath the giant concrete slide. That problem was corrected in the weeks after the floodwaters subsided. Consumers would end up spending $140,000 to repair the fifty-six-year-old dam.

The raging river receded almost as quickly as it rose; within a few days, everyone who had been evacuated during the flood was allowed to return home. Nesselroad was one of the lucky ones; the swollen river did not flood his house. He found his fishing boat a few weeks later in the woods near a campground, twelve miles downstream from his house.

Stewart and Betty Montgomery were not as fortunate. Their riverfront home near Newaygo, just downstream of an area known as Devil's Hole, was one of many that sustained heavy damage in the flood. The Montgomerys, who were fishing in Michigan's Upper Peninsula when they heard about the Muskegon River flood, rushed home to find four feet of water in their home. The water damaged several classic cars, a Harley Davidson motorcycle, and all of their furniture. The Montgomerys spent weeks stripping the interior of their house down to the wall studs and replacing carpet, insulation, and drywall. "Living along the river is not all fishing and scenery," Stewart Montgomery said. "It's a constant battle."[11]

By the end of September, the Flood of '86 had become a memorable chapter in the annals of Muskegon River history. "You get the feeling the river will never be the same after a flood, but three weeks later it was back to normal. It's amazing how it healed itself," Nesselroad said.

A post-flood editorial in the *Muskegon Chronicle* reflected on the event, saying, "a story that has been repeated countless times throughout the ages. It's about how relatively helpless we human beings are when nature decides to unleash its enormous powers and go on a rampage."[12] With the river back within its banks, life quickly returned to normal for most people in communities along the river. The same could not be said for the river; the flood's effects would be felt downstream for years to come.

In the summer of 1987, anglers who frequented the south branch of the lower river, near Muskegon, noticed dramatic changes where it flows through a marsh in the Muskegon State Game Area. Sand was blanketing parts of the river bottom where salmon and other fish laid their eggs on beds of gravel. Where was the excess sand coming from? A reservoir of sand that had accumulated behind the Newaygo Dam before it was removed in 1969.

Floodwaters that increased the river's flow carried tons of sediment that had been trapped behind the Newaygo Dam for more than a century downstream until the river's current slowed. When the dam was removed, experts predicted that it would take the river fifty years to transport all that lingering sediment downstream. Those calculations did not account for a record flood. The raging river carried a huge volume of sand downstream of Newaygo in a matter of months. But when the swollen river hit the bottleneck created by the U.S. 31 bridge, the water backed up and dumped much of its load of sand in the marsh.

Muskegon fisherman Stan Peterson fished the middle and south channels of the Muskegon River for thirty-five years, until the torrent of sand made parts of those waterways too shallow to float a boat. A legend among local fisherman, Peterson would launch his sixteen-foot aluminum boat at Richards Park, just downstream from the marsh, and head east up the river to his favorite fishing hole. Peterson fished that stretch of river for half his life before old age forced him to hang up his rods in the mid-1990s. "I was catching salmon and steelhead pretty regularly in the south branch," Peterson said in 1999. "But it's gone to pot. . . . It's all filled in with sand."[13]

The south branch of the lower Muskegon is now a wide, shallow river channel, the bottom covered by a thick blanket of sand that creates the appearance of an underwater desert. On most days, it was impossible to float a canoe down the section of the south branch visible from U.S. 31. The boat launch at Richards Park in Muskegon, where the river's middle branch once flowed, was high and dry. A section of the middle branch that flows beneath the Causeway between Muskegon and North Muskegon has been evicted by a sandbar. Most of the water that flowed down the south branch diverted to the north branch in the mid-1990s, slicing new courses across the marsh to relieve pressure caused by sand that filled in natural channels.

The volume of water flowing through the marsh in 1990 was evenly divided between the Muskegon River's south and north branches. By 2002, just 10 percent of the river's water flowed through the south branch; the north branch carried the other 90 percent into Muskegon Lake. Roads built through the marsh were effectively tilting this massive natural feature. To experience this phenomenon, pour water into a large, shallow cookie sheet. Hold the pan level and then tip one side slightly upward. Feel the water rush to the other side of the pan? That was what was happening in the lower Muskegon River marsh—the huge sheet of water that flowed through the marsh was tilting to the north as sand filled in the southern half of the huge wetland.[14] Why did this matter? The sandstorm was burying important habitat for fish, birds, amphibians, reptiles, and mammals. Over time, the roads and bridges that have boxed in the marsh could force all of the river's water into the north branch, transforming a lush wetland into little more than a pipeline for water. Rediske explained the ramifications in his 2000 study:

> Two of the key features of the lower Muskegon River watershed are its habitat diversity and quality. Habitat diversity is reflected in the variety of upland and wetland environments present in the watershed. Forested and meadow/shrub communities are present in the upland areas while wetland environments including open water marshes, emergents, hydrophilic shrubs, and lowland forests are found in the flood plain. These environments contribute to the diversity of flora and fauna in the area. The flooding and sedimentation in the lower Muskegon River watershed have reduced both habitat quality and diversity. The loss of wetland trees and shrubs significantly impacts the nesting and habitat areas that support many species of birds and small mammals. In addition, this change in vegetation will impact the aquatic environment with respect to a reduction in woody debris, increased transpiration/evaporation and an elevation of the [water] temperature.[15]

And there is always the possibility of another massive flood. With the north branch carrying nearly all of the river's water into Muskegon Lake, that channel will place far more stress on the U.S. 31 and Causeway bridges every time storm water runoff increases the river's volume and velocity.

"You could make a good case for changing the U.S. 31 bridge" to permit more water to flow through the levee, says Mike Wiley, an aquatic ecologist at the University of Michigan. "It's real clear to me that we've built a cage by changing the way water and sediment can move through there. Because of the highway, the river is aggrading [building up] faster and is now shifting quickly from south to north. It's happening at a startling rate."[16]

What would it take to restore the natural flow of water through the marsh? Replacing the existing highway and levee with a bridge built on concrete pilings would do the trick. But in an era of tight state budgets, that was not likely to happen. At a minimum, Wiley says, the state should bore several holes beneath the U.S. 31 bridge to restore natural water flow and reduce siltation upstream of the highway. Otherwise, "eventually, the south channel will fill in with sand and the north branch will be the only channel. If there is one large channel, it's a less hospitable environment for fish. It becomes a pipe [for water] more than a processing unit. It won't be as productive a place."

The U.S. 31 bridge has already reduced the turtle population in the marsh. Each spring, dozens of turtles migrated to lay their eggs on dry ground ended up on the highest point in the marsh—the highway—and faced a gauntlet of cars traveling more than seventy miles per hour. It was often a hopeless, bloody mismatch. "Turtles migrating across the highway are killed by cars in substantial numbers, especially during the spring egg-laying season," according to a Muskegon River Assessment published in 1997 by the Michigan Department of Natural Resources.[17] Muskegon resident Gale Nobes said he has counted as many as thirty dead turtles along the highway during the spring. "I think some people go out of their way to hit them," said Nobes, chair of the Muskegon River Watershed Assembly.[18] He figured that the only way to keep turtles from crossing the road was to erect a small fence along the two-mile-long bridge, one tall enough to turn back the map, spotted, and wood turtles that live in the marsh and try to cross the highway. But initial estimates put the cost of the turtle barrier at $500,000, and there was no obvious source of money to pay for it.

Lange said that the marsh where he hunted ducks in the 1950s and '60s was hardly recognizable in 2004. A well-spoken man with a proper demeanor and passion for the Muskegon River, Lange said the river has paid a terrible price for "progress." The middle branch of the lower river, which constituted the waterway's main branch in the 1940s and '50s, has been suffocated by sand that has washed downstream. And sixty-five acres of the marsh just above Muskegon Lake was turned into a sports complex. At the urging of Muskegon city officials, Consumers Energy agreed to seal its former ash dump, plant grass, and turn what once was a lush marsh before it became a dump site into something city officials call useful and beautiful: soccer fields. "When I look at the marsh as I drive across the Causeway going to North Muskegon, the areas that used to be marsh are no longer marsh—they're filled in," Lange said in 2004. "The marsh is smaller now than it was before the highway was built and there was all that fill put in. That's what they call progress—more electricity from the Cobb plant, more highways, and less marsh."[19]

The U.S. 31 highway bridge symbolized nature being slighted in the name of "progress." There was no debating the fact that the bridge caused profound, harmful changes in one of the Great Lakes' most important estuaries. But like the dams that dominated vast stretches of the Muskegon River and its tributaries, the U.S. 31 bridge was built before many of Michigan's landmark environmental laws were on the books. It was unlikely that the state or federal governments would now permit such an obtrusive structure to be built in this distinctive natural area.

Harmful as it was, construction of the U.S. 31 bridge also marked a turning point in the history of the river—it was the last major structure built in the Muskegon's main channel. Five years after the bridge opened, the Newaygo Dam thirty miles upstream was removed. After 130 years, the era of using the Muskegon almost exclusively as a working river was over. The resurrection of this magnificent waterway had begun.

7.

PARADISE FOUND

> With expansive gravel bars, slow deep holes, runs and over fourteen miles of spawning gravel, it's no wonder the mighty Muskegon is home to so many trout and game fish species.
>
> —Chad Betts, Muskegon River fishing guide

DENSE FOG ENVELOPED THE COAL-COLORED RIVER, CRIPPLED OUR vision, and caused a momentary wild thought that this fishing trip might lead us into the abyss. Mist from saturated air that made it difficult to distinguish river from sky dripped off our waterproof jackets and chilled our bare hands. With dawn nearly an hour away, we headed into a mighty river we could barely see to pursue huge salmon that could only be heard as the fish leaped out of the water. Paddles lightly slapped the water as the guide directed the drift boat a hundred yards up the river. He steered against the current and dropped anchor when the boat was stationed in the prime spot for casting a fly rod, just upstream and to the side of a deep, dark eddy in the river. For a while, the only sounds we heard—aside from our own hushed voices—were the river gurgling over small rapids and what sounded like small cannonballs landing in the water. Only when the rising sun illuminated the river did we catch a glimpse of huge chinook salmon leaping out of the water like porpoises as they prepared for a spawning ritual that lures thousands of anglers every autumn to this stretch of the Muskegon River.

As the rising sun melted the fog, we saw a large eddy in the river where our guide, Matt Supinski, said the salmon were staging before swimming further upstream to spawn on beds of gravel before dying. "There are probably two hundred fish in that hole," Supinski said. I was skeptical. Supinski instructed my son and me—novice anglers—to cast our wet flies into a thin line of floating foam that extended the length of the hole along the river's edge. Within thirty minutes we hit pay dirt: a twenty-five-pound male chinook struck a fly and the battle was on. For the next fifteen minutes, my son, Eric, mustered every ounce of strength in his thirteen-year-old body in his tug-of-war with the powerful fish. The reel screamed, and his fly rod bent as the fish raced downstream, trying mightily to dislodge the small hook lodged in its jaw. Exhausted by the battle, the fish finally surrendered. Supinski netted the fish and gently raised it out of the water, and we snapped a few pictures. Instead of keeping the fish, Supinski released the green-hued beast back into the river. Unless it was caught and kept by another angler, the four-year-old fish would complete the spawning run and make his contribution to what has become Michigan's most productive salmon stream.[1]

"You can have the same kind of fishing experience here that you could have in Montana, Vancouver, or Alaska," Supinski says. "Why go to Alaska and stand shoulder to shoulder with forty-seven other guys trying to catch salmon when I can catch a thirty-pound salmon here and have the river to myself? As far as the steelhead, I don't think there's a better place in the world than here in the Muskegon. The trout fishing here is just as good as going down the Snake River in Idaho. That's what makes this a world-class river: You can catch thirty-pound salmon, steelhead, and trout."[2]

This was not empty rhetoric from a guy who makes his living taking people fishing on the Muskegon River. Government data and scientific studies backed his claim. Moreover, Supinski had the credentials that warrant paying attention to what he said. A stocky man with a biting wit and a hot temper, Supinski has fished for salmon, trout, and steelhead in rivers all over the world. He authored three books on fishing, has written for many of the nation's most prestigious fishing publications, and writes salmon/steelhead columns for several magazines.

A former hotel executive who made enough money by his late thirties to check out of corporate America and pursue his lifelong passion for fishing,

Supinski could have set up shop on any river in the world. He chose the Muskegon, where he bought seven acres of land along the river in 1995 and opened his Gray Drake Lodge and Outfitters in Newaygo. After a decade of living and working on the Muskegon, Supinski had no regrets. No wonder. He could walk out his back door and catch massive salmon, chrome steelhead, and gorgeous brown and rainbow trout. Giant lake sturgeon occasionally swim past his dock as the behemoths head upstream to spawn. A state survey in 2000 found that anglers caught nearly 200,000 fish that year in a forty-mile stretch of the river between Croton Dam and Muskegon Lake; most of the fish caught—147,436—were steelhead. Anglers from all over the world, many from Japan, pay Supinski and other guides hundreds of dollars per day to lead them to salmon, steelhead, and trout. "The Muskegon," he said, "is a world-class river without people knowing about it or being managed as a world-class river."

Other knowledgeable anglers who have fished Michigan's great trout and salmon rivers—the Pere Marquette, Manistee, Au Sable, and Boardman—shared Supinski's assessment. Legendary fly fishermen Carl Richards and John Krause declared in their 1996 book, *Hatches of the Muskegon River II,* that the Muskegon River below Croton Dam was "one of the finest trout fisheries in the country and certainly the best in the Midwest."[3] Bob Nicholson, a veteran angler and river guide who was something of a legend among Pere Marquette River fishermen, said the Muskegon's greatest attribute was its diversity of fish species. Salmon, steelhead, smallmouth bass, brown trout, rainbow trout, sturgeon, and walleye lived in the lower Muskegon. "It's a hell of a fishery. I think it's as good as it gets," Nicholson said. "If you know what you're doing, you can go out on the Muskegon River twelve months of the year and have a great time."[4] The Muskegon was not a trout stream in the traditional sense because, unlike the Au Sable and Pere Marquette, it did not support a self-sustaining population of rainbows, brookies, or browns. Trout would likely vanish from the lower Muskegon if the state stopped stocking the fish. The river's salmon population was nearly self-sustaining in 2005, although the state still stocked thousands of those fish each year to ensure their survival.

Scientists who have studied Great Lakes salmon streams have said the Muskegon is one of the best. "The Muskegon River is the largest producer of wild chinook, and also contains the largest walleye population in southern

Lake Michigan, which is supported largely by stocking," according to a 2004 report by fish researchers Doran Mason and Ed Rutherford.[5] The Muskegon supported the only genetically pure strain of walleye in the Great Lakes. Eggs from walleye in the Muskegon were used to stock many rivers that empty into the Great Lakes. However, the river's walleye population has struggled over the past two decades. State fish biologists have not figured out why so few walleye reproduced on their own in the river in recent years.

Clean, clear water and abundant fish have made the fourteen miles of river between Croton Dam and Newaygo the most popular and healthiest section of the Muskegon. Slicing a winding channel through a deep, wooded valley teeming with wildlife, this stretch of the river featured several small rapids; vast expanses of transparent water where you could see fish, mussels, and crayfish with the naked eye; and deep holes where opaque, cola-colored water provided refuge for countless species of fish. The resurrection of this majestic, biologically vibrant section of river began in 1969, the year the Newaygo Dam was removed. Removing the dam represented a turning point in the river's history, but it was not without controversy. At the time, opponents predicted that removing the dam would destroy the river. They could not have been more wrong.

THE NEWAYGO DAM STRANGLED A SEVEN-MILE STRETCH OF THE MUSKEGON River for 115 years. Originally built in 1854 to power the Big Red Mill, the Newaygo Dam was the first built across the main branch of the Muskegon River. As logging ground to a halt in Michigan in the late 1800s, the Newaygo Dam failed. The first attempt to rebuild the structure was a disaster—the dam washed out as water levels rose in the reservoir behind it. A new dam was completed in 1903 but had to be rebuilt again just thirteen years later when the utility now known as Consumers Energy—which built the Croton, Hardy, and Rogers hydroelectric dams further upstream—converted the Newaygo Dam into a hydroelectric facility. By 1960, the Newaygo Dam had clearly outlived its usefulness. Other hydroelectric dams on the river generated far more electricity, as did new coal-burning power plants. With no use for the dam, Consumers offered to sell the structure to the city of Newaygo for one dollar; city officials balked at the offer, saying that maintenance costs outweighed any economic benefits that could be realized by owning the dam. With no suitors to purchase the obsolete dam, Consumers in 1967 transferred ownership of the structure to what is now called the Michigan Department of Natural Resources (DNR).

Department officials were eager to remove the Newaygo Dam. For years, government fish biologists had argued that the dam suppressed fish populations upstream of Newaygo. Fish from the lowest thirty miles of the river and Lake Michigan—with the exception of a newly introduced population of chinook salmon—could not jump over the relatively short dam. To compensate for the dam's harmful effects on fish populations, the DNR for years paid for walleye caught below the Newaygo Dam and trucked the fish to reservoirs behind the Newaygo, Croton, Hardy, and Rogers Dams. It was an exercise in futility.

In 1956, anglers caught the limit of 10,000 walleye in the river below Newaygo Dam; that figure plummeted to 2,493 in 1963 and 645 in 1966. The walleye population crash was blamed on the 1949 arrival in Lake Michigan of alewife, an exotic species accidentally imported to the Great Lakes in the late 1800s. Small but prolific, the six-inch-long alewife became the dominant Lake Michigan fish species by the mid-1960s. Alewife also moved up rivers flow into the Great Lakes, eating thousands of tiny walleye that hatched each year in the Muskegon River. Faced with a dwindling number of fish in the river, the DNR discontinued the walleye transfer program in 1967. That decision came as the agency was drawing down the Newaygo Dam reservoir as a prelude to removing the structure. "There simply haven't been enough walleyes running the last several years to justify the manpower and cost of the project," said Max Hunt, a DNR fisheries supervisor, in a newspaper article.[6]

The state of Michigan began stocking salmon in Michigan rivers in the mid-1960s to control the exploding alewife population. Salmon feast on alewife, which had no natural predators in the area after sea lamprey decimated lake trout in the Great Lakes. But the success of the salmon stocking program depended heavily on rivers, fish nurseries where chinook and coho were planted each spring and would return four years later to spawn before dying. Against this backdrop in October 1968, the state opened bids for the removal of the Newaygo Dam. State fish biologists said the project would create more spawning habitat for salmon and walleye by restoring the river's natural flow through Newaygo.

Although the Newaygo Dam was obsolete and posed an obstacle to fish passage, the state's plan to remove the structure ignited a fierce community debate. Many Newaygo residents and a few anglers lobbied to save the dam. Jeff Steele, owner of Steele Sporting Goods in Newaygo, disputed the state's claim that removing the dam would increase the natural reproduction of salmon in the river above Newaygo. Steele argued that chinook salmon would never become a self-sustaining species in the river. He also predicted that removing the dam would expose a small waterfall that would prohibit walleye from migrating upstream of Newaygo. Restoring the natural flow of the river also would eliminate boating near Newaygo, Steele warned, because water levels in the free-flowing river would be too low to float a boat.[7]

There were also purely sentimental arguments for preserving the Newaygo Dam. After the state approved a contract to remove the dam, Grand Rapids resident John Scheeres and his wife wrote a letter to the *Newaygo Republican* calling the project a mistake:

> This last Saturday I made another of the most pleasant trips that it has been my privilege to make. It was to Newaygo once more to see a sight that until lately one would have to go to the Northwest to see . . . the king salmon trying to fulfill the purpose that the good Lord put him on this earth to do. We have been there nearly every Saturday for a couple of months, bringing friends from Ontario, Canada, eastern Michigan, Washington state and a number of people from our home city of Grand Rapids. . . . We have heard from several of your folks that you plan to remove the dam at Newaygo. In our opinion that would be a very sad mistake. It seems to us that you would be removing the very thing that brings so many people to your little city to see, the thing that no one has to offer but you. We could see making steps of a sort to help the salmon in their journey, but please don't take away the beautiful sight you have for the people of this state and of all that come your way.[8]

Contrary to such dire predictions, removing the Newaygo Dam represented one of the most beneficial actions—ecologically and economically—ever carried out on the Muskegon River. The state still planted 150,000 chinook salmon every year in the Muskegon River below Croton Dam, but the fish produced between 300,000 and 400,000 offspring in the river every year. The river's salmon were thriving. Walleye could be found in the river all the way up to Croton Dam. And average water levels in the river below Croton were sufficient to float canoes, kayaks, and small fishing boats. Boating in the river could certainly be hazardous—there were many shallow areas, and large boulders often lurked just beneath the surface in the deeper water. Removing the dam also put Newaygo on the national map in the 1990s as a hotbed for salmon, trout, and steelhead fishing.

Some people who supported keeping the dam continued to blast the state's action after the project was completed. Removing the dam "ruined the riverfront property for the people who live along the river between Newaygo and Croton," wrote Janet L. Strahl, a Western Michigan University student, in a 1971 research paper. After the dam was removed, Strahl said, flooding increased downstream, damaging waterfront homes. That may have been true, since dams can help control flooding by storing storm water runoff. But flood control was never the intended purpose of the Newaygo Dam or any other dam on the Muskegon River. "It is too bad the [DNR] could not have found a means, possibly an effective fish ladder, for the fish to get upstream, without taking such a drastic step, since this measure has certainly ruined the one great attraction our little city had: the Newaygo Dam," Strahl wrote.[9]

The Newaygo Dam may have been a community landmark, but it was hardly missed four decades later. The state spent $84,000 to remove the Newaygo Dam, a pittance in light of subsequent economic and ecological benefits, which have reached into the millions of dollars. The state still spends about $230,000 annually to stock chinook salmon and walleye in the river between Muskegon and Newaygo, but those efforts also have paid huge dividends. Anglers spend about 110,000 person days fishing that section of the river each year, and the fishery alone is valued at $4.9 million.[10] That does not include the vast sums of money spent by tens of thousands of people who paddle and float that section of the river each year, nor does it account for the intrinsic value of having a large, scenic river rippling through Newaygo.

After the dam was removed, water levels dropped several feet in the seven-mile-long reservoir, and fish from Lake Michigan returned to the river above Newaygo. Yet no one foretold just how profoundly the removal of this one dam would improve the lower Muskegon River.

The dam removal was the first in a series of events that created the lower Muskegon's nationally recognized salmon and trout fishery. In the late 1980s, Consumers Energy changed the way it operated Croton Dam so that the amount of water passing through the structure was always close to the river's natural flow. Stabilizing the river's flow downstream of the dam reduced erosion of sandy stream banks and improved fish habitat. That led to increased natural reproduction of salmon and steelhead. "From Newaygo to Croton, the river is laced with gravel and its aquatic life is diverse," Supinski wrote in his 2001 book, *Steelhead Dreams: The Theory, Method, Science, and Madness of Great Lakes Steelhead Fly Fishing*. "Steelhead up to twenty pounds are common on this classic looking, Western style river. Its crystal clear waters and vegetation look like a giant spring creek."[11]

LOOKING THROUGH A GLASS SLIDER IN HIS A-FRAME COTTAGE IN A PLACE known as Cottonwood Flats, Sam Nesselroad had nothing but praise for visionary state officials who pushed to remove the Newaygo Dam. Before the dam was removed, the low-slung area near Newaygo where Nesselroad's cottage was located was submerged under the backwaters of the Newaygo Dam. This stretch of free-flowing water teemed with fish and wildlife after the dam was demolished: salmon, steelhead, and walleye could be seen swimming in the transparent water a stone's throw from Nesselroad's deck. Kingfishers swooped down from sugar maples and shimmering aspens that lined the river, their tiny bodies cruising just above the water. In the early morning hours, deer emerged from the wooded ravine on the other side of the river to drink its cool, clean water. Tens of thousands of people converged on this stretch of river every summer to float in tubes, canoe, and kayak. Nesselroad soaked up the river's majesty as he stood at his sliding glass door, smoking a cigarette while watching two fishermen attempt to land the giant salmon parked on a gravel bed, preparing to spawn. This was Nesselroad's nirvana.

Now retired from a job in a motorcycle manufacturing warehouse and a successful motorcycle racing career, Nesselroad's life was centered on the river. The interior of his cozy home was a veritable shrine to the river's bounty. Fishing poles were mounted horizontally between exposed rafters that soared to the ridge of the A-frame home. There were fly rods and spinners, classics and the best that modern technology has to offer the serious angler. A dining room wall was devoted to Nesselroad's prize catches: chinook salmon, steelhead, rainbow trout, walleye—all caught in the river that flowed past his home.

In Nesselroad's living room, much of one wall was lined with wooden disks the size of laundry baskets: these log ends, bearing the distinctive stamps of nineteenth-century lumber barons who owned the valuable white pine, were cut from logs that sank more than a century ago while being floated downstream to sawmills in Newaygo and Muskegon. In the refrigerator, sharing space with packages of lunch meat and a bottle of wine, were jars of bright orange salmon eggs—Nesselroad stockpiled the eggs to use as bait on future fishing trips. It seemed that everything except the television in Nesselroad's living room was geared toward the river. With no phone or computer, this humble, soft-spoken man isolated himself from an increasingly technological society—telemarketers, the Internet, and computer viruses are not part of his world. A simple existence allowed Nesselroad to spend most of his waking hours thinking about the river and his next fishing trip.

On this autumn day, however, Nesselroad was content to watch the two fishermen in a drift boat cast over and over for two large chinook salmon hovering near the bottom of the crystalline river. The fish were engaged in a spawning ritual that would drain them of their energy and soon claim their lives if the fishermen did not strike first. The anglers were obviously frustrated—they could see the fish, but the chinook refused to bite. After several unsuccessful casts, the men gave up and allow the current to carry their boat downstream. Nesselroad took a hit on his cigarette, exhaled a small cloud of smoke, and cracked a little smile. He knew the joy of fishing the Muskegon, even when it did not bring tangible results. "I've dedicated the rest of my life to being happy. I love the river. This is a rare river. It's clean, big, and navigable. From here you can navigate all the way to Chicago or Mexico."[12]

The Muskegon River is part of a vast, natural network of water that links the Great Lakes to the Atlantic Ocean and the world. As Nesselroad said, a person could travel by boat from Newaygo to Chicago, Montreal, the Atlantic seaboard, and beyond—even to Mexico. But it is not possible to travel from Newaygo to Big Rapids, a mere fifty miles upstream, by way of the

Muskegon River. Three hulking hydroelectric dams—Croton, Hardy, and Rogers—block the way. Someday in the distant future, when those dams are removed, anglers in Big Rapids and other communities further upstream will reap the benefits of bold environmental restoration projects that have created one of the nation's best salmon and steelhead fisheries in the lower Muskegon River.

8.

POLLUTION REVOLUTION

> After the wastewater system was built, it was just beautiful to go out on the lake, sit there for a couple of hours, and catch a bucketful of perch.
>
> —AL LEMKE, MUSKEGON LAKE ANGLER, 2004

THE ANNALS OF AMERICAN HISTORY ARE RICH WITH MEMORABLE decades, blocks of time defined by war, poverty, political upheaval, crime, pop culture, and revolutionary social movements. The Roaring '20s, the World War II years of the 1940s, the violent, turbulent '60s, and the self-centered '80s—during which a corrupt stockbroker in the film *Wall Street* defined the decade's overriding theme when he declared, "Greed is good"—have been seared into our collective memory. Then there were the 1970s, one of the most eclectic decades in American history.

The '70s were marked by events that defined turmoil and the trivial: a staggering defeat in the Vietnam War, President Richard Nixon declaring "I am not a crook" just days before resigning over the Watergate scandal, and, on the cultural front, the emergence of a dance craze known as disco. There was more to the '70s, however, than the mounting casualties of a misguided war, a disgraced president, and the big hair, silk shirts, and bell-bottom pants that were the trademarks of disco. The decade also ushered in one of this nation's most significant environmental laws, the federal Water Pollution Control Act of 1972, a precursor to the Clean Water Act of 1977.

Enacted in response to municipal and industrial discharges that poisoned scores of America's rivers and lakes, the Clean Water Act was the most ambitious national effort to regulate the amount of pollutants that could be discharged into the nation's navigable waters. One of the law's earliest success stories played out in Muskegon, where the Muskegon River pools into a 4,149-acre drowned river mouth known as Muskegon Lake before flowing into Lake Michigan. Its waters fouled over the course of a century by sawmills, factories, and municipal wastewater that left fish smelling like chemicals and the water smelling like sewage, Muskegon Lake would become the focal point of a pollution revolution that would transform the dirty foundry town of Muskegon and its filthy lake into a recreational paradise.

AL LEMKE SPENT MUCH OF HIS LIFE CAVORTING ON THE LOWER MUSkegon River and Muskegon Lake. Lemke and his childhood friends would spend hot summer days swimming and ogling girls on the beach at Richards Park, where the south branch of the river meets the lake. When he was not swimming, Lemke could be found fishing off boat docks for northern pike that hid in the lake's dark, cloudy water. Although the lake was severely polluted by then, Lemke could not recall any obvious signs of contamination in the fish in the 1940s and early '50s. Something changed, however, during the six years he spent in Europe as a corpsman in the U.S. Air Force.

Upon returning home in the early 1960s, Lemke went to his fishing hole on the north side of the lake in search of northern pike. He could catch fish, but they were no longer suitable for eating. "You'd pick up the fish and the smell would just about knock you over. They smelled like rotten eggs. We never ate them. We didn't ever take them home," Lemke said. The water had become so polluted that it was hazardous even to run a fishing boat across the lake. "When the water splashed up, it would burn your face and eyes."[1]

Lemke became familiar with one of the worst sources of pollution in Muskegon Lake when he took a job in 1969 at the S. D. Warren paper mill (now called Sappi Fine Paper North America). For seven decades the mill—and most other local industries—dumped all wastewater into the lake, each day fouling the lake with millions of gallons of sewage laced with toxic chemicals. The paper mill was known for turning part of the lake milky white when it discharged millions of gallons of wastewater laced with remnants of the white clay used to coat glossy paper. "Everything went into the lake," Lemke said.

As a boy growing up during the 1960s, Rich O'Neal spent many a day fishing at a site between the paper mill and a terminal where tankers unloaded gas and oil, just a short walk from his house. At the time, the lake was not particularly inviting. In fact, its appearance was downright appalling. The water was always murky and sometimes took on the color of milk. Oil that foundries and refineries dumped into the lake cast huge, colorful rainbows across the water's surface. And if O'Neal and his buddies strayed too close to the spot where Ruddiman Creek empties into the lake, there was a good chance they'd see human feces floating on the water.

Despite the foul condition of the lake, several species of fish managed to survive—perch, walleye, and suckers, to name but a few. O'Neal often caught perch from the banks of the lake's south side, an area that was lined with sawmills during the nineteenth-century logging boom. But the joy of catching perch was often dashed when O'Neal would take the fish home to be filleted and cooked. When fried, the pungent smell of chemicals wafted out of the fish and filled the kitchen. There was no need to conduct sophisticated scientific tests to determine that fish in Muskegon Lake were affected by toxic wastes that industries dumped into the lake—the proof was in the frying pan. "We couldn't eat the fish because they smelled so bad. That was a childhood memory that still sticks with me."[2]

A series of photos and a brief essay in the May 23, 1970, edition of the *Muskegon Chronicle* documented the problems in Muskegon Lake:

> Years ago, Muskegon was a lumber town nestled on the edge of a crystal clear lake. . . . Lumbermen built docks and dumped wood chips and sawdust into the lake. What harm could it do? The lake was big and the city needed the business.
>
> Then the trees went . . . and the heavy industry moved in. And the new foundries and plants built docks and dumped cinders and waste metal into the lake. What harm could it do? The lake was large and the city needed the business.
>
> Today, Muskegon is an industrial town nestled on the edge of a no-longer crystal clear lake. And it's a lake that's getting smaller because of all the gradual filling of its edges.

> Is it too late to save Muskegon Lake? The Save Our Lakes Committee says no . . . but we've got a long way to go.[3]

As the article correctly stated, the environmental torture of Muskegon Lake began in the 1800s, when sawmills that lined the lake dumped countless tons of sawdust, logs, and slabs of scrap wood into the lake. When the logging orgy that cleared the Muskegon River Valley of trees began to fade away, the few lumber barons who remained in the area turned their attention to new forms of commerce.

Muskegon's most successful lumberman, Charles Hackley, made it his personal mission to create a new wave of industrial development in the post-logging era. Working with other community leaders starting in the 1890s, Hackley helped the city of Muskegon secure two hundred thousand dollars in bonds to promote industrial development. The first company to benefit from the industrial development fund was the Central Paper Company mill, which began operating in 1899 and later became S. D. Warren and, most recently, Sappi Fine Paper. During the first two decades of the twentieth century, several other companies—foundries, a knitting mill, and a furniture company—built factories on or near the shores of Muskegon Lake. Still, not until the United States entered World War II in 1941 did the second wave of Muskegon's industrial era hit its stride.

The war generated numerous defense-related orders for foundries on the Muskegon Lake shoreline. The Continental Motors Manufacturing Company, which produced tank and airplane engines, increased its payroll from seven hundred to five thousand workers. Other foundries along the lake also benefited from the war economy; by the war's end in 1945, thirty-six thousand people were working in Muskegon industries, up from fourteen thousand before the war.[4] A community that had struggled to redefine itself after logging's demise had a renewed sense of pride. Life in Muskegon in the early 1940s was good, provided you could ignore the wretched air pollution that darkened the sky and water pollution that turned the surface of Muskegon Lake into a chemically induced rainbow.

Muskegon's third wave of economic development—the chemical manufacturing industry that prospered in other parts of the nation—drove the environmental abuse of Muskegon Lake to its apex in the 1960s. Chemical plants built along streams that flowed into the lake dumped toxic wastes into unlined storage lagoons and nearby surface waters. The poisonous compounds seeped through sandy soils, contaminating billions of gallons of groundwater and surface waters that flowed into the lower river and Muskegon Lake.

By the time the federal Water Pollution Control Act was enacted in 1972, vast areas of the lake bottom contained dangerous concentrations of toxic chemicals. The muddy lake bottom, once home to a thriving community of organisms known as benthos, was becoming a biological wasteland dominated by bloodworms and other pollution-tolerant organisms. Tiny, desirable benthos at the base of a food chain that supports fish and wildlife could not survive pollution that depleted oxygen from the water and poisoned the lake bottom. Many species of fish tainted with chemicals were unsafe to eat, the number of fish and animals in the lake was plummeting, and the practice of filling in shallow areas of the lake with sawdust and foundry slag had obliterated hundreds of acres of coastal wetlands that provided habitat for fish and wildlife. Muskegon Lake had hit rock bottom.

THE LAKE'S SAVIOR ARRIVED IN 1973 IN THE FORM OF A MASSIVE, INNOVATIVE wastewater treatment system that is so huge astronauts have reportedly spotted it from outer space. The new facility, which replaced Muskegon's inadequate sewage treatment plant on the banks of Muskegon Lake, was built several miles up the river at a cost of $50 million. The Muskegon County Wastewater Management System spans eleven thousand acres and has the capacity to treat 42 million gallons of wastewater daily. The facility's completion finally terminated industry's practice of dumping toxic wastes directly into Muskegon Lake—the norm until 1973. With the new system, wastewater from every industry and every house without a septic tank was processed before being discharged into the Muskegon River.

Unlike most treatment facilities, which use chemicals and biological agents to kill pathogens and neutralize toxins, the Muskegon County system uses the earth as a living filter. The facility stores wastewater in two massive lagoons, each covering 850 acres, where bacteria consume some of the contaminants. After solid materials settle in sludge on the bottom of the lagoons and tons of chemicals evaporate into the air, the wastewater is used to irrigate 5,000 acres of corn, alfalfa, and soybeans. That water then filters through the soil, is captured in drains, and is discharged into the Muskegon River. The county wastewater system has represented an unqualified success in terms of improving water quality in Muskegon Lake. "That wastewater plant did a lot of good for the lake. Before it was built, you could drive around and see dead fish all around the lake. You couldn't eat the perch. It was impossible. They smelled like oil," said Ed Subler, a legendary Muskegon angler who has fished the lake since the 1920s. "The water in the lake was murky, and you couldn't see down in the water at all. Now the water is very clear. . . . I eat everything I catch in the lake."[5]

Despite lingering contaminants in some fish and lake bottom sediments, water quality in Muskegon Lake has improved significantly since the wastewater system was built. Data collected by government agencies that monitor the system's performance have shown that the facility rarely discharges excessive amounts of pollutants into the Muskegon River. Fred Eyer, a longtime district water quality supervisor with the Michigan Department of Natural Resources, praised the wastewater system in a 1992 newspaper interview. "When you look in Michigan, [the wastewater treatment system is] unique. When you look nationwide, it's unique. When you look worldwide, it's still unique. The county should be thankful it has a treatment system that can treat substances as well as it can."[6] The facility has subsequently drawn visitors from communities all over the world, many of whom have borrowed its design when building their own wastewater treatment systems.

The unusual facility has not been immune to controversy. Egelston Township Supervisor John Flickema, who supported building the facility in his community, was recalled from office for endorsing the project. Nauseating odors from the facility triggered lawsuits in the 1970s and '80s. And the wastewater collection system that carries raw sewage several miles east of Muskegon has been plagued by repeated pipe breaks that have dumped millions of gallons of untreated sewage into Muskegon Lake. In 1999, a ruptured sewer main dumped 25 million gallons of untreated sewage into the lake four days before the opening of Michigan's trout, walleye, and pike fishing season. The release forced the cancellation of a walleye fishing tournament and prompted health officials to warn people to stay off the lake until bacteria counts returned to safe levels.[7]

Despite its flaws, the Muskegon County Wastewater Management System deserves credit for the dramatic improvements in Muskegon Lake's water quality. Fishing tournaments resumed on the lake within a decade of the sewage treatment plant's completion. The bowed white sheets of sailboats now float across the water on many summer evenings, and anglers flock to the lake to fish for walleye and perch.

Like the removal of the Newaygo Dam four years earlier, completion of the Muskegon County Wastewater Management System represented a turning point in an emerging effort to restore the tattered Muskegon River ecosystem. The locals were justifiably proud. Just two years later, the community that rallied to clean up its lake would be sharply divided over a lucrative economic development proposal that tested the resolve of residents who professed a commitment to restoring and protecting the lake.

North Star Steel was a Minneapolis-based company looking to expand its Midwest operations with a new mill in 1975. The company settled on a site on the south shore of Muskegon Lake, where officials proposed building a $50 million mill. The project, which would have created five hundred jobs with an annual payroll of $15 million, seemed like a no-brainer for Muskegon, an economically depressed community suffering from a high unemployment rate. But there was a catch: to build the mill, North Star officials said the company needed to fill in fifty-six acres of Muskegon Lake to create a site large enough for the new factory.

The proposed fill infuriated local environmentalists, who in the late 1960s began fighting every proposal to dump material in Muskegon Lake. Filling the lake was a time-honored tradition—lumber mills that lined the lake in the 1800s often created additional storage space by turning hundreds of acres of wetlands into land along the shoreline. Filling the shallow, mucky areas along the Muskegon Lake shoreline with sawdust, dirt, or discarded steel was the quickest and easiest way to ensure access to the deep areas of Muskegon Lake that were ideal for nineteenth-century lumber schooners and the huge freighters that became the lifeblood of industry in the late twentieth century.

The North Star Steel project was Michigan's spotted owl controversy of the 1970s, a classic case of jobs versus the environment. Supporters of the mill said that it would pull Muskegon out of a prolonged economic slump; opponents refused to surrender, urging North Star to build the mill at an old city landfill on the east end of Muskegon Lake and holding their ground against the proposal to fill in part of the lake. Opponents of the mill filed a lawsuit in federal court to block the project, lobbied federal officials, and protested the project at public hearings. A local labor group countered by presenting petitions bearing the signatures of ten thousand people who supported the project. William Jackson, owner of a local chemical manufacturing firm and founder of the environmental group Save Our Lakes, was among the more than one thousand people who attended an October 1975 community forum on the North Star project. Jackson, a chemist, summed up the feelings of many opponents during the five-hour-long meeting: "Since 1967, we have successfully combated every industrial fill that has been attempted [on Muskegon Lake] and we cannot in good conscience condone this one. It would be a short range economic benefit but a long term detriment. And environmentally, we think it would be a disaster."[8]

Two days later, an editorial in the *Muskegon Chronicle* vilified North Star's opponents for inundating federal agencies and the company with letters urging that the plant be built elsewhere. The newspaper urged project supporters to write letters in favor of the project to the U.S. Army Corps of Engineers, the agency that would decide whether North Star could fill in part of Muskegon Lake. The newspaper even included the name and address of the corps official in charge of the project. In its editorial, the newspaper issued a dire warning: "If we lose the mill you can bet your unemployment check, safely, that we'll be written off the prospect list by developers all over the country. Down in Lansing [the state capital] they'll just draw a red ring around Muskegon's location on the map and kiss us off—forever."[9]

On November 8, 1975, frustrated North Star officials announced that the company would build its mill in Monroe, a waterfront community on the east side of Michigan. Muskegon city officials called the decision a tragedy. Robert VanLente, a Muskegon resident who had sued to block construction of the steel mill, declared a victory for the environment. "While the loss of the mill is unfortunate, it is not tragic. Muskegon is on the move. She is cleaning up and her quality of life is improving," VanLente said in a newspaper article.[10]

The passage of thirty years has provided some answers to the raging debate over the North Star project. Muskegon remained an economically depressed community in 2005, with one of the state's highest unemployment rates. On the flip side, Muskegon Lake became a playground for sailors and anglers and supports a bustling tourism economy. By the turn of the twenty-first century, anglers and scientists from near and far were heaping praise on the lake's thriving, diverse fishery.

A group of scientists from the University of Georgia who came to Muskegon in 2002 to study sturgeon that migrate up the river each spring were astounded by Muskegon Lake's population of flathead catfish—a large, ugly fish considered a delicacy by many southerners. The gill nets the scientists used to trap sturgeon routinely captured flatheads weighing twenty pounds, sometimes more. The news generated little excitement among local anglers, most of whom were more interested in catching perch, walleye, and salmon than fish with whiskers. The Georgia scientists were stunned to learn that anglers were not in hot pursuit of huge flathead catfish in Muskegon Lake. "If the people in Georgia could see this, they would say it's incredible," said Eugene Hoyano, a fisheries technician. "I'm not sure the fishermen around here know what a great resource they have in these catfish. They're excellent fighters and the fillets are delicious. These aren't your typical bottom feeders [like channel cats] as flatheads prefer to feed on bait fish such as shad, suckers and bluegills."[11]

Sailors and pleasure boaters also flocked to Muskegon Lake after the water cleared up. The number of boat slips on Muskegon's portion of Muskegon Lake increased from 571 in 1980 to 1,578 in 1995. The site where North Star wanted to build is now home to a popular 263-slip marina.[12] Attractive parks, condominiums, and office complexes now occupy parts of the Muskegon Lake shoreline formerly dominated by foundries and other factories that fouled the air and water. In 2004, a high-speed car ferry began shuttling tourists between Milwaukee and Muskegon, landing at a site on Muskegon Lake near where North Star wanted to build its steel mill.

After nearly two centuries of industries abusing Muskegon Lake for profit, the city has ensured that such abuse will not happen again in the foreseeable future. In 1981, Muskegon city officials adopted a land use plan that called for residential, commercial, and recreational development—but no industrial development—along the Muskegon Lake waterfront. That shift from industrial- to residential- and recreation-related development has drawn people to Muskegon Lake to fish, sail, and hang out at marinas. However, marinas and condominiums are not environmentally benign. Marinas often need to be dredge lake bottoms to provide deep enough water for boats, a process that can destroy aquatic vegetation that supports fish. Still, Muskegon clearly is benefiting environmentally from the transformation of its lakefront.

All is not well with the lake, at least not yet. The past practice of using Muskegon Lake as a dumping ground for industrial waste and human sewage has left the lake with a toxic hangover. In the 1980s, severe sediment contamination, tainted fish, and the loss of wildlife habitat earned the lake a spot on the International Joint Commission's list of forty-two Great Lakes areas of concern. The lake is far cleaner today than in 1970, but it is far from pristine. Muskegon's industrial heritage has saddled the waterway with vexing environmental problems.

In 1999, Rick Rediske was on a mission to determine whether sediment on the bottom of Muskegon Lake was still laced with toxic chemicals. It was old news that the lake bottom sediments contained a witch's brew of toxic and cancer-causing chemicals, calling cards from the factories that had lined the lake for more than a century. But Rediske and his colleagues from Grand Valley State University were stunned by what they found: tar balls, dozens of them, on the bottom of the lake.

At a sampling site near Terrace Point, where a former coal gasification plant had been demolished and the site transformed into a ritzy office building, restaurant, and marina, scientists found numerous tar balls the size of golf balls. The first hint of trouble came when they dropped anchor in about fifty feet of water and a small oil slick came to the surface. "We had heard there were tar balls in parts of the lake, but finding that much coal tar in the lake was a surprise. That's something you don't want in the lake," Rediske said.[13]

Despite those problems, Muskegon Lake is far cleaner than it was in 1970. Nevertheless, in 2005 advisories remained in effect urging people to limit their consumption of some species of fish and wildlife caught in the lake. Contaminated sediments on the lake bottom restricted dredging in the lakes, and large areas of fish and wildlife habitat had been eliminated. The good news was that water quality in the lake had improved enough to prompt scientists to develop scientifically-based targets that, if met, would allow Muskegon Lake to shed its dubious status as a toxic hot spot.

Muskegon Lake and its feeder streams have provided a myriad of environmental surprises and prompted numerous incidents of moral indignation for Rediske and others who live near the polluted waterways. One of the most extreme sources of pollution entering Muskegon Lake was found in the early 1990s: Ruddiman Creek, a small stream that runs through much of Muskegon's urban area.

At the beginning of the twentieth century, Ruddiman Creek was notorious for transporting raw sewage, oil, and chemicals into Muskegon Lake. Rediske was outraged when he discovered in 1998 that Ruddiman Creek essentially constituted an open sewer flowing through a residential area. Elevated levels of bacteria from human or animal feces routinely fouled the creek, and bottom sediments were contaminated with dangerous concentrations of sixteen different toxic chemicals, including lead, mercury, cyanide, arsenic, and other cancer-causing compounds. Muskegon city officials blamed the bacteria problem on raccoons that live and defecate in storm sewers that empty into the creek, but people living near the creek were skeptical of that claim.

Scientists determined that pollutants in the creek bottom mud came from twenty-seven facilities—gas stations, dry cleaners, foundries, and plating firms—that discharged chemical wastes into storm sewers. Meetings were held with people who live near the creek, including parents of children who played in and around the toxic stream. All involved agreed that immediate action was necessary to protect public health. That was in 2000. A $10.6 million sediment cleanup in Ruddiman Creek began in late 2005. By then, scientists had discovered extreme pollution in Ryerson Creek and Four Mile Creek, two other streams flowing into Muskegon Lake.

Frustrated residents have lobbied—in some cases begged—state and federal officials to promptly clean up the most polluted streams in the Muskegon River watershed. Theresa Bernhardt, a neighborhood activist who chairs the Ruddiman Creek Task Force, has on numerous occasions expressed her frustration over the slow pace of cleanup work in the creek. "I'm tired of waiting," Bernhardt said during a public meeting in 2000. "Every day that we wait is another day that residents are exposed to this."[14] Worried that her children were still playing in the creek's toxic mud, Bernhardt eventually moved her family further away from Ruddiman Creek. She remained active in efforts to clean up the creek.

When it comes to contaminated sediments, Muskegon Lake and Ruddiman Creek are not unique. Such sediments are a problem at dozens of sites in the Great Lakes, with cleanup estimated to cost at least $5 billion and take decades to complete. Cash-strapped government agencies were unlikely to begin digging contaminated mud off the bottom of Muskegon Lake anytime soon. Given that, the best-case scenario was that the amount of pollutants entering the lake from local industries and communities upstream would not increase appreciably in the coming years.

History has proven that the Muskegon River and Muskegon Lake could recover from extreme abuse by humans, but it is a slow, costly, and often incomplete process. That may be the most powerful incentive to do everything possible to prevent future water pollution in the Muskegon River system. The fact that pollution, like water, always flows downhill represents an ominous reality for Muskegon Lake, which acts as a giant kidney that filters pollutants out of the river before it enters Lake Michigan. The lake will be one of the main barometers of environmental health in the Muskegon River system in the coming decades as more people move into the river valley and developers build more homes, shopping centers, and parking lots.

Unlike humans, who could seek a kidney transplant if that essential organ failed, there was no way to replace the cleansing powers of Muskegon Lake. Construction of Muskegon County's mammoth wastewater treatment system represented a huge step toward cleaning up the lake. The future health of the lake would be determined in large part by the health of the river that flows into it. The burning question was whether the more than four hundred thousand people who live in the watershed would make the lifestyle changes needed to protect the river and the quality of life enjoyed by their neighbors downstream.

9.

SACRED COWS

> To those who live here, it's alive, a part of us. The old dam . . . is loved by all.
>
> —Fred Mare, Newaygo County physician, in a 1982 essay marking the seventy-fifth anniversary of the construction of Croton Dam

On a hot August night in 1989, a crowd of four hundred people packed a small, stuffy school gymnasium in Newaygo County's Croton Township to vent the kind of anger usually reserved for companies attempting to build landfills or halfway houses near established neighborhoods. For more than two hours, one local resident after another stepped up to the microphone to berate government bureaucrats viewed as missionaries of disaster. Angry residents presented state officials with petitions bearing the signatures of fourteen thousand people opposed to changes they feared would hurt their property values and destroy the character of Newaygo County, a scenic, tranquil area where small towns are scattered among abundant lakes and forests in the heart of the Muskegon River basin. The uproar was unprecedented in the former logging community. Never before had so many locals spoken out so passionately in defense of the status quo. Then again, 1989 marked the first time anyone had ever suggested removing three beloved hydroelectric dams in the Muskegon River.

The Croton, Hardy, and Rogers dams were built in the heart of the Muskegon River in the early 1900s. By the end of the century, those dams and the huge ponds created by harnessing forty miles of scenic river had become community treasures. Cottages lined the banks of Croton and Rogers Ponds, and the four-thousand-acre pond behind Hardy Dam had become a recreational hot spot, attracting anglers, boaters, and campers from across Michigan who came to play in the deep, still waters and the lush woods that surround the reservoir. The fact the dams and reservoirs existed at the expense of the Muskegon River was not an issue in the community until John Robertson, then chief of fisheries for the Michigan Department of Natural Resources (DNR), did the unthinkable. In a 1989 newspaper interview, Robertson suggested removing the Croton, Hardy, and Rogers Dams along with several other hydroelectric dams on the Manistee and Au Sable Rivers. Robertson called the dams "concrete and steel monsters" that destroyed long stretches of Michigan's finest rivers while generating just 2 percent of the state's electricity. His comments came as Consumers Energy, owner of the Croton, Hardy, and Rogers dams, was seeking to renew its fifty-year federal license to operate the facilities. "I think these dams deprive the public of more value than they provide . . . and they should ultimately be removed. In their time, these hydroelectric facilities provided for the development of this state and they were incredibly valuable. But environmental issues weren't a concern 70 years ago."[1]

Some people labeled Robertson a hero; others called him a heretic. Conservationists praised him for daring to take up the controversial cause of dam removal. Residents of communities near the Croton, Hardy, and Rogers reservoirs were united and passionate in their determination to save the dams. Their collective reaction to Robertson's call to remove the structures could have been summed up in four words: "Over our dead bodies." Robertson's crusade ultimately failed. In 1994, the Federal Energy Regulatory Commission (FERC) granted Consumers Energy a license to operate Croton, Hardy, and Rogers dams through 2034. However, the federal agency for the first time required Consumers to minimize the dams' impacts on the river by mimicking the Muskegon's natural flow downstream of Croton Dam, thereby reducing erosion of stream banks. The government also ordered Consumers to study whether the dams increase water temperatures and decrease oxygen concentrations in the river (they do) and find ways to reduce those impacts.

DAMS HAVE LONG BEEN THE FRIED LIVER OF MANMADE STRUCTURES—people either love or hate them. Middle ground is rarely an option when it comes to debating the benefits and environmental costs of keeping dams in rivers. Dams are a source of clean energy and provide secondary benefits such as flood control, recreational activities, and water for irrigation and consumption. The downside is that dams fundamentally alter rivers, creating barriers that disrupt natural water flow; alter water temperatures; block the movement of sediment, fish, and nutrients; and often increase soil erosion downstream. Thousands of fish died annually in the Croton, Hardy, and Rogers dams, chewed up in spinning turbines or crushed by extreme hydraulic pressure as they pass through the structures.

The emotional debate Robertson triggered was not the first time dam removal has sparked public outrage in the Muskegon River basin. The first attempt to remove the Big Rapids Dam in 1966—which was botched and only partially completed—and the successful removal of the Newaygo Dam in 1969 were extremely controversial. Many residents of those communities argued for keeping the dams. In the late 1990s, Big Rapids city officials encountered a second wave of opposition when they sought funds to remove what was left of the city's hydroelectric dam.

Big Rapids Mayor Ed Burch was among a group of local leaders in 1999 who wanted to see the Big Rapids Dam rebuilt, three decades after a contractor demolished the top two-thirds of the structure before running out of money and fleeing town. "Instead of taking it out, I thought we should keep a low-head dam in the river and make real big rapids," Burch said.[2] He changed his stance when the state refused to allow the city to restore the dam; instead, the Michigan DNR forced the city to remove the dangerous structure, which contributed to the deaths of several people who tried to canoe or tube over it.

With the Big Rapids dam removal completed in 2001, the city raised $450,000 in donations to build a pedestrian/bike trail along a four-mile section of the restored river. The dam removal and Riverwalk project changed the community's attitude about the river, Burch said. "People are using the river more—to canoe, go tubing, fishing, or kids just playing in the water. When our two daughters were married, we had the rehearsal dinner at North End Park, overlooking the river. What a great place to have a dinner."

Removing the dam restored a mile of whitewater rapids in the heart of the city and improved fish habitat above and below the dam. The free-flowing river scoured its channel, removing a blanket of sand and exposing beds of gravel that some species of fish need to spawn. After all was said and done, Burch counted himself among the converts who belatedly embraced removal of the city's historic dam. "Big Rapids is here because of the river, not in spite of it. I don't think anybody visualized that the river could be this great after the dam was taken out."[3]

Removing dams is a tricky business—politically, economically, and environmentally. Communities often hesitate to support the removal of dams, the work is costly, and, if carried out improperly, pulling a fortified structure out of a river can send tons of sediment downstream, endangering fish and other aquatic organisms.

"There are few issues that excite more controversy amongst a significant portion of the engineering and environmental community than the issue of removing a functioning dam," according to a 2003 article by the American Society of Civil Engineers.

> The parties often find themselves polarized with the one extreme seeing dam removal as an act of sacrilege while the other side sees it as an act of salvation. While there may be much sentiment attached to an older and nonfunctioning structure there is generally a modicum of common sense that tells all of us that when a dam has outlived its physical life span it should be removed. However, a proposal to remove a functioning dam seems to some to be an act that defies common sense.[4]

Dams played an integral role in the development of the United States, powering the Industrial Revolution by generating electricity for sawmills, grist mills, and numerous other industries. Dams provide water for agricultural irrigation and create reservoirs that provide recreational activities and in some cases drinking water. In 2000, the United States had seventy-five thousand dams standing more than six feet high. The National Research Council has put the number of all dams in the U.S. at 2.5 million.[5] Michigan has twenty-six hundred dams, ninety-four of them in the Muskegon River and its tributaries.

Dams have been used in various parts of the world for five thousand years, but not until the 1980s did removing dams come into vogue. More than 450 dams have been removed in the United States over the past century, with most removals taking place since 1980.[6] The pace of dam removals intensified in the 1980s because many small dams built early in the twentieth century had become old, obsolete, unsafe or had reservoirs filled with sediment. Most dams removed over the past century were small structures that stood less than five feet high. Fewer than 200 dams over five feet high were removed in the United States during the twentieth century.[7]

The pace of dam removal in the United States picked up during the 1990s, when studies began finding that the environmental costs of keeping those structures often outweighed the economic benefits. In 1999, the 160-year-old Edwards Dam was removed from the Kennebec River in Maine. It was the first operating hydroelectric dam in the United States ordered destroyed by the FERC, the agency that licenses large hydropower facilities. The project restored eighteen miles of free-flowing river and allowed ten species of sea fish to migrate further up the river.

Since 2000, large dams have been removed in North Carolina, Washington, and Michigan. Consumers Energy, which owns the hydroelectric dams on the Muskegon River, removed the ninety-year-old Stronach Dam from the scenic Pine River in 2003. The project uncovered three miles of rapids above the former hydroelectric dam in northern Michigan, which in turn contributed to an increase in the trout population.[8]

Environmentalists and fishing groups pressed for more dam removals on the grounds that many of the structures were outdated, dangerous and caused severe ecological harm to rivers and streams. "The rapid aging of dams (especially small ones) and the costs of maintaining old dams practically ensures that dam removal will continue at a brisk pace for the foreseeable future," according to a 2002 article in the journal *Bioscience* by N. Leroy Poff and David D. Hart.[9]

In most cases, age, usefulness, and safety were the determining factors in whether a dam was removed. The expected life span of the average dam is fifty years; older dams often do not meet current safety standards and are living on borrowed time, according to the American Society of Dam Safety

Officials. One-quarter of all large dams in the United States—nearly twenty thousand structures—are more than fifty years old; by 2020, that figure will reach 85 percent.[10] The Association of State Dam Safety Officials estimated in 2002 that the United States had twenty-six hundred unsafe dams. Repairing, replacing, or removing unsafe, privately owned dams had an estimated cost of $36.2 billion.[11]

In 2004, the governors of Pennsylvania and Michigan called on President George W. Bush to increase federal funding to repair or remove unsafe dams. In a letter to the president, Michigan Governor Jennifer Granholm said that Michigan had at least twenty dams with serious deficiencies, eleven of which could cause significant flooding and loss of life if the structures burst. "The nation's dams have been overlooked at significant cost to property owners, public safety and the environment. For quite some time we have heard from dam owners, particularly owners of small dams, many of which are small municipalities, who want to do the right thing but are unable to because of the expense," Granholm wrote.[12]

Some states, particularly Wisconsin and Pennsylvania, took an aggressive approach to removing obsolete and dangerous dams. Wisconsin, which has thirty-eight hundred dams, has removed eighty dams since 1960, fifty-six of them since 1980. The average cost of removing those structures was $115,000 per dam, far less than the average estimate of $700,000 needed to repair each of those dams.[13] Between 1996 and 2002, Pennsylvania removed seventeen dams from the Conestoga River at a cost of less than $1 million. Removing those dams allowed American shad to return to the Conestoga after an eighty-year absence. The restored fishery is expected to generate as much as $3 million annually for the local economy.[14]

Denny Caneff, executive director of the River Alliance of Wisconsin, said persuading communities to remove dams is often a tough sell. Old dams are often local landmarks, homeowners around a reservoir are reluctant to give up waterfront property, and people commonly fear that removing a dam will expose huge, unsightly mud flats that create breeding grounds for insects and disease. "Dam removal is pretty tricky sometimes. People get pretty attached to what they think is their lake or pond [behind the dam]. People connect to rivers in ways that they don't connect to other natural features. When trying to remove a dam, you have to inform people that the river will be nice once the dam is removed. Let them imagine what's possible."[15]

Michigan lagged behind other states when it came to removing obsolete and dangerous dams. Between 1998 and 2004, just thirteen dams were removed in the state. But there were signs of change. The successful removal of the Big Rapids Dam remnant in 2001 has increased interest in dam removal elsewhere in Michigan, said Sharon Hanshue, the dam expert for the Michigan DNR. Newspapers, engineering journals, and lake association newsletters published numerous articles about the Big Rapids project. Michigan's dam safety unit also has became aggressive in pursuing removal of obsolete and unsafe dams. Prior to 1998, the state was more inclined to press for the repair of old dams than to force removals, Hanshue said. In its 2003 and 2004 budgets, the Michigan DNR devoted all of its two-hundred-thousand-dollar fund for inland fisheries grants to dam removal projects. Most of those grants funded engineering studies, the first step toward dam removal, Hanshue said.

> It's not a lot of money, but it's a step in the right direction, and it overcomes the major obstacle for many small dam owners—coming up with the money for engineering studies. We've actually started to move the rock up the mountain. I'm starting to sense momentum in this state toward dam removals. The city of Big Rapids got the word out about the dam removal. I think that project also opened some eyes and showed that removing a dam doesn't have to be funded only by the state.[16]

The state of Michigan released a 2003 position paper on dam removal that was nothing short of revolutionary in a state that since its inception in 1837 has been ruled by industry. According to the paper, "Dams that no longer serve a purpose should be removed for safety, economic and environmental reasons. . . . Selective dam removal is an integral component of successful watershed management. The Michigan Department of Natural Resources promotes river restoration through the selective removal of dams that no longer serve a useful purpose."[17] If old age and obsolescence were criteria for removing dams, twenty-five of the ninety-four dams in the Muskegon River and its tributaries were prime candidates for removal. Dams in the Muskegon River system that are more than fifty years old, obsolete, or unsafe include the Nartron, Hersey, Marion, and Falmouth dams, all of which were obsolete and disrupted trout streams, and the Morley

Dam, a defunct hydroelectric dam on the Little Muskegon River that has not produced electricity since 1995. Several other small dams that maintained artificially high water levels in lakes were of questionable value. The Rowe Dam no. 2 on Penoyer Creek, a defunct hydroelectric dam built in 1915, was used to maintain a private pond at the expense of a trout stream. It was one of several small dams that disrupted publicly owned streams for the private enjoyment of a few people.

Insufficient funds and a lack of political will have been the primary obstacles to removing dams in the Muskegon River system and elsewhere in Michigan. Several communities have rallied to save local dams on the grounds that they are historic structures. Residents of the village of Marion, in the upper Muskegon River system, organized in 2000 to fight a state proposal to remove a historic dam and millpond, a remnant of the town's nineteenth-century logging heritage. "There was a lot of outrage," said Jim Blevins, editor and publisher of the weekly *Marion Press,* in a 1999 interview. "Our biggest fear if we lose the dam is that we'll end up with a swamp, a muddy mess where the mill pond is now. Basically, the state wants to take out every dam in the Muskegon River watershed."[18]

Unwilling to wage a bruising court fight over the dam, state and federal officials worked with village leaders to find an alternative. The solution: a $4.5 million project to divert the Middle Branch River around the dam by building a dike along one side of the sediment-choked millpond. Removing the dam would have cost about $500,000, but the politically expedient alternative allowed Marion to keep its dam and millpond. The project also would liberate five miles of the Middle Branch River, a blue-ribbon trout stream, and eliminate thermal pollution downstream of the dam.

Community leaders in the village of Hersey, on the banks of the Hersey and Muskegon Rivers, battled for more than a decade to save the town's crumbling dam from the wrecking ball. State officials allowed the structure to remain in place despite warning village leaders that the dam was in danger of collapsing. In a 1999 newspaper article, an engineer in the state's dam safety unit said that the agency did not force the village of Hersey to remove its dangerous dam because state officials did not want to "take a heavy-handed approach." Milton Day, a Hersey village trustee at the time, said, "We want to put the water back in our little pond. It just needs some repairs like a lot of old structures."[19] By 2004, however, village leaders had changed their tune and began working with state officials and the Muskegon River Watershed Assembly to bring about the removal of the dam.

Given the political difficulty of removing small dams such as those in Marion and Hersey, imagine the fierce battles that lie ahead when large dams on the Muskegon River are targeted for removal. The Croton, Hardy, and Rogers dams still produce electricity and show no signs of structural weakness. But the dams will not last forever. The facilities are licensed to operate through 2034, at which time the structures could be relicensed, decommissioned and left in place, or removed from the river.

The sheer size of Croton, Hardy, and Rogers dams will make removal of those structures far more complex than yanking the Big Rapids or Newaygo dams out of the river. Because the three hydroelectric dams have fundamentally changed the lower Muskegon River, there will be an increased risk of creating environmental problems if or when those structures are removed. The dams prevent harmful exotic species such as sea lamprey from migrating up the river beyond Croton Dam; the structures also keep contaminated Lake Michigan salmon from reaching the upper river, where toxic chemicals in their body fat could harm bald eagles that feast on the fish. And Hardy Dam, which draws frigid water from deep in its 65-billion-gallon reservoir, sends unusually cold water downstream, a phenomenon that helps support a nationally recognized trout fishery downstream of Croton Dam.

State officials contend that the upper and lower river, currently divided by the hydroelectric dams, need to be ecologically connected. Until the 47 miles of river below Croton Dam are connected to the 172 miles of water above it, the Muskegon will remain a dysfunctional river.

There were two ways to connect the upper and lower river: remove the hydroelectric dams or install costly fish ladders at those structures. "Fish passage at the hydroelectric dams would benefit the entire river," according to Richard O'Neal, a fisheries biologist with the Michigan DNR.

The concept of reconnecting the fractured river was one of the reasons the Great Lakes Fishery Trust in 1999 designated the Muskegon a "first-priority river." The trust has spent millions of dollars on scientific studies designed to boost fish populations in the Muskegon River and in turn the

Great Lakes. The Muskegon played a crucial role in the Great Lakes sport fishery because it was Michigan's most productive salmon river, producing between three hundred thousand and four hundred thousand chinook annually. However, not everyone has jumped on the fish passage bandwagon.

Officials at Consumers Energy, which owns the Croton, Hardy, and Rogers hydroelectric dams, were skeptical about the state's fish passage plan. Their objections were to be expected: installing fish ladders could cost the utility millions of dollars. In addition, however, some respected scientists warned that installing fish passage devices over the dams was a dangerous proposition that could have dire consequences.

Consumers Energy officials and some local residents and business owners have also argued that ponds created by the dams are a more valuable source of recreational activities than a free-flowing river would be. After all, houseboats could not float on the free-flowing Muskegon, and there are hundreds of houseboats on Hardy Pond. State officials claim that a free-flowing river is more valuable, ecologically and for recreation-related activities, than a dammed river.

O'Neal, the state's point man in the debate over dams on the Muskegon, says Croton, Hardy, and Rogers dams were never intended as barriers to exotic species. And he said there were ways to liberate the river from the grip of dams and prevent exotic species from migrating upstream. Low-sill dams could be built across the river, allowing it to flow freely while blocking lamprey and other exotics from expanding their territory. O'Neal said that the economic, environmental, and recreational benefits of removing the hydroelectric dams—indeed, all dams—from the Muskegon River system would be immense.

> As a division [of the DNR], we're looking for free-flowing systems. We want these streams in their natural state. That's the best thing for these streams. Hydroelectric dams impound forty miles of the main stem of the Muskegon, the highest-gradient, most productive stretch of the river. At one time, walleye and sturgeon had free rein in the river: they could move from Lake Michigan all the way to Higgins Lake. But now we have dams in the way, and we have to be careful about providing passage because of lamprey and fish contaminant issues.[20]

The ecological significance of connecting the upper and lower sections of the Muskegon cannot be overstated. Restoring forty miles of fast-flowing river would provide terrific fish habitat and increase the amount of oxygen in water downstream of the Hardy and Croton dams. Oxygen concentrations in the river below the dams plunge to dangerously low levels each summer, which jeopardizes the health of fish. Elevated water temperatures in the reservoirs and immediately downstream of the hydroelectric facilities—coupled with decreased oxygen levels each summer and fall—put the Croton and Hardy dams in violation of Consumers' federal operating permits about 20 percent of the year, according to a 2003 study performed for the utility, although the "Rogers [Dam] consistently meets the water quality requirements of its FERC license."

> However, temperature values greater than the monthly average maximums did occur at both Hardy and Croton. At Hardy, the discharge water temperature often did not meet the FERC license requirements during the months of November and December in the years 1998 through 2001. While maximum water temperatures were exceeded in these months, the temperature conditions present would not be life-threatening to the cool-water and warm-water fish species present in the Hardy tailrace. Croton temperatures were often above the FERC licensed water quality requirements during the months of July through October each year. Following comparison of the hourly dissolved oxygen data for each [dam] discharge with the requirements set forth in the FERC licenses, it was determined that dissolved oxygen levels below their respective limits at both Hardy and Croton occur throughout the summer months.[21]

The thermal pollution downstream of Croton Dam endangers a steelhead fishery that attracts anglers from around the world to the lower Muskegon River. When the river's water temperature rises above sixty-nine degrees Fahrenheit, as it often does in the summer, juvenile steelhead are among the first fish to suffer. Because baby steelhead live in the river for three years before heading out into Lake Michigan, high water temperatures in the summer could reduce their numbers. Maximum daily water temperatures below Croton Dam routinely exceeded sixty-nine degrees during the summer months.

Research by scientists at the University of Michigan and at the Michigan DNR found that the density of juvenile steelhead in Bigelow Creek, a cold-water stream that flows into the Muskegon near Newaygo, was seven times greater than in the river's main channel. Fewer than ten thousand juvenile steelhead survive their first three years in the lower Muskegon and move into Lake Michigan; that was only a fraction of the steelhead that hatch in the river. The Little Manistee River, a smaller stream north of the Muskegon with a similar amount of fish spawning area, sends four times more juvenile steelhead into Lake Michigan annually. The difference: the Little Manistee remained a cold-water stream in the summer, while the Muskegon heated up as warm water from the top of the Croton Dam reservoir streamed into the river. One possible solution: pipe colder water from the bottom of Croton Pond into the river downstream of the dam, which could help the Muskegon keep its cool during the dog days of summer.[22]

In 1989, when the Michigan DNR held hearings to discuss renewing the operating licenses for the Croton, Hardy, and Rogers dams, no local resident came forward to advocate removing the historic structures. Quite the contrary. Local residents, business owners, and community leaders praised the dams and the way Consumers Energy operates the facilities. The support was not surprising, considering that Consumers is the county's largest taxpayer and that the operators of hundreds of cottages and several campgrounds, stores, and gas stations rely on the dam reservoirs for their livelihood and recreational activities. "Without Hardy Dam, we probably wouldn't be here in our business. The dam attracts so many people in the summer. . . . Without the summer business, we couldn't save enough for the wintertime, the four lean months of the year," said Judy Chesley, owner of Hilltop Grocery in Newaygo.[23]

Many residents near the dams had strong emotional ties to the structures. The August 12, 1981, edition of the *Fremont Times-Indicator* marked the fiftieth anniversary of the construction of the Hardy Dam by praising the structure as if it were a living, breathing organism. An article in the newspaper by Dave Hewitt said, "He is a shepherd, the shepherd of the Muskegon River, and his name is Hardy Dam. It isn't just the power. There is the scenic wonder over which he is master."

Matt Supinski, a fishing guide who works on the river below Croton Dam, believed that building fish ladders at the hydroelectric dams would be a waste of money. If fish ladders were installed, Supinski said, it was unlikely that salmon and steelhead would survive the forty-mile swim across the warm waters of the Croton, Hardy, and Rogers Dams. Removing the dams, in Supinski's view, would be sheer lunacy.

> If you remove those dams, it would fill the river with silt and wipe out the salmon and steelhead fisheries. It would be a disaster for a hundred years. Those dams are like having a giant charcoal filter in the river. They filter the sediment out of the water, and the bottom water released from Hardy dam is ice-cold. It would have been nice if the dams had never been built, but once they are there, you've stuck with them forever. Right now you've got a world-class salmon fishery, a world-class steelhead fishery, and sturgeon spawning in the lower river. Why screw it up?[24]

Supinski's opinion was the prevailing point of view among residents who live along the river and around the dam reservoirs. Most of those people have a vested interest in protecting the status quo: removing the dams would eliminate the dam reservoirs, which might lower property values and could jeopardize the lower river's fantastic trout and salmon fisheries.

Paul Seelbach, one of Michigan's top river researchers, said that people could not imagine the Muskegon without the Croton, Hardy, and Rogers dams because the structures have lorded over the river longer than most Michigan residents have been alive: "What people cannot see, because it's buried beneath the dams, is the potential of the river. It's huge."[25]

Envisioning the Muskegon River without hydroelectric dams does not require all that much imagination. Take a few hours to canoe the lower river, from Croton Dam to Newaygo. Soak up the natural beauty of the river as it courses through a deep, forested valley and meanders past wetlands and towering bluffs. Keep an eye on the river's transparent water—you are likely to see dozens of fish pass by in the course of the fourteen-mile trip. Gaze into the dark forests that shelter parts of the river, and you might see deer bounding through the woods. Shift your attention to the river's edge, where turtles sun themselves on rocks by the dozens and otters frolic on downed logs. And when the river's rippling current eases and there are no boulders or fallen trees to avoid, look toward the heavens and observe the avian ballet performed by kingfishers, osprey, hawks, bald eagles and great blue heron.

This was the most vibrant and arguably most scenic stretch of the Muskegon in 2005. Submerged beneath the Croton, Hardy, and Rogers dam reservoirs lie forty miles of river just like it, only better. Removing those dams would unleash a powerful river with miles of whitewater and a rocky bottom that could produce an additional 1.9 million chinook salmon and 362,000 steelhead annually.[26] *That's* hard to imagine.

10.

A TANGLED WEB

> Protecting the river in one political unit won't do any good if the town next door doesn't do its job.
>
> —Gale Nobes, chair of the Muskegon River Watershed Assembly

They gathered at the edge of Muskegon Lake on a frigid autumn morning, a dozen Good Samaritans trying to restore one small piece of a river's tattered ecosystem. Standing in the shadow of a towering smokestack at the B. C. Cobb power plant, the fifteen volunteers—anglers, teachers, government employees, utility workers, retirees, and homemakers—gave up a Saturday morning to drop wild rice seeds in a frigid lake. The conditions seemed ideal: the lake was calm and there were enough people to complete the job quickly. But there was a big problem: the surface of the lake was frozen. You cannot plant rice on ice.

For the first half hour, the volunteers made like human icebreakers. They crashed through the cardboard-thick ice in waders, each step creating another hole. They plunged shovels and steel rakes through the lake's glass ceiling, uncovering a shallow, marshy area where stands of wild rice once grew as thick as fields of sweet corn.

Before planting the rice, there was a brief ceremony in which the seed was blessed, following the tradition of Odawa Indians, who lived in villages on the lake's shoreline until the mid-1800s. The rice planters then got into formation, a line of people in neoprene waders that stretched 150 feet into the lake. On cue, they marched forward, casting handfuls of inch-long, mortar-shaped rice seeds into the water until their five-gallon pails were empty. This was the only way to restore the wild rice that dominated the shallows of Muskegon Lake and other parts of the Muskegon River system before lumber mills, marinas, and powerboats annihilated the towering plants.

For centuries, wild rice was a primary food source for the Odawa Indians who lived along the lake. Captains of the first lumber schooners that plied the Muskegon River in the 1800s knew wild rice meant the water was shallow and the lake bottom ruled by muck, conditions capable of stopping a boat dead in its tracks.[1] Restoring native stands of wild rice in the lake 160 years later would prove difficult.

Gale Nobes stood on the edge of the lake, a century after logs stopped flowing down the river, and surveyed his troops. He longed for the day when wild rice flourished again in the Muskegon River, in places such as Houghton Lake, Muskegon Lake, and the Maple River. But his tireless efforts to make it happen were routinely dashed by this brutal reality: nature no longer calls all the shots in this river. Powerful, human-induced changes were at work. That became painfully evident when Nobes returned to the rice-planting site the following spring. His optimism soon gave way to grief and rage.

The rice seeds had taken root in the lake bottom, but the plants were sheared off just below the water's surface. It looked like a lawnmower had skimmed through the marshy area—the rice looked like an underwater cornfield after the fall harvest. A few of the culprits were still picking at the crumbs of their wild rice feast.

Mute swans are large, stunning white creatures that can grow to forty pounds and are known for aggressive behavior. The birds should not be in this lake, eating stalks of native rice. Imported to northern Michigan in 1920, mute swans are one of more than 180 exotic species of plants and animals living in the Great Lakes region and complicating efforts to restore rivers, lakes, and wetlands.[2]

Nobes, a soft-spoken man whose calm demeanor belies his passion for preserving nature, was beside himself. Violent thoughts crossed his mind. "Mute swans eat the rice like crazy, but there's nothing we can do about it because even though they are an exotic species in Michigan, they are protected under the federal Migratory Bird Act."[3]

It was not unusual to see dozens of mute swans in the marsh that links the Muskegon River to Muskegon Lake, their shocking white heads rising above the vegetation as they cruise through narrow channels. The only way to prevent the swans, native ducks, and Canada geese from chowing down on the rice was to erect a fence around the plants, but that was not the image Nobes wanted to create. His goal was to plant enough rice seed to create self-sustaining stands of this native, ecologically important plant species. Instead, he had to cordon off areas of the lake to keep ravenous birds away. The fence was ugly but necessary.

A conundrum, indeed. But Nobes refused to concede defeat. The first chair of the Muskegon River Watershed Assembly, Nobes was a veteran foot soldier in a campaign to restore the river so that future generations can experience the joy of fishing, swimming, and boating in a river with lush wetlands and miles of water so clear you can see a fish approach before it strikes your line.

Nobes was a charter member in a small fraternity of conservationists who began working in the river system in the late 1980s. They started by placing logs and rocks along the banks of Cedar Creek, a trout stream that flows into the river near Muskegon. Erosion had caused the sandy banks to slide into the creek, suffocating prime trout habitat. At the time, Nobes was clueless about the challenges that would lie ahead for people who would attempt to restore a thoroughly manipulated river that drains a landmass the size of Rhode Island. "I didn't realize how daunting a task it was," he said.[4] Until the 1990s, efforts to restore the Muskegon occurred only sporadically and focused on isolated problems in the river: removing the Newaygo Dam, repairing eroding stream banks in Cedar Creek, building a new sewage treatment plant to clean up Muskegon Lake. There was no comprehensive plan to restore and protect the entire river. There was not even any money available to document the most critical environmental issues facing the river, let alone fix them.

That changed in 2000, when the struggling river restoration effort caught the attention of a wealthy philanthropist and officials at a private trust dedicated to improving Great Lakes fish populations. Civic groups are usually fortunate to have one benefactor who lends financial support to projects that often have more good intentions than money. The Muskegon River restoration project was blessed with financial support from two well-heeled foundations.

PETER WEGE WAS INCREDIBLY WEALTHY, BUT YOU WOULD NEVER KNOW it by his demeanor. He did not live in a huge mansion or drive fancy cars. Wege put his money where his heart was: health care, the arts, and the environment. Wege had long championed environmental causes in western Michigan. In 1969, he started the Center for Environmental Study, a Grand Rapids group that exposed plating companies illegally dumping toxic wastes into the Grand River. Wege's interest in environmental causes dated back to 1943, when the young military pilot had the misfortune of trying to land a plane in Pittsburgh, at the time a notoriously polluted steel mill town. Although it was daytime, "the smoke from the foundries was so thick I couldn't see the ground. The airport had to turn on the lights so I could see the runway. That was a very important day in my life," Wege said. "That was the day my environmental psyche began."[5]

Born into wealth in 1920—the only child of Peter Martin Wege, who founded Steelcase, the world's largest manufacturer of office furniture—the younger Wege never let his lofty status in the community interfere with his passion for environmental causes. A humble but outspoken man, he often angered his fellow corporate executives in the conservative western Michigan community of Grand Rapids with his activism. Some of his corporate counterparts considered him a fanatic, said Terri McCarthy, Wege's assistant at the Wege Foundation. The criticism never fazed him, she said: "Peter's message never changes. It's always, 'Clean air, clean water.' He's always brimming with that desire to save the planet."[6] Wege walked the walk when it came to environmental stewardship. The devout Catholic drove a hybrid sedan that got sixty miles per gallon, recycled his household garbage, and demanded that the publications his foundation underwrote were printed on recycled paper. He coined the term *economicology,* the merging of economics and ecology, which he believed must become an overriding principle to sustain the planet's natural resources: "Caring for creation is not an idle statement, but a credo to guide us on a daily basis," Wege said in his 1998 book, *Economicology: The Eleventh Commandment*. "For even though all living creatures are affected by pollution, only man has the ability to do something about it."[7]

When he learned about a burgeoning effort to restore the Muskegon River, Wege (pronounced WEGG-ee) pulled out his checkbook, convened a meeting of the state's top scientists, and issued a challenge. Develop a plan for preserving the Muskegon River system that could be used as a model for managing watersheds all over the Great Lakes basin, Wege told the scientists.

As it happened, the Great Lakes Fishery Trust was looking to spend millions of dollars developing a plan to restore one Michigan river. The trust wanted scientists to create a model for watershed restoration and protection that could be applied to other rivers. The Muskegon River would be the poster child for that effort.

The trust was established in the early 1990s as part of a settlement with Consumers Energy over massive fish kills at its Ludington Pumped Storage Plant. The trust used millions of dollars from that settlement to support research and restoration projects designed to improve Great Lakes sport fish populations. The Fishery Trust selected the Muskegon as a priority river because the waterway supports healthy populations of trout, salmon, and walleye and had the potential to support far more fish if the upper and lower rivers were linked, according to executive director Jack Bails. The trust provided nearly $5.5 million for scientific studies documenting critical problems facing the Muskegon and examining how to preserve the river in the face of increasing development pressure. Wege contributed another $2 million. The race to save the Muskegon in the face of increasing land development was on.

The days of volunteers dabbling in narrowly focused restoration projects gave way to teams of top-notch scientists and a watershed assembly with two full-time employees tackling the daunting task of restoring and protecting the sprawling, complex river system.

Wege, who was in the twilight of his life when he formed the Muskegon River Watershed Partnership in 2000, longed to educate people about the need to protect the Great Lakes by preserving the rivers that flow into the lakes. The five Great Lakes hold 20 percent of the world's fresh surface water, support a $4 billion fishery, and provide drinking water for 40 million people.

Rivers are a critical part of the Great Lakes ecosystem, arteries that link land and water. The Muskegon River's 2,725-square-mile drainage basin accounts for about 5 percent of the Lake Michigan watershed; the river in 2001 was the number one source of chinook salmon in the lake. "We want the Muskegon River project to become a model for all the watersheds flowing into the Great Lakes," Wege said. "Why reinvent the wheel?"[8]

Ecological restoration was a relatively new concept in the United States in 2000, a trend born of tough environmental protection laws adopted in the 1970s to clean up the nation's tortured waterways. The Muskegon was not the first Michigan river to be targeted for an environmental makeover. It did, however, represent the state's largest watershed management effort, said Bails, a former deputy director of the Michigan Department of Natural Resources.[9]

The notion of restoring nature would seem to be without controversy. After all, who could oppose healing Mother Earth? The reality was much more complex. Reversing environmental damage can be astronomically expensive, fraught with uncertainty and is often controversial due to conflicting social values. But it is possible to restore rivers, even those that have been severely polluted or altered, to a semblance of their natural condition.

Efforts to restore the Rouge River in Detroit in the 1990s yielded tremendous improvements. By reducing the volume of untreated sewage and storm water runoff entering the river, the Rouge project improved water quality and fish and wildlife populations in a river that had been left for dead in the 1970s. The national demonstration project provided a test of whether communities could restore a severely polluted urban river. It was an overwhelming success. The Rouge is still far from pristine, but it is also a far cry from the river that routinely became an open sewer following periods of heavy rainfall.[10]

The Rouge was one of the earliest attempts to restore a Michigan river by attacking problems across an entire watershed. Communities in the Rouge watershed restored wetlands, reduced the use of lawn chemicals, and separated miles of combined sewer pipe that dumped untreated sewage into the river after heavy rainfall.

The Muskegon River restoration effort would follow a similar holistic approach but on a much grander scale—the Muskegon's watershed is nearly six times larger than that of the Rouge. Size matters when it comes to restoring rivers. Quite simply, it costs more to restore large rivers and waterways that have been radically altered by human activities. That point has been driven home in Florida, where the state and the U.S. Army Corps of Engineers spent $518 million on a fifteen-year project to restore a 43-mile stretch of the Kissimmee River. The Kissimmee, which flows between Orlando and Lake Okeechobee, once was a winding, unpredictable 103-mile river. Between 1961 and 1972, the corps turned the river into a 56-mile drainage ditch to keep floodwaters away from Orlando and Disney World.

The corps began restoring the Kissimmee in 1998 at the request of state officials. Once completed, the project will restore forty square miles of wetlands. The first stretch of river to be liberated has made a dramatic recovery since dams were removed and the Kissimmee was allowed to rediscover its natural, meandering channel. "The benefits to the restored stretch of the river have been instant and obvious," according to a *Washington Post* article.

> Oxygen levels are increasing, so native fish such as largemouth bass and black crappie are returning. So are skinny-legged wading birds—great blue and tricolor and black-crowned night herons, glossy and white ibis, roseate spoonbills with dazzling pink coats. Shorebirds and waterfowl are back, too. By contrast, in the unrestored ditch, there are few fish but gar and bowfin and few birds but cattle egrets.[11]

In 2002, the Kissimmee project represented the most ambitious river restoration ever attempted in the United States. It has earned widespread praise from conservation groups and scientists who lobbied for restoring the river.

Lou Toth, an employee of the South Florida Water Management District who worked on the Kissimmee project, said in a 2002 newspaper interview that the plan succeeded because it was simple: blow up dams, buy out ranchers who had settled in the river's dried-up wetlands, and let the river reclaim its natural course. "This is about as pure as a restoration project can get," Toth said. "It's not about making all the stakeholders happy. It's not manipulating nature and managing different parts of the system for different things. We just went out and did our best for the environment."[12]

Ecological restoration projects can also backfire, leading to disastrous, unintended consequences. The first attempt to remove the Big Rapids Dam from the Muskegon River in 1966 was a colossal failure. The contractor failed to contain sand and silt that had accumulated behind the structure over the course of a century. When he dynamited the dam, one million cubic yards of sediment were flushed downstream, clogging the river channel and flooding dozens of homes.

Three years later, the state of Michigan removed the Newaygo Dam. The project succeeded, at least in terms of removing the dam and allowing fish from Lake Michigan to reach another fourteen miles of river upstream of Newaygo. But state officials left much of the sediment behind the dam in place when the structure was removed, and the 1986 flood carried the sediment downstream much faster than was predicted, burying miles of riverbed under a blanket of sand.

In some cases, ecosystem restoration can create situations that were never imagined. Other well-intentioned projects are crippled by bad planning or faulty science. That was the case in South Florida, where a $7.8 billion plan to restore the Everglades—once a mammoth, free-flowing river of grass—sparked intense criticism just two years into the thirty-year project. The Comprehensive Everglades Restoration Plan was supposed to increase water levels and improve wildlife habitat in the Everglades, vast areas of which were sucked dry by water diversion projects built to reduce flooding in cities and benefit the state's lucrative sugar industry. The linchpin of the restoration plan: capture one trillion gallons of fresh water flushed into the ocean each year and store it in reservoirs until it can be distributed, when needed, to farms, homes, and the Everglades. But the project was based on unproven technology, and federal officials were not sure it would work.

A series of *Washington Post* articles in 2002 revealed numerous flaws in the project that had some supporters of the plan predicting it would amount to a monumental failure. "It's all falling apart before my eyes," Richard Harvey, the U.S. Environmental Protection Agency's South Florida director, said in an interview. "We were all singing 'Kumbaya.' Now we're singing 'Can't Get No Satisfaction.'" U.S. Fish and Wildlife Service biologist Bob Gasaway was more blunt. "I don't see a shred of evidence that all this money will help the environment."[13]

Similar rumblings of criticism began to surface in the Muskegon River basin in 2004, four years after Wege and the Great Lakes Fishery Trust contributed millions of dollars to restore the river. The Muskegon River Watershed Assembly, the group Nobes helped form to restore and protect the river, was the most common target of the verbal salvos.

THE WATERSHED ASSEMBLY OPERATED ON A SHOESTRING BUDGET FOR the first two years of its existence. That changed in 2000, when Wege and the Fishery Trust pumped hundreds of thousands of dollars into the organization.

Wege wanted the money to result in more than a series of academic studies: he wanted prompt action that produced tangible improvements in the river.[14]

That has proven to be a much more daunting task than assembly officials expected. The assembly spent months organizing, appointing board members, forming committees, and hiring its first full-time executive director, Gary Noble. Since then, the group has focused much of its attention on increasing public awareness of problems facing the river and trying to build a consensus for river protection among government agencies at the local, state, and federal levels.

The assembly produced a video history of the river, published newsletters, developed a Web site, worked with scientists studying human-caused changes to the river, helped reestablish small plots of wild rice, and assisted with stream bank restoration projects that improved fish habitat and reduced erosion along more than a half mile of the Muskegon's most important tributaries. The group also received two hundred thousand dollars in grants to help plant and maintain miles of permanent vegetative filter strips along farms that adjoin Tamarack Creek, a cold-water stream that flows into the Little Muskegon River. The filter strips were expected to reduce the amount of polluted storm water that drained off farm fields and fouled Tamarack Creek with agricultural chemicals, fertilizer, animal waste, and excessively warm water.

Though the assembly has been involved in numerous river restoration projects, some property owners along the Muskegon have suggested that the organization has not done enough to improve the river's physical condition. Noble, a former Amway marketing executive with a degree in resource management, bristled at the criticism. He said the assembly has established a reputation as a "credible source" for information about the river, created partnerships with several government agencies involved in river work, and increased public awareness of problems affecting the river. According to Noble, the assembly's primary role is to educate the public and local units of government about changes needed to protect the river and then to help make those changes happen. "My goal is to restore the natural wonder of the river," he said. "We can't restore it to presettlement condition; we're trying to maintain functional hydrology and functional natural systems. Our job is to work with local units of government to maintain a level of functionality in these river systems."[15]

Noble has already had to fend off opponents of Nestlé's controversial Ice Mountain water bottling plant near Big Rapids. Opponents of the Ice Mountain project, which pumps millions of gallons of groundwater from the Muskegon River basin each year and sells it across the Midwest, claimed that the water bottling operation would lower water levels in nearby lakes and streams that flow into the Little Muskegon River. Critics wanted the Watershed Assembly to take a stand against the project, but the group's board of directors refused. Noble said the assembly is not an advocacy organization: "We're an advocate for the river, but we're not an advocacy group."[16]

Noble said the assembly would work with Nestlé and other companies that demonstrated an interest in restoring the river: "We don't agree or disagree with the Ice Mountain project," Noble said. "Our point is that it's better to work with groups and industries rather than to be confrontational, whether it's Ice Mountain, Consumers Energy and its hydroelectric dams, or farmers." For their part, Wege and officials at the Fishery Trust praised the Watershed Assembly's work on Muskegon River issues.

Criticism of the Watershed Assembly highlighted the politically complicated nature of environmental restoration work. Alan Steinman knew well how difficult it could be to restore impaired ecosystems. The director of the Annis Water Resources Institute at Grand Valley State University worked on the Everglades restoration and served as director of the Lake Okeechobee Restoration Project.

Steinman said his work in Florida represented a crash course in understanding the minefield of political, economic, and scientific issues that must be navigated when tackling ecosystem restoration projects. In 2000, the agency he supervised at the time was sued for allegedly mismanaging the allocation of freshwater from Lake Okeechobee. Steinman eventually resigned after months of fierce controversy and personal attacks that culminated in an anonymous death threat. "I had worked until 9 P.M. one night and when I got into the office the next morning I had nine voice mail messages waiting for me," Steinman said. "That's when I decided I couldn't live like that. Unless you work in that kind of environment, there's no way to convey in words the experience."[17] Steinman ended up at Grand Valley State and soon found himself involved in the emerging effort to restore the Muskegon River, a project certain to generate controversy. Two suggestions sure to ignite fierce debate: The Michigan Department of Natural Resources wanted fish ladders or other fish passage devices installed at the Croton, Hardy, and Rogers dams so that fish in the lower river could migrate further upstream. The agency also wanted to remove several small dams in the Muskegon River's tributaries that were considered obsolete or unsafe.[18]

Dams in Michigan are as treasured as water control structures in Florida, regardless of whether the structures are obsolete, dangerous or fail to serve any useful purpose. Steinman believed the Watershed Assembly was taking the correct approach to restoring the river, even if critics did not like the pace of progress. "We're approaching the Muskegon River the way we should . . . from a holistic perspective. That's a real advantage, but we have to make sure we don't screw up this opportunity."[19] Scientists must understand which problems pose the greatest threats to the river before government officials can take steps to protect it, according to Mike Wiley, a University of Michigan ecologist who led a comprehensive study of the Muskegon. He argued that tackling piecemeal restoration projects before scientists understand how the whole river system functions would be counterproductive:

> We don't know much about a lot of rivers. When these studies are done, the Muskegon River will be one of the most intensely studied rivers, at least from an ecological standpoint. Even if nothing else happened, having the information on what is true about the river is a very important contribution unless we want resource management to be driven by politics. We're going to be able to say, "If you take this action, it is likely to have a large or small effect on the river system." Without this data, the debate about the river is based on generalities and politics. You want the management actions you take to be focused on the thing you're managing—the river—and not human needs.[20]

Even if, by some miracle, a public consensus could be reached on the best ways to restore the Muskegon, there was the all-important issue of cost. People often asked what it would cost to restore the river and when the work would be finished. The answers: A fortune, and no idea.

No one has put a price tag on the cost of restoring the river. However, a 2002 river management plan produced by Grand Valley State provided some insight. The university's researchers concluded that controlling non-point source pollution from diffuse sources—overheated water from dam reservoirs and polluted runoff from farm fields, parking lots, and residential developments—in just two of the Muskegon River's ninety-four tributaries would cost a staggering $43 million.[21]

Doing nothing to reduce non–point source pollution in Tamarack Creek and the Middle Branch River would cost more in the long run because the problem would only get worse, according to John Koches, the lead investigator on the Grand Valley State study.[22] The cheapest option was to prevent pollution from happening—cleaning up polluted streams costs about thirty times more than preventing pollution, according to the Michigan Department of Environmental Quality.[23]

Because the Muskegon's watershed is so huge, the Grand Valley State study recommended tackling pilot pollution reduction projects in the Tamarack River and Middle Branch River watersheds. If successful, the techniques used to protect those streams—planting miles of vegetative buffer strips along waterways near farms, stabilizing eroding stream banks, and erecting miles of fence to keep livestock from defecating in the water—could be applied throughout the watershed.

"We assume that the costs estimated for the Middle Branch and Tamarack Creek are indicative of what we can expect throughout the Muskegon River watershed," Koches said. "The fact that we have a plan—a plan that identifies and prioritizes these problems—puts us ahead of most other watersheds when it comes time to compete for resources needed to solve these problems."[24]

Restoring the Muskegon's damaged sections and preserving its spectacular natural features could easily cost hundreds of millions of dollars. Finding common ground on the most pressing issues facing the river may prove as difficult as securing the funds needed to fix those problems. Policymakers, scientists and riverfront property owners could not even agree on the best way to solve the most basic problems, such as whether human intervention was needed to stem the tide of sediment bleeding into the Muskegon from the river's sandy banks.

11.

HUNGRY WATER

It's terrible, the amount of sand coming down the river.

—Stan Peterson, Muskegon River fisherman, 1999

Hundreds of bank swallows flew loopy, counterclockwise missions over a sharp bend in the river where the Muskegon gnawed at a steep bank while making a ninety-degree turn to the west. The small birds created a swirling, vertical gray cloud as they swooped down from a wall of sand that jutted straight up from the river. Over and over, the birds dove down from the sandy bank, snatching defenseless mayflies out of the air and then circling back to the bluff. It was late afternoon, and the Hex Hatch was on.

Thousands of mayflies, *Hexagenia limbata,* were rising from the river's darkening waters as the setting sun cast long shadows over the valley. This was a thing of beauty for a trout angler. Mayflies are an indication of clean water; the insects with the small bodies and oversized, transparent wings are a delicacy for trout, which reside only in clean water. George Trueman knew that the cloud of insects indicated the river that passed by his cedar-sided house was healthy. The other half of this equation, however—the presence of bank swallows—concerned the retired office furniture executive.

Swallows congregated on barren bluffs and cliffs where the soil was soft enough to permit the winged drillers to bore fist-sized caves to hold their nests. The sandy river bank just downstream of Trueman's house was been laid bare by the ever-changing river and passing boats that sent small waves crashing into a bluff with the appearance and consistency of brown sugar. Over the course of several years, Trueman said, fluctuating water levels in the Muskegon have washed away a large part of this bluff, ripping tons of sand and dozens of huge trees off the bank and depositing those materials in the river. Only then did the swallows arrive.

The five-inch birds quickly transformed this open wound along the river's edge into something resembling a giant peg board as long as a football field and as tall as a three-story building. The wall of sand was an ideal place for swallows to nest and a nightmare for property owners whose land was sliding into the river, inch by agonizing inch. Each time the river rose or waves from a passing boat lap at the shoreline, a little more sand washed off the bank and into the river. And George Trueman's blood pressure soared: "I'm very concerned about the river. I see it getting hurt bad by erosion. You see a four-foot wake from a jet boat hit that bank down there, and you can see that man is speeding [erosion] up big-time. I'm amazed no one is stepping up and saying, 'We've got to stop this.' I don't think we need to do more studies to save the river. I think we should be patching up eroding stream banks."[1]

Trueman knew that it was possible to stop the river from slicing into its sandy banks. He did it. He placed thousands of bowling ball–sized rocks at the base of the bluff in front of his house, creating a rock retaining wall that kept the river from cutting into the base of the steep bank and thereby preventing the upper portion from sliding into the water. His neighbors five houses downstream lacked the time or money to build a rock retaining wall and were at the river's mercy. Over about five years, the river washed away nearly twenty linear feet of their land, depositing tons of sand, huge trees, shrubs, and large mats of grass in the water. This was just one of hundreds of erosion sites hemorrhaging sand and silt into the 219-mile-long river.

A canoe trip down the river revealed major erosion sites at almost every turn, open wounds on the land that marred the scenic waterway like chicken pox on a small child. In the 1990s, officials in Osceola County, which encompasses much of the upper Muskegon River basin, identified

608 erosion sites in the river and its tributaries. Osceola is just one of nine counties in the Muskegon's watershed.

Whether the sediment washing off these eroding stream banks was harming the river—by burying gravel beds where fish spawn or on a larger scale by making the river warmer, shallower, wider, and more prone to flooding—was the subject of an intense debate that pitted scientists against property owners who saw a hungry river continuously gnawing at their property. Were these erosion sites the result of human activities or part of the river's evolution, a natural function of flowing water continuously changing as it rose and fell and shifted from side to side within the river valley? That was the sixty-four-thousand-dollar question for scientwasts faced with the question of whether human intervention was required to curb the torrent of sand bleeding into the river. The answer was not as obvious as it seemed.

Rivers are meant to move dirt—it is one of the primary functions of water flowing downhill. The constant flow of sand and silt down the channel is what allows rivers to change shape and evolve, creating new fishing holes and filling in others by moving sediment from one spot and depositing it somewhere else. It was no surprise that the Muskegon River moved tremendous volumes of sand down its channel every day. Much of the river flowed through a thick layer of sand deposited in north-central Michigan thousands of years ago by the same glaciers that formed the Great Lakes.

At issue was whether the amount of dirt washing off the land and into the river was excessive and harmful. The tangled issue of soil erosion and sedimentation in the river frightened waterfront property owners (who feared loss of land) and anglers (who feared excessive amounts of dirt washing into the Muskegon would suffocate prime fish habitat). The issue frustrated scientists. They could not say conclusively whether more sediment washed into the river in 2000 than was the case in 1840, before logging scarred the landscape and dislodged tons of sand and before dams strangled the river, trapping huge volumes of sediment in reservoirs while causing erosion downstream by altering natural water levels.

Even if researchers eventually determined that excessive amounts of sand were washing into the river, there was no simple way to correct the problem short of lining the entire river with rocks or steel retaining walls. That was a fool's proposition, financially, aesthetically, and ecologically.

When considering the issues surrounding soil erosion and sedimentation in the Muskegon, one must remember that the river was divided into sections. Three hydroelectric dams in the river's midsection have created huge reservoirs that trap virtually all sediment transported by the upper two-thirds of the river. There were hundreds of eroding stream banks along the Muskegon and its tributaries above Rogers Dam, but the sand and silt washing into the river from those sites settled in the slack water ponds behind the Rogers, Hardy, and Croton dams. Little if any of that sediment made it through the three reservoirs downstream and to the river's mouth. Yet the lower river valley had plenty of sand to feed a hungry river.

The amount of sand the lower forty-seven miles of river deposited into Muskegon Lake in the late 1990s was almost beyond comprehension. Each day, the river dumped 334,000 pounds of sand (measured as dry weight) into Muskegon Lake. That worked out to 122 million pounds per year, give or take a few tons.[2] A 1997 state study concluded that the river was deluged with a disproportionate amount of sand and silt from eroding stream banks, farm fields, and construction sites: "The river may be receiving [the] sediment load of a watershed five times as large as the actual basin. This does not include additional, substantial sediment load from bank erosion that is the result of past deforestation practices and destabilization of flows. Road crossings also increase erosion of sediment into the stream through improper construction and direct runoff from roads."[3]

The author of that report, Michigan Department of Natural Resources fisheries biologist Rich O'Neal, said that sediment in a river constituted a problem only when it disrupted biological communities, changing the way fish, insects, or invertebrates lived and reproduced. Those types of harmful changes have been under way in the Muskegon for more than a century, the result of logging, dams, agricultural runoff, and urban development. Still, O'Neal said that he saw no sense in spending money to stabilize eroding stream banks until scientific data show that doing so would benefit the river. In the Muskegon River Management Plan released in 2003, O'Neal wrote, "At this time it would be inappropriate to attempt bank erosion control on the hundreds of [erosion] sites located on the main stem upstream of Big Rapids. Many, or possibly all, of these are the result of natural channel processes. In addition, if hydrologic conditions in the watershed are unstable, bank erosion control will be less effective, or not effective, until hydrologic conditions are stabilized."[4]

Hydrology is the movement of water in and out of a river's drainage basin. When farmers installed underground pipes to drain fields and when construction workers paved roads and parking lots, the rate at which water flowed off the land and into the river accelerated. That phenomenon—altered hydrology—caused water levels in the river to rise more often and faster after it rained and following periods of snowmelt. Higher water levels in the river meant increased erosion of stream banks.

In the late 1990s, more than a dozen eroding stream banks in the Muskegon River were stabilized. Phil Dakin, former director of the Timberland Resource Conservation and Development Council, worked on many of those erosion control projects. He believed that eroding stream banks must be stabilized where human activities have accelerated naturally occurring erosion.

> The question posed to erosion control projects managers is: Why don't we just leave the streams and rivers alone to do what they have done for millions of years? Because, when man stepped on the earth the natural forces were no longer free to do their artistry on the landscape. We are no longer involved with a natural erosion system [in the Muskegon River] since it has been greatly altered for several hundred years [*sic*] by man's land use changes.[5]

Mike Wiley, a University of Michigan aquatic ecologist who knew the inner workings of the Muskegon River as well as anyone, said that soil erosion and sedimentation would not be such a hot topic if people did not crowd the river by building homes and cottages within a stone's throw of the water. Wiley contended that larger setbacks would give the river the room it needed to move within its valley, which was as much as a mile wide in some areas:

> The river is behaving pretty much like we might expect it would, and people whose banks are eroding are losing their property and aren't very happy about it. The Muskegon River sits on the largest pile of sand in eastern North America. Rivers erode the landscape—that's what they do. If the river is in

> the middle of a giant sand pile, what will it erode? People have to recognize that if their property is endangered by an eroding bank, it doesn't mean the river is endangered by the eroding bank or that the fish are endangered by the eroding bank. Erosion is a problem for property values, but it's not a problem for the lower river. The best predictor of where the river is going to go is where the river has been.
>
> People ought not be near the river valley because rivers will move [laterally] toward the valley walls. People think the river is like a dog on a leash, and we can control where it goes—we can't.[6]

Controlling the amount of sand and silt that washed into the river has been complicated by human-created changes—logging, dams, and land development—that made parts of the Muskegon more prone to erosion. Because dams trapped sand and silt in reservoirs, water flowing out of the structures carried little to no sediment. As a result, the rivers downstream of dams generally have more energy to move dirt and cause erosion. The absence of sediment in the water gave the Muskegon more energy to cut deeper in its channel when the water level was low and more power to scour its banks when rainfall and snowmelt swelled the river. Scientists called the phenomenon hungry water. The Muskegon was more than a hungry river—it was ravenous.

The river exhibited its appetite in the spring of 2004, when sturgeon researcher Paul Vecsei put a "No Wake" sign atop a low-slung bank about three miles upstream of Newaygo. He wanted anglers in jet boats to slow down as they passed an area where sturgeon spawn. He was careful to place the sign a safe distance back from the water's edge—about five feet away. Over the next month, torrential rains dropped a foot of water on the area, inundating the Muskegon River basin and bloating the river out of its banks. When Vecsei returned in late May to check on the sign, he found it lying in the water, barely clinging to the low bluff that had been stable just four weeks earlier. The swollen river had ripped tons of dirt from the land and transported it downstream.

Such stories were common on the Muskegon. Anyone who spent more than an hour canoeing the river was likely to see several major erosion sites. Long, eroding banks could be seen near the river's headwaters at Houghton Lake and at hundreds of locations along the river and its numerous tributaries. One erosion site in the upper Muskegon, at a former state forest campground, looked like a small version of the famous dune climb at Sleeping Bear Dunes National Lakeshore in northern Michigan. The twenty-foot-high bluff that spanned more than five hundred linear feet has not a single blade of grass. The site was a popular playground for people who paddled that section of the river—the proof was in the trail of footprints on the sandy bluff.

In the thirty years he has lived on a floodplain along the lower Muskegon, Stewart Montgomery has watched sand and silt fill in parts of the river in front of his house. The result: a wider river that has shifted laterally by more than two hundred feet in some areas. Residents of Devil's Hole, a small neighborhood below Croton Dam, have gained about two hundred feet of land between their homes and the river as it has shifted sideways over the past two decades. Montgomery had a front-row seat from which to observe these changes. He was bothered by what he saw:

> The river is thirty feet wider now than it was in the 1970s, and it's shifted to the west. Twenty years ago, I could throw a golf ball across the river. Now I can't hit a golf ball across it with my driver. The river is filling with sand and getting wider . . . and shallower, and no one is doing anything about it. It's a simple thing to protect the river. They could pull the old logs out of the river and put them along the bank [to slow erosion]. I did it with my bank, and it's worked.[7]

Montgomery was forced into action in the spring of 2004, after the rain-swollen river washed away part of a bluff beneath the road that leads to his house. He hired several men who, over the course of a week, filled fourteen hundred sandbags and placed them along the edge of the river. Montgomery then paid to have tons of clay dumped over the edge of the road, re-creating the bluff that had been washed away by the raging river.

But Wiley said that fortifying the river's banks with rocks, sandbags, trees, tires, metal sheet piling, concrete walls, or piles of bricks—all of which are used and disfigured the Muskegon's shoreline—was a simplistic approach to a complex problem.[8]. Sedimentation was a natural, dynamic part of how a river functioned. Controlling erosion at one site by hardening the riverbank would shift the problem downstream, where the sediment-starved hungry river would scour even more of its channel and banks to feed its voracious appetite. And then there was the issue of money. Stabilizing only the worst erosion sites along the river would cost millions of dollars, and no individual or government agency had offered to foot the bill.

Until and unless the eroding banks were stabilized, tons of sand and silt would continue flowing down the river each day, suffocating parts of a sprawling estuary in the Muskegon State Game Area and filling the east end of Muskegon Lake. Evidence of sand choking the lower river was evident at the Richards Park boat launch in Muskegon. Prior to 1990, many anglers launched their boats at that site and headed up the river's middle and south branches to fish for salmon and steelhead. By 1999, the boat launch was high and dry. A sandbar, now covered with weeds, had reduced the middle branch of the river to a trickle. Most days, the south branch of the river through the marsh was too shallow to float a canoe.

CONSERVATION GROUPS HAVE STABILIZED SEVERAL OF THE WORST eroding stream banks in the Muskegon, but that work pales in comparison to aggressive erosion control programs launched in other Michigan rivers. The Pere Marquette Watershed Council has dredged hundreds of tons of sand out of traps dug in the bottom of the Pere Marquette River. Those traps—long, rectangular depressions dug in the bottom of the river channel—captured sand flowing downstream. Excavators then used backhoes to remove the sand. The watershed council spent hundreds of thousands of dollars waging war on sand because the sediment buried gravel beds where fish laid eggs and filled deep holes where trout congregate.

In 2003, a sand trap in the Little South Branch of the Pere Marquette was dredged, yielding 11,356 cubic yards of sand—enough to cover a football field with a layer of sand seven feet deep. That volume of sand accumulated in the trap in just ten years. Absent human intervention, erosion and sedimentation of the river would devastate the Pere Marquette's famous trout fishery. Dick Schwikert, president of the Pere Marquette Watershed Council, made clear his group's disdain for sand in a 2003 newsletter:

> Sand is the result of the natural process of erosion with the wind and rain (and snow here in Michigan) slowly breaking the earth into smaller pieces

> and moving it toward the oceans. It's been going on for a long time but man's appearance on earth is speeding up the process . . . through farming, logging, construction, you name it. And while man has introduced many chemicals, including PCBs, PBB, dioxin, etc., sand itself is far and away Michigan's greatest pollutant. . . . Logging didn't cause the sand in the rivers, it just made it easier for it to find its way into our streams.[9]

Scientists knew that excess sand harmed trout streams. In the 1970s, biologists with the Michigan Department of Natural Resources and U.S. Forest Service performed a study that involved dumping 4,233 cubic yards of sand over five years into Hunt Creek, a trout stream in northern Michigan. They found that it took twenty-one months for the first batch of sand to move one mile downstream. Most of the sand settled in the creek's deeper pools, decreasing trout habitat by 90 percent. At the end of the experiment, the stream bed and water surface had risen nine inches and the stream was warmer and more than a foot wider than before the sand was added. The result: the brook trout population declined by half.

> The decline in habitat quality induced by increased sand bed load caused a decrease in brook trout survival rates, which reduced trout numbers. When there was less food, there were fewer fish. This study has demonstrated that a relatively small sand bed load . . . had a profound negative effect on brook trout and their habitat. Moreover, it demonstrates that reduction of [sand] bed load can improve trout populations and trout habitat considerably.[10]

Hunt Creek recovered most of its natural channel six years after the experiment ended. However, some of the excess sand remained, and the survival rate of brook trout in the stream remained depressed a decade later.

Reflecting on the Hunt Creek study, Schwikert said, "Sand destroys what trout like: deep pools, gravel riffles, cold water. It sandblasts the large woody debris smooth, like driftwood. It scours and buries the substrate, fills the pools and channels and covers over the gravel.[11]

The Hunt Creek study led to a follow-up experiment on Poplar Creek, a trout stream that was part of the Pine-Manistee River system. When a sand trap was constructed in Poplar Creek, it reduced by 86 percent the amount of sand moving down the creek while increasing the number of trout by 30 percent. Sand traps clearly captured a portion of the sand moving down the stream. But Schwikert noted that artificial sand traps are not a panacea: "For a trap to be effective and efficient, you must prevent further erosion upstream; no use spending money to continuously remove sand if it continues to pour in above the trap. Also, traps are ineffective for naturally soft, erodible stream beds or in low-gradient streams."

Government agencies have reduced erosion on sandy banks in remote sections of the Manistee River by using helicopters to place fallen pine trees along the river's edge. The result: less sand washed into the river, the channel narrowed, and the river flowed faster, creating the energy needed to move sand downstream.

In the 1990s, members of the Muskegon chapter of Trout Unlimited had tremendous success stabilizing several eroding banks along Cedar Creek, a fine trout stream that flows into the lower Muskegon River. Over the course of a decade, Trout Unlimited members placed thousands of tons of rock at the base of several eroding banks along the picturesque, winding creek. They also placed huge bundles of trees along several bends in the creek and anchored the trees to the bottom. The results were impressive: reducing erosion and increasing the creek's energy by narrowing the stream allowed Cedar Creek by 2003 to reclaim some of the deep, cold holes and gravel beds that trout need to survive. Stretches of Cedar Creek that were buried under a blanket of sand a decade ago featured gravel and deep holes, and it was not uncommon to see large trout swim through areas of the creek that once resembled underwater deserts.

Gale Nobes worked on many of the Cedar Creek bank stabilization projects. Yet the chair of the Muskegon River Watershed Assembly was not sure that the same approach would work in the much larger Muskegon River. Before hardening the river's eroding banks with rocks, trees, or other structures, some big-picture decisions had to be made about how the river would be managed in the coming decades: "If erosion is a problem that man created, or made worse, we ought to fix it," Nobes said. "If it's a natural phenomenon, we ought to leave it alone. The trick is knowing the difference. If we put logs into the Muskegon River [to stabilize eroding banks] like they did in the Manistee River, we have to decide how we are going to manage the river. Do we manage it for fish, and which species, or do we try to make it a natural river?"[12]

George Trueman has come to dread spring. It is the peak period for fluctuating water levels and steelhead fishing on the lower Muskegon. Dozens of jet boats zoom up and down the river each day, many driven by professional guides racing toward popular fishing holes. Many guides headed out on the river in their noisy jet boats well before sunrise—some as early as three in the morning. Jet boats are noisy and, if you believe many longtime residents along the lower Muskegon, have increased erosion of the river's sandy banks. "They're kicking nature's butt with these jet boats. They're assaulting the river," Trueman said.[13] It was a relatively recent phenomenon.

By the mid-1990s, the lower Muskegon had shed its reputation as strictly a working river; it had become known as one of the finest trout and salmon fisheries in the lower forty-eight states. As anglers flocked to the Muskegon—spurred in part by articles in national publications that raved about the river's bountiful steelhead, majestic trout, and gigantic salmon—a cottage industry was born.

River guides, experts who earned three hundred dollars or more per day to help less skilled anglers catch fish, quickly seized on the economic opportunities created by the Muskegon's resurgent fishery. As competition increased, the river guides naturally looked for an edge over their business rivals. Enter the jet boat—a large, flat-bottomed aluminum boat with a powerful motor capable of quickly transporting four adults up the river. Because jet boats have a shallow draft and powerful motors propelled by water, not a propeller, the vessels could travel in as little as three inches of water. Speed and versatility made jet sleds an overnight sensation in a river where low water levels and excessive sedimentation combined to make some areas impassable for boats with propeller motors.

Around 2001, according to Trueman, erosion of the towering, sandy bluff near his house began to intensify. That was about the same time that jet boats became popular with river guides on the lower Muskegon. As the boats speed upriver against the current, they leave a trail of waves lapping against the river's sandy banks. "Every time these boats go by, the wake they create takes another bite out of the bank," Trueman said.[14]

Matt Supinski, a fishing guide who has lived and worked on the Muskegon since 1995, disagreed, arguing that jet boats have been made a scapegoat for many of the river's problems: "The only harm jet boats do is they wake people up. Jet boats don't cause any ecological damage to the river; they don't throw a wake any larger than a boat with a prop."[15]

Vecsei, the sturgeon researcher, could not believe the state of Michigan had not imposed no-wake zones in areas where sturgeon and steelhead were known to spawn.[16] A known sturgeon spawning area was just upstream of Trueman's house. Frustrated by his inability to get local or state agencies to impose a boat speed limit or no-wake zones on the river, Trueman took matters into his own hands in 2003. He made a floating sign that read, "Slow, no wake zone." Within two weeks, the sign vanished. Trueman said it turned up a couple of miles downstream.

Irritated by noisy jet boats and what he perceived as a lack of action on the state's part to regulate jet boats and reduce stream bank erosion, Trueman considered moving away from the Muskegon. "I don't know how much longer I can take the noise," he said. Trueman grew tired of waiting for scientists and government agencies to complete the studies that could determine the best way to deal with soil erosion and sedimentation in the river. On one particularly busy day in 2003, Trueman called the local sheriff's department to complain about jet boats roaring past his house. When the deputy arrived, Trueman could not believe his eyes. The officer was driving a jet boat. Enraged, Trueman considered calling the state game warden who patrolled the river for the Michigan Department of Natural Resources. But Trueman knew his anti–jet boat tirade would fall on deaf ears—the state's game wardens also patrolled the river in jet boats. Said Trueman, "They just don't get it."[17]

Although Trueman and others focus their wrath on jet boats as the major source of stream bank erosion, other culprits exist. Urban development was slowly but steadily transforming the sparsely developed Muskegon River basin, with hundreds of acres of farmland, forests, and open space being converted each year into subdivisions, shopping centers, and parking lots. Development generates more than property tax revenue and jobs. Impermeable surfaces associated with urban development—roofs, roads, and parking lots—divert a larger volume of storm water runoff into the river than do forests or farmland. The surge of water that drains off streets and parking lots and rushes into the river following rain showers elevates stream levels and ultimately increases erosion. Preventing urban development and the additional storm water it diverts to surface waters from overwhelming the river will be one of the greatest environmental challenges facing the Muskegon for the foreseeable future.

12.

FATAL ATTRACTION II

> The battle to preserve the Muskegon River must be fought and won on land.
>
> —Rich O'Neal, Michigan Department of Natural Resources biologist

Cedar Creek used to meander freely through a northern Michigan valley dotted with wetlands and small lakes, an artery of cold water that delivered trout to the Little Muskegon River. Just one bridge spanned the creek, and reaching the top of a hill overlooking the assemblage of lakes, swamps, and springs required a grueling hike up a hillside covered with downed trees. Aspiring land developer Don Bollman hiked this trail in his search for a suitable place to build a private resort with lakes, lush golf courses and waterfront homes in the heart of the Muskegon River Valley. Once atop the hill, the former professional baseball player—a minor league pitcher whose promising career was cut short at age twenty by a car accident that caused severe burns over much of his body—stood in awe of the natural beauty beneath him. "I couldn't believe it," Bollman recalled. "In front of us was as pretty a lake as eyes could ever behold, and through the trees in the distance, another and then . . . another lake. From this point you could see for over two miles down the valley, all wilderness."[1]

Standing along the sluggish stream the next day, Bollman concluded that he could turn four small lakes in the valley into one large lake by damming Cedar Creek. Bollman did what any good developer would: he bought the land—six thousand acres in all—and transformed the natural landscape to meet his entrepreneurial needs. The Canadian Lakes resort was born.

The development, which is said to resemble a remote part of Canada, is Michigan's largest private resort. Since Bollman began working on the project in 1962, Canadian Lakes has evolved into a $180 million recreational oasis that features five golf courses, five artificial lakes spanning twelve hundred acres, more than six hundred homes and cottages, an airport, tennis courts, and pools. Bollman's crowning achievement was his family home overlooking Canadian Lakes—a massive hilltop castle built with concrete grain silos at each corner.

Canadian Lakes was a testament to one man's determination to build a first-class resort community. But there was a dark side to this story that was never mentioned in the resort's brochures: the Canadian Lakes project ruined Cedar Creek. "The cumulative impact of the Canadian Lakes development upon the cold-water fisheries of the historic Cedar Creek and the Little Muskegon River has been adverse and significant," according to a report by the Michigan Department of Environmental Quality. "The coldwater fishery of Cedar Creek has been destroyed and that of the Little Muskegon River has been impaired."[2]

Canadian Lakes has been a boon to the local economy and provides a haven for retirees. But it is also a monument to the types of harmful development practices that threatened other parts of the Muskegon River system in 2005 as urban sprawl transformed more farmland and open space into subdivisions and strip malls.

In fairness to Bollman, the development of Canadian Lakes—and the damming of Cedar Creek—did not violate any environmental laws. Most of the resort's artificial lakes were developed before Michigan had laws protecting wetlands like the one through which Cedar Creek flowed. Bollman's use of dams to create the Canadian Lakes also was far from unique. Dams have been built to maintain artificially high water levels in hundreds of Michigan lakes.

Cedar Creek was not the first stream in the Muskegon River basin to be harmed by development, nor will it be the last. Forty years after Bollman started developing Canadian Lakes, the race was on to save another Cedar Creek that flows into the other end of the Muskegon River.

"ASK ME IF I CARE," READ THE BUMPER STICKER ON A GRAY FILE CABINET in James Muston's office. Muston, the plainspoken supervisor of Cedar Creek Township, obviously cared about the rural, fast-growing community he managed and called home. That was the only explanation for the fact that he remained in a thankless job for nearly thirty years. Muston held one of the most important positions in the Muskegon River watershed. His thirty-six-square-mile township about eighty miles southwest of the Canadian Lakes development included the other Cedar Creek in the Muskegon River system. The Cedar Creek in Muston's community happened to be one of Michigan's top five brook trout streams.[3]

Winding through farm fields, steep ravines, and part of the Manistee National Forest before spilling into a nearly impenetrable marsh on the outskirts of Muskegon, this Cedar Creek was an ecological gem. It also lay in the path of a tidal wave of growth moving northeast from the Lake Michigan coast and heading up the Muskegon River valley.

Muston witnessed his rural township undergo dramatic changes over the course of three decades. When Muston was first elected supervisor in 1976, an acre of land in the township sold for an average of seven hundred dollars. In 2005, land commonly went for seven thousand dollars or more per acre. Muston said that some people have paid as much as twenty-four thousand dollars for a 1.5-acre lot, their small piece of paradise. But the river of people streaming into the township threatened the rural nature that made the area attractive. According to Muston, township officials could do little to stem the tide of growth. "The 1990 census showed a 28 percent increase in population. The 2000 census showed a 14 percent increase," Muston said. "We've been averaging twenty to thirty new homes a year for the past ten years. People are moving to the township from bigger cities because they want to get out in the country to have some more room. Then they grumble when someone builds across the street. They say it's destroying the rural character of the township, which was the reason they moved here. I tell them, 'You can't stop progress.'"[4]

The population of Cedar Creek Township doubled between 1970 and 2000. Although the township was home to just 3,109 residents in 2004, that number was expected to continue increasing as urban sprawl moved across the township like lava flowing downhill—a slow, unstoppable force.

Since 1960, population growth in the Muskegon River watershed has been spreading north and east, from Muskegon toward Newaygo and Big Rapids. Since 1978, urban development in the watershed increased 60 percent, while the amount of land used for agricultural purposes decreased 17 percent. The amount of farmland in the watershed decreased by 61,003 acres between 1978 and 1998, while 48,162 acres of land were developed for residential, commercial, or industrial uses. The bulk of the new development—78 percent—was residential, and most of it occurred in forests and open fields. The population of the watershed in 1960 was 220,800; that number swelled to 447,257 by 2000 and was projected to reach 508,000 by 2020.[5] More people mean more stress on the ecosystem, particularly in the form of sewage. In 1960, residents in the river basin discharged roughly 10.5 billion gallons of wastewater into sanitary sewers and septic tanks; that figure could reach 18 billion gallons by 2020.[6] Most alarming was the fact that the largest growth surges have occurred near some of the most fabulous and fragile trout streams in the watershed: the Clam River, Hersey Creek, the Little Muskegon River, Tamarack Creek, and Cedar Creek.

The Cedar Creek near Muskegon became a test case in 2002 to determine whether scientists and government officials could restore stream hydrology—the natural movement of water in and out of a waterway—in a relatively small area within the Muskegon River basin. Scientists figured that if they could not maintain functional hydrology in Cedar Creek, the odds of achieving it across a landmass spanning 2,725 miles were not good.

Cedar Creek was chosen for the grand experiment because it was a phenomenal trout stream facing increasing pressure from growth. The creek also resembled a scaled-down version of the Muskegon River system. The winding, tea-tinted stream, rarely more than thirty feet wide, meanders through fifty-seven square miles of farm fields, thick forests, and steep ravines before spilling into the huge marsh near the mouth of the Muskegon.

The biomass of brook trout in Cedar Creek far exceeded the average for Michigan rivers. At one site in Cedar Creek, biologists documented 65.4

pounds of brook trout per acre, which ranked fifth among all Michigan trout streams. A second site, which registered 50.7 pounds of brook trout per acre, ranked twelfth.[7] Despite its thriving trout and salmon fishery, the creek long remained a well-kept secret. That has changed as more people moved into the area. The days of clean water, abundant trout, and feisty salmon in Cedar Creek may be numbered.

Urban development in the Cedar Creek drainage basin increased 73 percent from 1978 to 1998, as 1,134 acres of farmland and open space were turned into single-family homes and subdivisions.[8] The most notable development in the township in the past decade was Stonegate, a 520-acre golf course and residential complex built on a plateau near Cedar Creek and adjacent to the Manistee National Forest. Some conservationists feared that the 120-acre golf course could slowly degrade the creek by using a large volume of cold groundwater—which maintained the creek's average temperature of fifty-eight degrees—to irrigate lush fairways and greens. If that water is warmer than fifty-eight degrees when it eventually seeps back into the creek, it could slowly increase water temperatures and eliminate the trout.

Steve Vallier, the Muskegon County surveyor and one of the developers of Stonegate, said that the golf course would not harm Cedar Creek because it never came within one thousand feet of the stream. Additionally, all storm water runoff in the development was collected in a detention pond that slowly released it into the ground. According to Vallier, developers did all they could to keep the development from harming Cedar Creek, including leaving 150 acres of land in its natural state and limiting the number of residential lots to 174. However, he also said that it would be naive to think that Stonegate will have no effect on the natural surroundings: "No matter what, development always has an impact on the environment to some degree. Our job is to minimize that impact. We could have put in 340 lots but we decided against it. I think we've put measures in place so this development won't become a liability twenty or thirty years from now."[9]

Scientists predicted that the twenty-five-mile-long creek would deteriorate rapidly if development trends evident in 2000 continued. With more land paved for residential driveways and commercial parking lots, storm water runoff would flood the creek more often, sending increased amounts of sand, agricultural chemicals from farm fields, and oil and grease from streets and parking lots into the creek, the Muskegon River marsh, and Muskegon Lake. One study predicted that increased urbanization in the Cedar Creek watershed would eliminate three of ten species of fish currently found in the creek by 2020.[10] The ability—or inability—to preserve Cedar Creek in the face of increased urbanization will speak volumes about the fate of the entire Muskegon River system, according to Mike Wiley, an ecologist who led a huge study of the Muskegon River and Cedar Creek. "Cedar Creek is an interesting microcosm of the entire river. It's one of the tributaries that's in the path of a wave of development heading east from the Lake Michigan coast. It's an interesting system that faces an imminent threat."[11]

LAND DEVELOPMENT POSED THE GREATEST THREAT TO THE MUSKEGON River ecosystem at the dawn of the twenty-first century. The river that withstood a biological beating from logging in the nineteenth century and dams in the twentieth century faced a potential knockout blow from poorly planned urban development.

Turning open space into homes, shopping centers, and parking lots posed a greater threat to fish populations than did intense farming practices or the ninety-four dams remaining in the Muskegon and its tributaries. According to Wiley, growth and urban sprawl could negate many improvements achieved in the river over the past thirty years.[12] That was a frightening prospect in a river basin that was home to three of Michigan's fastest-growing counties in the 1990s and to numerous small communities that were ill equipped to manage an onslaught of development.

Urban areas accounted for about 3 percent of land use in the 2,725-square-mile river basin in 2002; agriculture accounted for one-third of land use; the rest was open space and forests.[13] Despite the relatively sparse development, growth had already scarred portions of the Muskegon's network of wetlands, streams, and lakes.

Nitrogen and phosphorous runoff from dense residential developments around Muskegon's Bear Lake and Hess Lake in Newaygo County has caused rampant weed growth and clouded the water. Researchers from Michigan State University classified the lakes in 2003 as eutrophic—aging prematurely and plagued by excessive nutrients and insufficient amounts of dissolved oxygen. Strawberry Lake, in a more rural area of the upper Muskegon River basin, was classified as mesotrophic, which meant it had a healthy balance of oxygen and nutrients. That was not surprising: only 20 percent of land within five hundred meters of the lake had been developed.[14]

Similar trends were documented in the wetlands and streams scientists used to gauge the Muskegon River's ecological health. Townline Creek and Laurel Marsh, in the sparsely developed upper river basin, were nearly pristine bodies of water that supported thriving communities of native fish, plants, and insects. In both cases, forests occupied the majority of land within five hundred meters of those waterways; no urban development had occurred near the creek or the marsh.[15]

At the other end of the watershed and water quality spectrum was Ruddiman Creek in Muskegon. Twentieth-century industrial development caused water and sediment contamination so severe that it posed health hazards to children who played in the tortured waterway. A $10.6 million cleanup to remove eighty thousand cubic yards of toxic sediment from the creek bottom began in 2005.

Land use was, and will remain, a critical issue for the Muskegon River and all of its components. The river's fate will be determined by how people use land that drains into the giant river system. Critical to the equation is the volume of water running off the landscape and into the river, the temperature and cleanliness of that water, and the rate at which the water moves from land to water. Hydrology is a major determinant of the Muskegon's flow, water temperature and purity, and biological diversity.

A team of scientists studying the Muskegon reported in 2002 that the diversity of fish species in the river system "decreased significantly from 1830 to 1978 and is predicted to continue to decrease significantly into the future."[16] Such forecasts caused trepidation among researchers who believed that the Muskegon entered a decisive period in its eight-thousand-year history. By 2020, scientists predicted, the Muskegon would either become more like the scenic Manistee River to the north or a mirror image of the severely polluted Grand River to the south.[17]

The Grand is Michigan's longest river but is far from the most grand. It had the dubious distinction of being the largest source of the pesticide atrazine, DDT compounds, and lead entering Lake Michigan from surface waters.[18] Sewer overflows plagued the Grand for decades and were still occurring as recently as 2004. Those overflows, coupled with polluted runoff from farms fields following periods of heavy rainfall, sent filthy, coffee-colored plumes of water into Lake Michigan in the resort town of Grand Haven. The Muskegon River, conversely, was the best salmon stream in the Lake Michigan basin. The challenge now and for the foreseeable future will be to manage growth in ways that protect the Muskegon's good name.

URBAN SPRAWL AND URBANIZATION DID NOT GENERATE CONCERN IN the Muskegon River basin until the 1990s. Growth was not an issue in the watershed for most of the past century because little of it occurred. When Michigan's logging era came to an end around 1900, the Muskegon River Valley entered a long period of relatively slow growth. Dozens of dams were built in the river and its tributaries during the first half of the twentieth century, and Muskegon was a boomtown during World War II, but most of the Muskegon River Valley missed the growth surge that took place in the Grand River basin.

The cities of Lansing and Grand Rapids subjected the Grand to far more pollution than entered the Muskegon River, at least upstream of the city of Muskegon. Grand Rapids and Lansing were home to numerous plating firms that over time dumped countless tons of toxic heavy metal waste into the Grand River. Agricultural operations, which can foul streams with chemicals and animal wastes, are far more widespread in the Grand River basin than in the Muskegon; two-thirds of the Grand's watershed is occupied by farms, double the percentage in the Muskegon River basin.[19] For much of the twentieth century, Lansing, Grand Rapids, and Jackson, near the headwaters of the Grand, dumped billions of gallons of untreated sewage into the river each year. Pesticides and livestock manure also washed off farms along the river's tributaries, fouling the water with toxic pesticides and bacteria-laden animal wastes.

The most severe pollution in the Muskegon River system occurred in Muskegon Lake, where industries used the lake as an open sewer for seventy-five years. Decades of pollution poisoned mud on the bottom of Muskegon Lake with several toxic chemicals, placing it among the forty-two worst toxic hot spots in the Great Lakes in the mid-1980s.[20] The gross industrial pollution that fouled many American rivers through the 1970s and caused Ohio's Cuyahoga River to catch fire was largely controlled in the Muskegon River basin by 1980. The Grand, however, continued to be fouled by sewage spills and agricultural wastes well into the first decade of the twenty-first century. The reason: Lansing, Grand Rapids, and Jackson had combined sewer systems that treated storm water as well as household and industrial sewage. Heavy rains overwhelmed the combined sewer systems, forcing city officials to dump huge volumes of untreated sewage into the river to keep it from backing up in residential basements. Grand Rapids and Lansing spent tens of millions of dollars to build sewage retention basins and separate their sewers in the 1990s. Though the volume of sewer overflows was greatly reduced by the end of the decade, sporadic problems continued into 2004. In that year alone, Lansing dumped 420 million gallons of untreated sewage into the Grand; Grand Rapids sent 196 million gallons into the river.[21] Sewer overflows have never been a major problem in the Muskegon River. A more pressing issue was storm water runoff. Untreated runoff from farms and urban areas can wreak environmental havoc by causing floods and inundating the Muskegon with sand, silt, and pollutants from diffuse sources. As land is paved for residential, commercial, and industrial uses, a greater percentage of storm water that once soaked into the ground is directed to rivers. The U.S. Environmental Protection Agency has said that non–point source pollution, runoff from farm fields and urban areas, is the nation's largest water quality problem and the main reason 40 percent of lakes and streams are too polluted for fishing or swimming.[22] Floods are a natural part of river hydrology. However, excessive flooding fueled by human activities can devastate rivers by increasing erosion of stream banks, which dumps more sand and silt in the river, burying prime fish spawning beds and harming other aquatic life. Over the past century, the volume of water flowing down the main branch of the Muskegon has increased by about 20 percent, a change scientists attributed to the land losing its ability to store water as development removes trees and covered soil with impervious surfaces.[23] "Hydrology is the number 1 issue that needs to be addressed in the Muskegon River," said state fisheries biologist Rich O'Neal. "If you work on preserving and restoring the natural hydrology, you're going to take care of a large portion of the problems."[24] But restoring the river's natural hydrology is not possible, according Gale Nobes, chair of the Muskegon River Watershed Assembly. Doing so would require filling in hundreds of miles of human-constructed drains used for decades to draw excess water off farm fields and roads. Said Nobes, "Until we figure out a way not to eat or drive, we're probably stuck with these drains."[25]

Maintaining the river's hydrologic condition may require tighter controls on land use. This is where river conservation efforts become dicey. Restricting growth is anathema in Michigan, where private property rights are of paramount concern and local governmental units have always called all the shots when it comes to regulating land use.

MICHIGAN ONCE WAS KNOWN AS NATIONAL LEADER IN CONSERVING natural resources. But that reputation has slipped in recent years, in part because of the state's inability to change a system of government that encourages urban sprawl.

The state constitution adopted more than a century ago established a home rule system of government that gave local governmental units control over all issues involving land use. The trouble now is that Michigan has 1,850 units of government—cities, counties, villages, and townships—empowered to plan for growth and make land use decisions. The result has been turf wars, because the quickest way for local units of government to increase revenue was to expand their tax bases by encouraging development. Given those conditions, urban sprawl has, not surprisingly, spread like crabgrass across the state. As environmental writer Dave Poulson once observed, Michigan may be the Wolverine State, but its residents behave more like groundhogs. "On average, the state of Michigan develops its land eight times faster than its population grows," according to a 2003 report by the Michigan Land Use Leadership Council. "The number of new households continues to significantly outpace population growth. From 1970 to 2000, the number of households in Michigan grew by 43 percent, while population grew by only 12 percent."[26]

Since the 1960s, Michigan residents have been fleeing cities for the suburbs or building cabins in the scenic northern half of the state. In 2003, Michigan's population was roughly 10 million people, and 9 percent of the state's 37 million acres of land had been developed. If current land use patterns continue, another 2 million acres of land could be urbanized by 2020; by 2040, there could be twice as much developed land in the state as in

1980.[27] Muskegon County had the highest rate of urban sprawl among all 83 Michigan counties between 1960 and 1990.[28] The trend was evident on the outskirts of Muskegon, where residential and commercial development was booming while the city's downtown lay in a shambles. The collective population of the communities that ring Muskegon surpassed the city's population in 1990. And in 2001, the downtown Muskegon Mall was razed because it could not compete with a new suburban mall.[29]

Other states—most notably Vermont, Florida, Oregon, Washington, and Maryland—have implemented programs that limited urban sprawl by restricting growth or requiring new development to pay for itself; by protecting farmland and environmentally sensitive areas; and by instituting regional land use planning that required mitigating the impacts of growth.[30] Similarly, several Michigan communities have formed regional planning organizations in an effort to reduce costly duplication of services. Brooks Township, in Newaygo, was the first municipality in the Muskegon River watershed to draft a land use plan aimed at protecting the area's natural resources. Over the past thirty years, the state legislature has passed laws aimed at protecting wetlands, sand dunes, and farmland. Still, Michigan had no mechanism in 2005 that allowed local governments to collaborate on managing growth across jurisdictional boundaries.[31]

With no infrastructure for managing growth on a regional basis, haphazard development will consume large tracts of Michigan's farmland and open space, according to a 2002 report on growth in western Michigan. The report warned that a 2,400-square-mile area that encompasses the lower Muskegon River and part of the Lake Michigan coast could become "L.A. on the lake." Los Angeles is the nation's poster child for urban sprawl and the problems it causes: loss of farmland and open space, traffic jams, increased air pollution, duplication of costly public services, and intense growth that harms lakes, streams, and other natural resources.[32]

Michigan's political, business, and environmental leaders have been saying since 1970 that dramatic steps must be taken to rein in urban sprawl. A 1992 report to Governor John Engler ranked Michigan's lack of land use planning to protect natural resources and the decay of cities as the state's top two environmental problems. Studies have predicted that by 2040, Michigan will lose 25 percent of its orchard land and 1.9 million acres of farmland; land available for hunting will decrease while the state's already bloated deer population gets even larger; and the amount of developed land will reach 6.4 million acres. All of those changes threaten the land-based industries—agriculture, tourism, forestry, mining, and recreation—that account for nearly one-third of the state's total economic output.[33] A 1995 editorial in the *Detroit Free Press,* Michigan's largest newspaper, summed up the views of many state leaders: "The three most critical environmental problems in Michigan are land use, land use and land use."[34]

Despite numerous studies and decades of rhetoric, state officials have done little to address the core issues that contribute to urban sprawl. In fact, the state has several programs in place—tax breaks for industries that build new facilities and grants to extend roads, municipal water, and sewer lines into undeveloped areas—that subsidize sprawl.

The Michigan Land Use Leadership Council convened in 2003 by Governor Jennifer Granholm explored ways to control urban sprawl. That panel drafted a long list of recommendations, but none dared challenge a primary cause of sprawl: Michigan's home rule form of government that encouraged patchwork development. One of the commission's least controversial recommendations—educating local government officials about how to curb sprawl by encouraging more compact developments—provided some insight into the difficult nature of controlling growth.

As part of a comprehensive effort to preserve the Muskegon River's greatest natural features in the face of growth, scientists at Grand Valley State University in 2003 produced detailed land use maps for all 140 units of government in the watershed. The maps showed how land use had changed between 1978 and 1998 in every township, city, and village in the Muskegon River basin. The maps were supposed to help local officials manage land use more effectively by steering development into areas that were not susceptible to environmental harm—precisely what the governor's land use council had recommended.

University researchers offered the maps to all local units of government free of charge and scheduled seven workshops to show township officials how to use the information to improve land use planning. Three of those workshops were canceled because of a lack of interest; attendance at the others was sparse. That concerned Rod Denning, a Grand Valley State research associate who was struggling to change the sorry state of land use regulations in some communities.[35]

Several townships in the Muskegon River basin had no zoning ordinances at the time, which meant people could build just about anything they wanted, wherever they wanted, as long as it was on their land. Some township officials in the watershed who introduced local zoning ordinances backed off when opponents threatened recall elections. "It's pretty old thinking, but that's where we're at in some of the communities," Denning said.[36] Residents in the Muskegon River basin were sharply divided on the issue of growth and whether it should be restricted to protect the river. Ted Houghton, a survivor of the Pearl Harbor invasion who has lived along the river for more than fifty years, said that he could not believe the amount of development along the Muskegon since 1970: "I used to be able to put my boat in at Croton and count the number of houses between there and Newaygo [fourteen miles downstream] on one hand. Now I'd have to have a book and tally sheet to count all the houses."[37] Houghton shared the viewpoint of many homeowners along the river below Croton Dam: the Muskegon was being overrun by noisy, jet-powered fishing boats and people who would get drunk and disorderly while floating the river in canoes and large tubes. George Trueman, a friend of Houghton's who lived a few miles upstream of Newaygo, said that he has seen people get out of canoes and tubes to urinate, defecate, and fornicate in the river and a wooded area across from his house.[38]

Police agencies occasionally conducted stings to bust underage drinkers on the river and ticket people who littered, but the problems persisted, and not just on the Muskegon—many Michigan rivers were overrun with rowdy drunks on summer weekends. State and federal agencies have restricted the number of canoes and kayaks on some rivers, such as the Pine and Au Sable, to strike a balance between competing recreational uses. For example, canoes, tubes, and kayaks were prohibited on certain stretches of the Pine River during the early morning and evening hours to accommodate anglers. However, there are no restrictions on the number of canoes, kayaks, or tubes allowed on the Muskegon—the river offers a recreational free-for-all.

Fishing guide Matt Supinski maintained that growth was good for the river:

> As far as growth is concerned, there are two schools of thought around here. There is the Old Bubba School: They don't want any outsiders coming in or

> any guides on the river. My viewpoint, which is shared by others, is that growth is good if properly managed. You bring people here from Chicago, they fall in love with the river, and they'll take care of it. You can never have too many people out on the river as long as you take care of the resource.[39]

Alan Steinman had the kind of office many people could only fantasize about. The director of Grand Valley State University's Annis Water Resources Institute in Muskegon did not have a particularly large workspace. It was all about the view. Steinman's office featured a wall of glass that afforded a spectacular view of Muskegon Lake. The view changed on a daily basis—the lake's surface was smooth as glass some days, whipped by strong winds into frothy whitecaps on others, and frozen solid during the winter.

Steinman viewed the lake as more than a pleasant diversion from the daily grind. For a scientist who cut his teeth working on the controversial campaign to restore natural water flows in the Florida Everglades, Muskegon Lake represented the bottom line in efforts to restore the Muskegon River. A healthy river will provide clean water for Muskegon Lake and support abundant fish and wildlife species. But if the river becomes overwhelmed by pollution, a lake that has made a dramatic recovery over the past quarter century could backslide to an era when excess nutrients caused unsightly, odorous algae blooms on the lake's surface. Disturbing signs of change in the lake are already apparent.

Scientists from the National Oceanic and Atmospheric Administration in 2004 found toxic blue-green algae blooms at several sites on the surface of Muskegon Lake. The concentrations of toxic microcystins in those algal blooms tested were some of the highest ever recorded in the world. NOAA senior ecologist Gary Fahnenstiel linked the toxic algae to zebra mussels, an exotic species imported to the Great Lakes from the Caspian Sea in the 1980s in freighters' ballast water.[40] Zebra mussels filter huge volumes of water each day; as they filter water, the fingernail-sized mollusks eat the beneficial algae and spit out microcystis, blue-green algae. Because zebra mussels eat many of the microscopic organisms that prey on microcystis, the blue-green algae proliferate. The result is blue-green algae blooms, some of which contain highly toxic compounds called microcystins.

If the Muskegon River becomes more like the severely polluted Grand River, Muskegon Lake could become more like Spring Lake, a thirteen-hundred-acre lake near the mouth of the Grand. Spring Lake was in critical condition at the dawn of the twenty-first century. Excessive amounts of phosphorous from lawn fertilizers, agricultural runoff, and leaky septic tanks triggered massive algae blooms that sucked oxygen out of the water. The algae blooms turned Spring Lake the color of pea soup, which did not bode well for the lake's tourism economy. Residents around Spring Lake decided in 2004 to spend $1.3 million to dump alum into the lake. The chemical treatment was expected to reduce algae blooms and increase water clarity by absorbing excess phosphorous.

Unlike Spring Lake, where property owners were engaged in a desperate race to save a polluted waterway, Steinman believed that residents in the Muskegon River basin have a chance to prevent pollution from ruining the river and Muskegon Lake and ultimately contributing to the demise of Lake Michigan.

> We have a tremendous wealth of information on the Muskegon River. The question is, what will we do with this information? Individuals have to get involved in efforts to preserve and protect the watershed, and politicians need to take the information that's been generated and move forward with comprehensive land use planning—especially township, village, and city officials who control land use. The onus is on them to take the information scientists have generated and do something progressive with it.[41]

Progressive was not a word critics used to describe a massive water bottling plant the state of Michigan permitted in the heart of the Muskegon River basin in 2001. The state's lack of water use regulations at the time or even the most basic information about groundwater quantity spurred fears that the Ice Mountain facility would unleash a water mining boom that could become a twenty-first-century version of Michigan's logging era, when greed ruled the day.

13.

LIQUID GOLD RUSH

> The concern about springs going dry is completely absurd. The record of the industry speaks for itself.
>
> —Deb Muchmore, spokeswoman for Nestlé's Ice Mountain bottled water plant in Mecosta

John Engler received a warm reception when he arrived in Muskegon to congratulate civic leaders who had raised $5.5 million to build a freshwater research institute on the banks of Muskegon Lake. The June 2001 dedication of Grand Valley State University's Lake Michigan Center provided the Republican governor a golden opportunity to preach the need to prevent diversion of Great Lakes water to other parts of the country. A wily politician despised by environmentalists, who accused him of selling Michigan's natural resources to corporations, Engler seized the moment.

"It is easy in Michigan to take fresh water for granted," Engler told the crowd of one thousand well-wishers at the ribbon-cutting ceremony. "Today, we need to guard that water like gold. It's clearly our most precious resource." Because Michigan was the only state entirely within the Great Lakes basin, Engler told the crowd that the state's residents had a "special responsibility" to protect the massive waterways, which contain 20 percent of the world's fresh surface water supply.[1] The governor neglected to mention that his administration had just finished courting a foreign company that wanted to bottle millions of gallons of Michigan groundwater annually and sell it across the Midwest.

The Perrier Group's plan to pump 210 million gallons of groundwater each year from a site near the headwaters of the Little Muskegon River—90 miles upstream of where Engler made his speech—and sell it as Ice Mountain Natural Spring Water ignited one of the most intense environmental controversies in Michigan history. The mighty Muskegon River, which survived the nineteenth-century logging frenzy and the dams that choked the river's arteries of water, had come full circle. The Muskegon would again play the role of guinea pig in an environmental drama involving the commercial exploitation of Michigan's natural bounty. Perrier was the protagonist.

The dawn of the new millennium found Perrier in hot water. The European company that made bottled water trendy in the United States with its stylish green bottles was having trouble finding a place to mine spring water in the Midwest, at the time the fastest-growing bottled water market in North America. Perrier's plan to build a bottling facility in Wisconsin met its Waterloo in Adams County, where residents argued forcefully that the project would endanger a trout stream. On November 22, 2000, Wisconsin Governor Tommy Thompson told Perrier to look elsewhere.[2] Company officials had already their sights set on Michigan.

Two weeks after Thompson told Perrier to hit the road, the company applied for a permit to sink wells in the resort community of Mecosta, Michigan. Officials in Governor Engler's decidedly probusiness administration embraced the Perrier project and crafted a plan to give the company a $9 million grant to build its bottling plant in Michigan. Dennis L. Schornack, an Engler aide, warned the governor in an infamous September 25, 2000, memo that courting Perrier could be politically disastrous in a state defined by water. "The amount of Perrier's proposed withdrawal will not have a significant adverse impact on the springs they are testing in Michigan. The key issue in this project is not the science, but public perception and how the governor will be perceived, particularly if Perrier is given a grant," Schornack wrote. He invoked the governor's words from the 2000 State of the State address, when Engler said: "The Great Lakes will never be for sale." In his memo, Schornack said, "Because Michigan is in the bottom of the basin bowl, Great Lakes water is defined to include groundwater. If the grant is given, Michigan won't just be giving away the water, it will be paying a private, and foreign-owned, firm to take it away. The rhetoric, should this get public attention, could get ugly, would be focused on the governor and could derail our efforts on Great Lakes water management."[3]

The Engler administration did not give Perrier the multimillion-dollar grant. It did not matter. In August 2001, after contentious public hearings and a lawsuit filed by residents who claimed the bottling plant would harm nearby lakes and streams and violated a state law prohibiting the diversion of Michigan water to areas outside the Great Lakes drainage basin, the state approved the Perrier project.

Perrier, which by then had adopted the name of its parent corporation, Swiss-based Nestlé Waters North America, finally had a Midwest beachhead for its bottled water empire. Much of the credit belonged to the Engler administration and to Mecosta Township officials, who gave Nestlé nearly $10 million in tax breaks on its $150 million bottling facility, which created 145 well-paying jobs.

Nestlé's Mecosta plant would be one of the largest facilities of its kind in Michigan, producing 56 million bottles of Ice Mountain water each month for thirsty consumers in a vast area stretching from Minnesota to Rhode Island, Michigan to St. Louis.[4] Nestlé was poised to earn millions of dollars annually selling Michigan groundwater, 15 percent of which (31 million gallons annually at full production) would be sold outside of the Great Lakes drainage basin.[5]

Diversions of Great Lakes water to other parts of the nation and world were long considered taboo by residents of the region, environmentalists, and politicians, including Engler. The governor said the Nestlé project did not constitute a diversion because the water would not be sent out of the state via a pipe, canal, or tanker. Nestlé would send millions of gallons of Michigan groundwater out of the Great Lakes basin in twenty-ounce bottles.[6] Critics argued that the Perrier project indeed represented a diversion of Great Lakes water and would make it more difficult, if not impossible, to block other diversions in the future.

"One of the questions at stake in the Nestlé case is where governments should draw the line on the many relatively small water withdrawals that could lower the level of Great Lakes," said Dave Dempsey, an environmental activist, author, and adviser to former Michigan Governor James Blanchard.

"No one has claimed that Nestlé's withdrawal, in itself, will have any measurable effect on the Great Lakes. But the water in the lakes is not infinite. At what point is the camel's back broken?"[7]

Controversial as it was, the Perrier project merely represented the detonator for Michigan's water war, which would be fought on many fronts. The Perrier case highlighted the selective memories of duplicitous politicians, both Democrats and Republicans, who championed environmental protection until it interfered with economic development. The fact that many of Michigan's previous economic booms—logging, dams, heavy industry, and chemical manufacturing—came at the expense of the Muskegon and other Michigan rivers did not factor into the debate about Perrier's proposal.

The Perrier project also exposed a gaping hole in Michigan law that permitted the wanton use of groundwater, one of the state's most precious resources. Groundwater withdrawal was the twenty-first-century equivalent of the nineteenth-century logging bonanza that eliminated Michigan's seemingly endless pine forests. When the Perrier project was approved in 2001, the number of state laws regulating groundwater pumping equaled the number of forest protection rules in place when logging crews laid waste to Michigan's forests: zero.[8]

TERRY SWIER PLANNED TO SPEND HER RETIREMENT RELAXING IN HER family's cottage overlooking the glistening waters of Horsehead Lake. The retired reference librarian never imagined that she would become the leader of a classic David-versus-Goliath struggle. Then again, Swier never imagined that Nestlé—a company she had boycotted two decades earlier over the company's practice of selling infant formula to poor women in Third World nations—would try to build a bottled water plant in the same county where she planned to spend her golden years.

Almost overnight, Swier was thrust into a hurricane of controversy that would divide her peaceful resort community in the heart of the Muskegon River watershed. The controversy would take a number of bizarre twists that included private eyes hired by Nestlé lawyers questioning the company's opponents and the FBI investigating a radical environmental group's failed attempt to blow up one of the company's wells. When Swier's group stopped the Nestlé project in court, albeit temporarily, a group of volunteers led by an accidental environmental activist had managed put the issue of groundwater withdrawal on the front burner of Michigan's policy-making stove. "We've learned an awful lot, and the vocabulary has changed for the people who live here. It's been hard. In the beginning, our sole motivation was to shut down Perrier," Swier said. "We figured Nestlé would leave if we showed the community was opposed, like they did in Wisconsin. But they didn't leave. We also learned this is not just a Mecosta County issue. This is a global issue. We need legislation so a private company can't come in and take the water and sell it."[9]

Swier was among a handful of area residents in conservative Mecosta County, population forty-one thousand, who learned about the Nestlé project shortly after the company applied for permits to sink wells on private land twelve miles east of its bottling plant. Opponents feared that Nestlé's wells would lower water levels in nearby lakes and the Dead Stream, which flowed into the Little Muskegon River, the largest tributary of the Muskegon River. They quickly formed a grassroots organization called Michigan Citizens for Water Conservation; Swier became the group's president.

Within six months, Michigan Citizens for Water Conservation filed a lawsuit to halt the Nestlé project. The case ignited an intense debate about who owned the water in Michigan, whether Nestlé's bottling plant constituted a diversion of Great Lakes water, and whether the project would harm the lakes and streams that comprise the headwaters of the Little Muskegon River, a state-protected trout stream. "When industry in Michigan drills for oil and natural gas in the forest, at least the state gets a dime on the dollar in royalties. With the water, we're not getting anything, and we're subsidizing Nestlé to take it," said Mark Kane, an outspoken activist and psychiatrist whose home is perched atop a bluff overlooking the Little Muskegon River.[10] His viewpoint was not shared by everyone in the largely rural area that is home to numerous Amish families and dozens of recreational lakes but few industries. "To have a company of this caliber is a godsend," Big Rapids Township supervisor Maxine McClelland said in a newspaper interview. "It's going to help our economic vitality for a long time."[11]

Nestlé's rationale for building its bottling plant in Mecosta County was simple: the midsection of the Muskegon River basin was a gold mine of groundwater fed by thirty-two inches of precipitation annually and stored in buried gravel beds called aquifers. According to Nestlé experts, aquifers in the area where the company wanted to pump spring water held 472 billion gallons of groundwater.[12]

Nestlé sank four wells on a private 850-acre hunting preserve known as the Sanctuary, a place where well-heeled hunters pay twelve thousand dollars apiece to shoot trophy bucks in a wooded area surrounded by a twelve-foot-high wire fence. The plan: pump four hundred gallons of water per minute from natural springs beneath the Sanctuary, pipe the water twelve miles through two stainless steel pipes to Nestlé's 750,000-square-foot bottling facility, and sell it as Ice Mountain Natural Spring Water.

The company's experts predicted the pumping operation would reduce the flow of water in the mile-long Dead Stream by 345 gallons per minute, or 18 percent. Nestlé's wells also would reduce the flow of groundwater into Osprey Lake, adjacent to the Sanctuary, by 26 percent; the flow at the lake's outlet would drop 56 percent.[13] Still, Nestlé officials maintained that the reduced water flow would not harm the Dead Stream or other lakes and wetlands that drain into the Little Muskegon and Muskegon rivers.

Under Michigan law, waterfront property owners were entitled to "reasonable use" of the water provided that their activities do not harm the interests of other property owners. That reasonable use doctrine also applied to groundwater in Michigan. After a twenty-day trial that featured 360 exhibits, Mecosta County Circuit Judge Lawrence C. Root ruled in 2003 that the Nestlé project interfered with the rights of other waterfront property owners by reducing flow in the Dead Stream by 29 percent, lowering the stream's water level by two inches, and causing the stream to become narrower. Root cited the testimony of scientists, hired by Nestlé's opponents, who said that lower water levels would increase water temperatures in the Dead Stream, harm fish populations, and reduce the ability of adjacent wetlands to filter pollutants.

In a ruling that surprised both parties in the lawsuit, Root said the only way Nestlé could avoid harming the Dead Stream was by ceasing to pump groundwater from the Sanctuary site. The judge ordered the company to shut down the wells within twenty-one days. Nestlé's lawyers promptly appealed the ruling, blasting Root's handling of the complex case, which could have had implications for other companies that use or sell Michigan's groundwater. "The court was misled by plaintiffs' predictions of stream and wetland level declines," Nestlé attorney Michael Haines said. "Those predictions have been proven wrong by the actual water level measurements taken at the site during the summer and fall, subsequent to the trial."[14]

From the outset, Nestlé officials tried to win the hearts and minds of Mecosta County residents by portraying the company's Ice Mountain facility as a "small water user in Michigan." The company's goal of pumping 210 million gallons of groundwater annually would make the Ice Mountain facility one of the largest consumers of groundwater in West-Central Michigan, but not the largest. Other companies in the region—a potato farm, a fish farm, a fruit-packing company, and baby food maker Gerber Products—used substantially more groundwater than the Ice Mountain facility would bottle. Farmers in Mecosta County collectively used 3.4 million gallons of water per day during the summer to irrigate their fields. And the Pfizer pharmaceutical manufacturing plant in Kalamazoo used 28 million gallons of water daily.[15]

Judge Root, however, rejected Nestlé's claim that pumping millions of gallons of groundwater and selling it as Ice Mountain Natural Spring Water was no different than other Michigan companies using groundwater to produce beer, soft drinks, vitamins, yogurt, or other products. State law "recognizes the value of water being incorporated into products from Michigan and sold wherever a market can be found. The key to this is that water is incorporated into a product to be recognized as being under the social value protected. However, if water is the product, the rationale loses its logical force in the face of the higher social value of preserving water as water," Root said in his ruling. "Given that water is a natural resource on its own, I believe the state has a rational basis on which to limit its removal as water from the state and/or the Great Lakes basin."[16]

If upheld, Root's ruling would shut down Nestlé's wells near the Dead Stream and make it much more difficult for companies to build new water bottling facilities in Michigan. But the case was far from over. The Michigan Court of Appeals ruled in Nestlé's favor, but only allowed the company to continue pumping from the Sanctuary site at a reduced rate of two hundred gallons per minute until the case was resolved. That reduced the company's extraction of spring water to 105 million gallons annually, which is no paltry volume—it is enough water to fill nearly fifteen Olympic swimming pools.

Even if Nestlé lost in court, the company might not close its Mecosta bottling plant. Nestlé sank a separate well at its bottling facility that was capable of producing ninety-two million gallons of water annually. But that water came from a deeper well and could not be marketed as "spring water." Federal law required that "spring water" be pumped from underground springs that rose to the surface. The water Nestlé pumped from the Sanctuary site was chemically identical to groundwater pumped from deeper wells. However, "spring water" was the focus of Nestlé's marketing strategy for its Ice Mountain bottled water; company officials said consumers preferred spring water over plain groundwater.[17]

The irony was not lost on Judge Root: "It is Nestlé's desire to capture 'spring water' that has resulted in the problems giving rise to this substantial litigation. There was no evidence that Nestlé couldn't put wells into deeper aquifers to get an ample supply of water to sell, albeit not spring water, a practice its own exhibits show many other beverage bottlers in Michigan already do, including beverage water bottlers."[18]

Communities in Michigan have relied on groundwater for drinking water for more than a century. Industries have used groundwater in the manufacture of numerous products; farmers and golf course operators used it to irrigate crops and maintain lush fairways and greens. Nestlé was not close to being Michigan's largest consumer of groundwater, but its plan to sell water outside the Great Lakes basin made the world's king of bottled water the lightning rod for a burgeoning water war.

Michigan's municipal water systems, industries, farms, food processors, and golf courses pumped an estimated 513 million gallons of groundwater daily in 2001. Half of Michigan's 9.9 million residents rely on groundwater for drinking water, using 254 million gallons daily.[19] In the Muskegon River basin, municipalities, industries, and farms pumped 26 million gallons of groundwater each day in 2001.[20] The Nestlé project, at full capacity, would add another 576,000 gallons daily, an increase of 2 percent. That mattered little to Nestlé's opponents, who staged protests outside the Ice Mountain facility and fought the project in the court of law as well as the court of public opinion.

Large-scale groundwater pumping was an obscure practice that generated little controversy in Michigan until Nestlé came knocking. The debate over groundwater use was largely concentrated in other areas of the country where water was scarce but has spread as demand for bottled water increased. Bottled water consumption in the United States skyrocketed from 415 million gallons in 1978 to 5.4 billion gallons in 2001. Nationally, the use of groundwater for drinking water and other domestic purposes more than doubled over a thirty-year period, from 8 billion gallons per day in 1965 to about 18.5 billion gallons per day in 1995.[21]

Robert Glennon, a law professor at the University of Arizona, warned of a looming global groundwater crisis in his 2002 book, *Water Follies: Groundwater and the Fate of America's Fresh Waters:* "Excessive pumping of our aquifers has created an environmental catastrophe known to only a few scientists, a handful of water management experts and those unfortunate enough to have suffered the direct consequences. . . . Ground water pumping steals water from our rivers and lakes, but because it does it very slowly, we do not notice the effects until they are disastrous." The abuse of groundwater has dried up parts of the Santa Cruz River in Tucson, Arizona, created huge sinkholes in Florida, and turned lakes near Tampa into mud flats that sink, cracking the foundations of homes.[22]

Because Michigan was surrounded by four of the five Great Lakes, it had a more abundant supply of groundwater than most states. Groundwater was one of the primary reasons that Michigan had more than ten thousand lakes and thirty-six thousand miles of rivers. Groundwater also provided the majority of base flow for many of the state's best cold and cool-water rivers, including the Au Sable, Manistee, and Muskegon. Groundwater was a renewable but not infinite resource that depended largely on rainfall and snowfall. Industrial and agricultural groundwater withdrawals in Michigan and other states have lowered water levels in small lakes, dried up streams, drained aquifers, and left residential drinking water wells high and dry. The most notable cases in Michigan, other than the Ice Mountain controversy, involved a Monroe County sand mining firm and a Saginaw County potato farm that lowered groundwater levels and, as a result, dried up nearby residential wells.[23] One of the great misconceptions about groundwater was that it was somehow separate from the surface water in lakes, streams, and wetlands. Groundwater and surface water were, in fact, one in the same. In Michigan, all water that fell on land or seeped into lakes and rivers from underground aquifers and did not evaporate eventually ended up in the Great Lakes. Groundwater pumping short-circuited that process. Whether or not the changes were visible, groundwater pumping affected surface waters. "Pumping groundwater can capture water from or intercept flow to streams and alter the area that contributes groundwater to the Great Lakes. Thus, groundwater withdrawals can divert groundwater that normally would discharge to the Great Lakes system," according to the U.S. Geological Survey.[24]

That statement shed some light on Nestlé's claim that its Ice Mountain project did not constitute a diversion of water out of the Great Lakes basin. While serving as Michigan's attorney general, Jennifer Granholm ruled in 2001 that the Nestlé project must comply with the federal Water Resources Development Act, a 1986 law that prohibited diversions of Great Lakes water out of the basin unless the governors of all eight Great Lakes states approved. Granholm's ruling meant that Governor Engler needed the approval of the seven other Great Lakes governors before the Nestlé project could proceed. Wrote Granholm, "I am concerned that if you decline the opportunity for consultation in this case, you may send a signal that there will be little or no scrutiny of new or increased uses of Great Lakes water that withdraw less than 5 million gallons of water per day, at a time when the governors and [Canadian] premiers are developing regional [water withdrawal] standards."[25]

Engler disagreed and ignored the attorney general's advice. Instead, Engler sent a letter to other Great Lakes governors arguing that the federal law required him to consult other governors only in cases where a company planned to "consumptively use" more than 5 million gallons of Great Lakes water daily. Nestlé's bottling plant pumped 576,000 gallons of groundwater daily, most of which was consumed within the Great Lakes basin. "If governors and [Canadian] premiers were to implement [Granholm's] interpretation of the Great Lakes Charter and the federal Water Resources Development Act, every new residential well and business use of water in the basin would require permission from all state and provincial leaders. Clearly, such a process would be costly impractical and hopelessly unworkable."[26]

Two years later, after Judge Root ordered Nestlé to turn off its springwater wells, Granholm, by then serving as governor, intervened on the company's behalf. The former attorney general, who opined in 2001 that the Nestlé project amounted to a diversion of Great Lakes water, asked the Michigan Court of Appeals to allow Nestlé to continue pumping spring water until the court case was resolved. The reason: jobs. Nestlé was poised to lay off all 120 workers at its Ice Mountain bottling facility if the company was forced to shut down its spring water wells. Granholm's move infuriated her supporters in the environmental community. "It felt like a stab in the heart," said Swier, who had considered Granholm an ally. The governor sought to appease her supporters by introducing legislation to regulate large-scale groundwater withdrawals. Her proposal and others like it would add more fuel to an increasingly heated debate over the use of groundwater.

GOVERNOR GRANHOLM INTRODUCED THE GREAT LAKES LEGACY ACT in 2004 to correct what she called Michigan's embarrassing lack of water protection policies. The proposed law would have required a state permit before anyone could withdraw 2 million gallons of groundwater per day over any thirty-day period or 100 million gallons per year. Existing operations, such as Nestlé's Ice Mountain facility, would have been exempt from the proposed rules.

Michigan in 2004 was the only Great Lakes state without a law regulating large-scale water withdrawals. Such laws were required under the 1985 Great Lakes Charter, an agreement among the Great Lakes states and Canadian provinces to prevent water diversions. "Michigan lacks even a rudimentary regulatory framework for water withdrawals. It is the only [Great Lakes] basin state that has not kept its 1985 promise to regulate withdrawals in excess of 2 million gallons per day," said Dennis Schornack, the former Engler aide, in a 2003 op-ed column in the *Detroit News*. "The point of Perrier [Nestlé] is that the laws of the Great Lakes states are profoundly lacking."[27]

The governor's Great Lakes Legacy Act initially enjoyed bipartisan support, but industry and agricultural interests labeled it unnecessary, intrusive, and economically harmful. Several months after Granholm and state lawmakers tried to regulate groundwater use, all they had to show for their effort was a law requiring an inventory of Michigan's groundwater and the formation of a council to study the use and potential abuse of the resource.[28]

Nestlé sought to further exploit Michigan's lack of water use regulations in 2005, when the company struck a deal to buy up to 1 million gallons of groundwater daily from the city of Evart's municipal wells and sell it as Ice Mountain water. The Michigan Department of Environmental Quality approved the project, prompting Governor Granholm to order a moratorium on new or expanded bottled water operations until the Legislature enacted a water withdrawal law.[29] Nestlé's bottling facility also became a flash point in the debate over Annex 2001, a proposed amendment to the Great Lakes Charter. Annex 2001 represented a response to a Canadian firm's 1998 proposal to pump 159 million gallons of water out of Lake Superior each year and ship it to Asia in freighters. The Nova Group was not the first company to propose diverting large quantities of Great Lakes water. Over the past sixty years, several companies have proposed diverting Great Lakes water to the parched southwestern states. None of those plans materialized, primarily as a result of the high cost of piping water across the country and over the Continental Divide. The final version of the Annex agreement, signed in December 2005 by the eight Great Lakes governors and the premiers of two Canadian provinces, restricted new diversions of Great Lakes water. But the agreement did not address bottled water, instead leaving it up to the individual states and provinces to regulated bottled water operations.[30]

Numerous scholars, legal experts, and politicians have warned that the Southwest's population boom and a soaring global population desperate for clean water will increase demand for Great Lakes water. "The pressure will be immense to use the Great Lakes, to pipe water from there," said Paul Simon, a former U.S. senator and expert on global water policy. "Right now, transporting water by pipe looks too expensive. But the cost factor will diminish as time goes by. If we don't find answers, it is almost inevitable we will be tapping into the Great Lakes."[31]

Politicians in the arid southwestern states knew that the Great Lakes represented a treasure trove of drinking water. Former U.S. House Majority Leader Dick Armey caused a stir in 2000 when he joked about using Great Lakes water to ease a three-year drought in his home state of Texas. Speaking at a Republican fund-raiser in Traverse City, Michigan, Armey told his fellow conservatives, "I'm from Texas and down there we understand that whiskey is for drinking and the water is for fighting over. If we get [federal control over Great Lakes water], we're not going to be buying it. We'll be stealing it. You are going to have to protect your Great Lakes."[32]

Former Michigan Governor William Milliken warned in the early 1980s of more attempts to divert Great Lakes water out of the region. Considered one of Michigan's most environmentally progressive governors, Milliken told lawmakers in a 1982 speech that attracting more water-dependent industries to Michigan would reduce the risk of Great Lakes diversions: "There is a growing threat of diversion of Great Lakes waters to other regions of North America. I, for one, strongly believe that jobs should be located where adequate supplies of fresh water exist, rather than attempting to move water to other regions. Michigan is encouraging industries to factor fresh water into their decision-making process. Our message is simple: 'Water. Enjoy it. Employ it.'"[33] Nestlé officials cited Milliken's comments as justification for the controversial Ice Mountain plant in spite of the fact that Nestlé was the world's largest food and beverage company and controlled one-third of the $6 billion bottled water market.

Though Michigan's groundwater has been free for the taking for more than 150 years, Nestlé spokeswoman Deborah Muchmore said that the company would not deplete the resource and flee, as lumber barons did in the early 1900s after the pine forests were leveled. In fact, Nestlé in 2005 was studying the possibility of building a second water bottling facility in Michigan. Ice Mountain has become a fixture in Mecosta County. The company was a blessing or a curse, depending on your perspective. Opponents proudly displayed bumper stickers reading "No Way Perrier" on their vehicles. Youth organizations and other civic groups sold Nestlé's Ice Mountain Natural Spring Water during fund-raisers. From 2002 through 2004, Ice Mountain donated more than 3 million bottles of Ice Mountain water and more than five hundred thousand dollars in cash to civic groups and schools in Michigan. Nestlé also committed five hundred thousand dollars to the Ice Mountain Environmental Stewardship Fund at the Fremont Area Community Foundation. The fund would pay for ecosystem research and restoration projects in the Muskegon River watershed. "We believe our business is sustainable indefinitely," Muchmore said. "It would be suicide for us to destroy the groundwater that is our product."[34] Kane and other Nestlé critics called the company's donations to civic groups an attempt to buy public support for its Ice Mountain facility.[35]

James M. Olson, the attorney who represented Michigan Citizens for Water Conservation in its lawsuit against Nestlé, said the company's five-hundred-thousand-dollar environmental fund paled in comparison to revenue from the sale of its Ice Mountain water products. "If this is sufficient, then water traders could purchase control over hundreds of millions of dollars worth of Michigan's water for a pittance," Olson said in a 2004 position paper. "This, of course, raises fundamental questions regarding the nature of water rights."[36]

Sales of Nestlé's Ice Mountain bottled water products totaled $212 million in 2003. Sales of all Nestlé bottled water products, marketed under fifteen different labels, reached $2.6 billion in 2003.[37]

In January 2006, Ice Mountain reached an interim settlement of its court case with Michigan Citizens for Water Conservation. The deal allowed Ice Mountain to pump an average of 218 gallons of water a minute (114 million gallons per year) from its four spring water wells. The interim agreement followed a state Court of Appeals decision that allowed the plant to continue pumping water but not as fast as it wanted. Ice Mountain officials said the settlement would save 200 jobs. The issue of what constituted a water diversion was not decided by the settlement—that issue was headed to the Michigan Supreme Court.[38]

Swier argued that the Ice Mountain project represented just the tip of the bottled water issue. She believed that more companies would come to Michigan to mine groundwater if Nestlé prevailed in court. "We don't want groundwater to become like logging in the 1800s," Swier said. "When the loggers came they just took what they wanted. A hundred years later, the problems caused by logging are still here. Are people going to look back one hundred years from now and say, 'The Michigan Citizens for Water Conservation said this would happen. Why didn't people listen to them?'"[39] Many people who lived near the Ice Mountain facility rejected the dire warnings that bottled water factories or other consumptive uses of Great Lakes water could ever make a dent in the massive waterways or the rivers and aquifers that feed the lakes. "I talk to people who are not concerned about Nestlé and the issue of water because they feel there's so much water in Michigan [that] we could never take it all," Swier said.[40]

Michigan's first Anglo-Saxon settlers said the same thing 150 years ago about the virgin pine forests, the arctic grayling, and the passenger pigeons. All are gone now, victims of greed, ignorance, and indifference. Unlike the European immigrants who transformed Michigan's landscape, we do not have the luxury of blaming environmental catastrophes on ignorance. We know that the planet's resources have limits.

Even if Nestlé ultimately prevails in the courts, Swier said her group has made a positive contribution to protecting Michigan's natural resources by forcing the issue of unregulated water withdrawals into the spotlight. "Every morning I wake up, look at the lake I live on, and tell myself I'll never take the water for granted again," she said. "I think that's what we've taught the people of Michigan—to not take water for granted."

EPILOGUE

CONNECTING WITH THE RIVER

> The Muskegon River is a fantastic river. It's one hell of a resource that needs to be fully developed.
>
> —Jim Truchan, former Michigan Department of Natural Resources biologist, 1995

Stewart Montgomery deftly maneuvered his fourteen-foot aluminum fishing boat up the Muskegon River, darting from one side to the other to avoid the barely submerged sandbars that often beach inattentive boaters. He knew precisely where to cut across the river's channel to remain in water deep enough to float his boat. His was the kind of knowledge gained by spending countless hours on the river: Montgomery has lived beside the Muskegon River for three decades and knows an eleven-mile section of the river near Newaygo as well as anyone.

A devout fisherman who has tested his skills against all of Michigan's great rivers—the Pere Marquette, the Au Sable, the Two Hearted, the Fox—Montgomery decided to settle with his wife along the banks of the Muskegon. "I floated this part of the river in the 1960s and decided I wanted to buy a place here. To us, it was seventh heaven."[1] As he navigated the river's sweeping bends and dangerous sandbars, Montgomery seemed to have one eye looking downstream and the other looking straight down. Every few seconds he would point out a fish swimming in the translucent water beneath us—walleye, suckers and occasionally a trout. He has tracked the seasons by the movement of fish in the lower Muskegon. He knew, on that sunny September day, that Chinook salmon would soon be heading up the river from Lake Michigan to spawn before dying. The salmon would be followed upstream by steelhead and, in the spring, by a handful of mammoth sturgeon that survived in the river despite two centuries of human activity that has wiped out much of their habitat. As those migrations were under way, numerous other species of fish would go about their business in the river. That endless biological symphony is one of the reasons Montgomery has stayed close to the river. "The sins of fishing," he joked.[2]

Montgomery has borne witness to some of the most dramatic changes in the Muskegon over the last half of the twentieth century. After the Newaygo Dam was removed in 1969, he watched the river transform from a sluggish backwater to a free-flowing gem that supports a world-class salmon and trout fishery. He survived the flood of 1986, when the river bared its teeth after torrential rains turned it into a raging beast that swept away homes and nearly demolished three hydroelectric dams. Most recently, Montgomery has watched the popularity of the lower Muskegon soar as word spread that the river's lower section is home to a stunning array of fish and wildlife and to breathtaking scenery.

What Montgomery can not fathom is why people who come to the river to fish, canoe, or float in tubes would do anything to harm it. It is counter-intuitive to damage the thing you enjoy. But that is precisely what has happened as the river's mass appeal has exploded among anglers and canoers. Montgomery has long feared that some of the worst elements of human nature—ignorance, laziness, and ambivalence toward nature—would bring about the demise of the Muskegon. His fears were warranted.

In 2003, after years of seeing tubers and canoers toss litter into the river and then ignore his demands that they pick up their trash, Montgomery conducted an experiment of sorts. He wanted to see how many soda and beer cans he could find while scuba diving in one of the river's deep holes near his house. He hauled more than a thousand cans out of the river in one day—Bud, Miller Lite, Coke, Pepsi, you name it. He has the photos to prove it: cans piled high in his fishing boat. On another one of his river diving trips, Montgomery plucked twenty-three shoes out of the Muskegon.[3]

It really did not matter whether Montgomery hauled a hundred or a thousand cans or shoes out of the river. His was a symbolic story that exposed laziness and ignorance at a minimum and at worst a callous disrespect for this magnificent natural resource. Ignorance and the notion that people can do anything they want to the Muskegon and its vast network of tributaries, wetlands, and lakes—maintain obsolete dams that create ecological dysfunction, allow lawn and farm chemicals to run into its waters, crowd lakes and streams with waterfront structures, and use the river as a trash can—without serious environmental and economic consequences pose what I believe are two of the greatest threats to the Muskegon.

Think, for a minute, about the different cultures that settled Michigan. The Native Americans who first inhabited the area managed to live in harmony with nature for more than two thousand years. They hunted wildlife, caught fish, grew and harvested corn, and occasionally started fires in forests. By the time the second wave of settlers, European immigrants from the eastern United States, began moving into Michigan in the late 1700s, the rivers remained pristine and the lush pine forests intact.

By 1900, Michigan's vast pine forests had been plundered, the rivers scarred by logs, sand and dams; lakes were fouled by sawdust from sawmills, and fish populations were depleted, victims of greedy anglers. During the twentieth century, more dams harnessed scores more Michigan rivers to generate electricity, and roads were built to carry automobiles across the landscape. Some of the European immigrants who felled Michigan's forests and skipped town when all the giant white pines were gone undoubtedly possessed a rape-and-pillage mentality. But ignorance about how human activities could devastate nature surely played a significant role in the devastation of Michigan over the past two centuries.

There is no evidence that the people who in the early 1900s built the dams that still choke much of the Muskegon River and its tributaries knew that those structures would warm the water, decrease oxygen levels in the water, and, in the case of hydroelectric dams, kill thousands of fish annually. Nor is there any indication that state highway officials who designed the U.S. 31 bridge over the river in Muskegon, which effectively dammed the river's sprawling estuary, knew it would have such a profoundly negative effect on the lower river's estuary.

Fortunately, the Muskegon has demonstrated incredible resilience. Parts of the river that were once choked by logs or submerged under reservoirs created by dams are now teeming with fish and other aquatic life. The river has rebounded in Newaygo and Big Rapids, where dams were removed and the river's natural flow restored. The Muskegon is a far healthier river now than it has been in one hundred seventy five years. But much more could be done to help the Muskegon reach its potential. It will never again be the pristine river the Native Americans discovered when they settled along its scenic banks. Still, it is possible to have a free-flowing, clean, biologically rich river system in the midst of a half million people. Achieving that will require making personal sacrifices and politically unpopular decisions.

For starters, too many dams remain in the Muskegon River system. Of the ninety-four dams in the river and its tributaries, more than thirty are obsolete or have outlived their life expectancy. All of those dams should be candidates for removal. Does it make sense to keep a retired hydroelectric dam built in 1930 in the Clam River, a blue-ribbon trout stream that flows into the upper Muskegon River, for the sole purpose of maintaining a swimming hole in the tiny village of Falmouth? Imagine the alternative: a blue-ribbon trout stream flowing through that village, a place where anglers, paddlers, and others converge to experience a vibrant, natural river.

Removing all dams from the Muskegon River and its tributaries would be the quickest way to restore the river's natural flow and reconnect a web of water disjointed by dams and lake-level control structures. But that would be impractical, at least in the short term. Communities have sprouted around the reservoirs created by some dams, such as Croton Dam. The three hydroelectric dams on the Muskegon's main branch are a source of clean energy (despite the fish kills and oxygen depletion they periodically cause downstream). And the lake-level control structures that maintain artificially high water levels on most lakes in the Muskegon River watershed are beloved among lakefront property owners, who might react violently to any efforts to remove the small dams. Surpassing the dams' negative effects on the river is the wave of urban development sweeping across the landscape. Thousands of new residents are moving into the Muskegon River watershed each year, generating human and chemical waste and sending more polluted storm water into the river as they transform farm fields and forests into subdivisions, shopping centers, school buildings, and parking lots. Given the reality that we cannot remove all dams from the Muskegon River system any time soon or prevent a flood of people from moving into the watershed, how do we go about restoring and protecting this ecological gem? Residents of the watershed who hope to restore the Muskegon need MEDS. Not conventional meds—more Prozac will not help the river. MEDS is an acronym for a set of guiding principles that I believe will help restore the Muskegon's greatest natural attributes and preserve it for future generations. It stands for Motivation, Education, Dedication, and Sacrifice.

Step one is educating residents of the Muskegon River watershed about this unique natural system. Alarmingly few people know that the Muskegon is 219 miles long and links Houghton Lake to Lake Michigan. Few people who live in the Muskegon River watershed understand what makes the Muskegon unique among Michigan rivers: its diverse ecological features and a water temperature regime not found in other large rivers in the state.

For people to feel connected to the river, they must be educated about what makes it special and why it is worth protecting. Every able-bodied resident of the Muskegon River watershed should spend at least one day canoeing, fishing, or swimming in the river. The allure of this river is so intense that few people exposed to its grandeur could, in good conscience, knowingly do anything that would harm it.

Ignorance and the lack of intellectual or physical contact with the river perhaps constitute its greatest enemies. After people are educated and motivated to protect the river, some will undoubtedly become zealots. Outstanding. The river could use a few more zealots working on its behalf.

People who attempt to bring about change will undoubtedly encounter opposition, especially when it comes to changing the way individuals interact with the river or the landscape that drains into the Muskegon. Only the most stubborn dedication to the river's health will survive the inevitable attacks from special interests willing to put financial gain ahead of the river's need for ecological integrity.

Taking a stand for nature and restoring natural features is difficult, often thankless, work. Consider the plight of Theresa Bernhardt, a Muskegon woman who fought so long and hard to bring about a cleanup of Ruddiman Creek, a horribly polluted stream that flows into Muskegon Lake. In 1995, Bernhardt was pregnant with her youngest child when some of her neighbors told her she should forgo thoughts of social responsibility—she planned to pick trash from Ruddiman Creek—because the creek had been grossly polluted by local industries. Stay away from the creek and mind your own business, her neighbors said. Bernhardt did the opposite.

Over the course of the next ten years, Bernhardt learned all she could about the source and extent of pollution in the creek. She then demanded action. Bernhardt became an environmental pit bull, a hero to those who wanted the creek cleaned up and a pest to lazy bureaucrats and those who feared that publicity about the pollution would harm property values in surrounding neighborhoods. Her efforts paid off in 2005, when the state of Michigan and U.S. Environmental Protection Agency launched a $10.6 million cleanup of polluted sediment in Ruddiman Creek. The cleanup would remove eighty thousand cubic yards of contaminated sediment containing 164 tons of pure lead, chromium, and other toxic wastes from the creek bottom. The goal: make the creek safe for people, fish, and wildlife.

After a decade of battling public apathy, bureaucratic inertia, and skeptics who told her she was wasting her time, Bernhardt stood proudly on the banks of the creek in July 2005 and watched as the first scoops of toxic mud were pulled from the creek. "Thank God for Theresa Bernhardt—she's the reason the creek is getting cleaned up," said Jim McCabe, who has lived near the creek for twenty-seven years.[4]

Bernhardt was one of those rare individuals who tackled a problem because it was the right thing to do. There was nothing in it for her other than the satisfaction of knowing that she did her part to make a small part of the world a healthier place. The Muskegon River needs many more people like Bernhardt, now and in the coming years, as increasing urban development serves up another major test of the river's tolerance for human activities.

Long overlooked by people who thought they had to go further north in Michigan to paddle a scenic river or catch mammoth salmon or chrome steelhead, the Muskegon River has been discovered. Abundant open space near the river and its numerous tributaries is becoming prime real estate as more people migrate out of the cities of Muskegon, Grand Rapids and elsewhere in search of serenity in the countryside. "The river isn't like it used to be; the river has grown up," Montgomery said.[5]

Convincing people to do what is best for the river, such as giving it the space it needs to flourish by building further from the water, will be a tall order. People are drawn to water, and those who pay big bucks for riverfront lots are going to want to see the Muskegon. You cannot blame them. Many people, given the financial means, would gladly live where they could look out the window and watch a lake, river, or ocean. There is something soothing, mysterious, and magical about water, particularly the eternal movement of a river.

That brings us to the most challenging part of the MEDS solution: Sacrifice. Are the roughly half a million people who live, work, and play in and around the Muskegon willing to make the personal sacrifices needed to preserve and protect the river? Here are several questions about personal sacrifice, each of which is based on actions that could be taken to improve some aspect of the river system.

- Would you be willing to stop using phosphorous-based fertilizer on your lawn, golf course, or farm fields to improve water quality in the river and its tributaries? Excessive amounts of phosphorous are devastating lakes and rivers around the country, fueling excessive algae and weed growth that prematurely age waterways, can foul water quality, make boating difficult, and choke out native plants. In some areas, excessive phosphorous is fueling the growth of toxic algae, which can pose health threats to fish, wildlife, and humans. The problem has already been documented in Muskegon Lake, near the mouth of the Muskegon River.[6] Phosphorous-free fertilizer may cost a bit more, but the environmental benefits are clear—cleaner water, fewer weeds, and less harmful algae in lakes and streams.
- Would you support removing a dam in your community if the structure was obsolete, unsafe, or proven to be harming water quality or fish in the river or one of its feeder streams? People often have a visceral reaction against removing dams. One reason: it is difficult for many people to imagine what a river or stream would look like if a dam and the reservoir it created were removed. People often fear that removing a dam will leave a mud pit that stinks and breeds mosquitoes. However, successful dam removal projects in Newaygo and Big Rapids and at scores of sites in Wisconsin and other states have demonstrated that removing a dam can create an aesthetically pleasing area along a free-flowing river. As far as the river is concerned, removing dams is an ecological no-brainer. Dams destroy sections of rivers by turning free-flowing water into lakes. It is that simple.
- Would you be willing to convert a strip of your manicured lawn or cropland into a vegetative buffer strip along the river or one of its lakes or

tributaries? Buffer strips help keep soil, pesticides, and herbicides from washing off the land and into the nearest surface water. Planting a buffer strip can mean less land on which farmers can grow crops, but federal subsidies are available to offset the lost revenue. For homeowners, planting a buffer strip might slightly reduce the view of the river, but there are low-lying plants that provide a natural barrier without obstructing the view.

In fast-growing communities, residents must ask themselves and their elected leaders if they are willing to control development for the sake of the river. Urban growth is inevitable in the Muskegon River watershed. The trick is to manage growth in a way that allows people to build new homes and shopping centers while minimizing environmental damage. Developers, for example, could install rain gardens to filter storm water runoff from new shopping centers and subdivisions. Rain gardens, which look like vegetated drainage ditches, are stocked with absorbent plants that soak up some of the pollutants that drain off the land after periods of rain or snowmelt.

Removing obsolete dams and controlling growth are two of the big-ticket challenges that must be confronted if we hope to protect the Muskegon River amid a growing crush of development in the watershed. Individuals can do scores of other things to prevent water pollution. Some examples: pick up your pet's waste and put it in a trash can or flush it down a toilet; build a gravel rather than concrete driveway to reduce storm water runoff; drive your boat slower in the river to reduce stream bank erosion; do not dump yard wastes or trash in or near waterways; never pour used motor oil or other chemicals on the ground; keep your septic system in good working order and have it pumped regularly; reduce your use of toxic chemicals at home and in the workplace; and landscape with native plants.

In the coming years, as homes and shopping centers sprout in the Muskegon River watershed and more dams become obsolete and unsafe, countless situations will arise in which individuals will be forced to choose between social activism and apathy, self-interest and the public good. Some people will be forced to decide between what is best for their pocketbook and what is best for the river. How they respond to those situations will reflect individual and community priorities. The river will always be there to hold us accountable for our actions.

MARK AND JEANETTE KNOPH COULD NOT FATHOM LIFE WITHOUT THE Muskegon River in their midst. The owners of the Old Log Resort, near the river's midpoint, have made a living along the banks of the Muskegon for more than twenty years. At first glance, the Knophs seem to have dream jobs: they are their own bosses, and they live and work along a scenic river. But appearances are a bit misleading.

The Knophs fled their jobs in Detroit in the mid-1980s—Mark worked in a steel mill, Jeanette was a nurse—to pursue their dream of owning a business in northern Michigan. Each summer, they work like dogs to keep their customers happy. They labor morning and night and are on call twenty-four hours a day, every day, hauling canoes to the river's edge in the morning and taking them out of the river at night. If a toilet becomes clogged in their resort's bathhouse in the middle of the night, guess who fixes it?

Though they occasionally grow tired of owning a business, the Knophs say that they never begrudge the source of their livelihood: the river. In fact, the river has been their source of solitude, a healing presence in their busy lives. "When we first bought this place, we didn't have time to canoe," Jeanette said. "Now, a lot of times we'll go out on the river for an hour just to get our equilibrium back, our sanity."[7]

In an era of cell phones, high-speed Internet, and increasingly fast-paced lifestyles, the river remains a soothing force. Go to its edge, focus on the beauty of the Muskegon and imagine all that lives in it, listen for its voice as the water slips over rocks and around trees. Let its current restore a sense of harmony in your life, if only for a few minutes. After you leave the Muskegon, return the favor—do your part to restore and protect the natural harmony of this spectacular, endangered river.

NOTES

PROLOGUE: FATAL ATTRACTION

1. Paul Vecsei, interview by author, April 18, 2003.
2. "The Road to Extinction," *Muskegon Chronicle,* June 1, 2003, 1A.
3. "Shadow of Its Former Self," 1A.
4. "Road to Extinction," 1A.
5. Martin Metcalf, "The Michigan Grayling," *Michigan History* 45 (June 1961): 140–63.
6. Andrew J. Nuhfer, *Evaluation of the Reintroduction of the Arctic Grayling into Michigan Lakes and Streams,* Research Report 1985 (Lansing: Michigan Department of Natural Resources Fisheries Division, 1992), 4.
7. Charles W. Creaser and Edwin P. Creaser, "The Grayling in Michigan," *Papers of the Michigan Academy of Science, Arts and Letters* 20 (1935): 604.
8. Metcalf, "Michigan Grayling," 153.
9. Nuhfer, *Evaluation,* 4–5. .
10. Ibid., 4.
11. "Last Century's Banner Trout Only a Memory," *Muskegon Chronicle,* September 12, 1999, 5A.

INTRODUCTION

1. Ernest "Jack" Sharpe [Newaygo Newt], "Muskegon River," unpublished poem, courtesy of the White Cloud Community Library.
2. Ernest Hemingway, "Big Two-Hearted River," in *Ernest Hemingway: The Short Stories* (New York: Simon and Schuster, 1995), 210.
3. Mike Wiley, interview by author, July 26, 2003.
4. "Muskegon River Valley Is Outdoor Paradise, Chicago Scouts Find," *Muskegon Chronicle,* July 6, 1929, 1A
5. Wiley, interview, July 26, 2003.
6. Richard P. O'Neal, *Muskegon River Watershed Assessment,* Report 19 (Lansing: Michigan Department of Natural Resources Fisheries Division, 1997), 20–21.
7. Ibid., 42–43; Sarah U'Ren, *Muskegon River Management,* vol. 1, *Management Plan,* Report MR-2002-4 (Muskegon: Annis Water Resources Institute, Grand Valley State University, 2002), 38.
8. O'Neal, *Muskegon River Watershed Assessment,* 11–15.
9. "A Shadow of Its Former Self," *Muskegon Chronicle,* September 12, 1999, 1A.
10. *Preliminary Population Projections—Michigan Counties to 2020* (Lansing: Michigan Department of Management and Budget, 1996), 3.
11. K. L. Cool, interview by author, February 20, 2000.
12. Jack Bails, interview by author, January 10, 2005.

CHAPTER 1. NATURAL WONDER

1. R. D. Ustipak, *An Analysis of Wild Rice at Houghton Lake, Michigan,* ed. G. F. Martz (Brainerd, Minn.: Cook Waterfowl Foundation, 1995), 2–3.
2. U'ren, *Muskegon River Watershed Project,*1:39.
3. O'Neal, *Muskegon River Watershed Assessment,* 31–32, 164.
4. Ibid.
5. John Mullett, surveyor's notes, 1837, in possession of Steve Vallier, Muskegon, Mich.
6. Frank Leverett and Frank B. Taylor, *The Pleistocene of Indiana and Michigan and the History of the Great Lakes* (Washington, D.C.: U.S. Geological Survey, Department of the Interior, 1915), 225.
7. *Encyclopedia of Michigan,* 2d ed. (St. Clair Shores, Mich.: Somerset, 1989), 59.
8. Charles E. Cleland, *Rites of Conquest* (Ann Arbor: University of Michigan Press, 1992), 20, 21. See also John R. Halsey and Michael D. Stafford, eds., *Retrieving*

Michigan's Buried Past: The Archaeology of the Great Lakes State, Bulletin 64 (Bloomfield Hills, Mich.: Cranbrook Institute of Science, 1999): 126–30; R. Ray Baker, "Ancient Earthworks Believed to Be Forts Are Found in State," *Muskegon Chronicle,* April 19, 1935, 1A.

9. U'ren, *Muskegon River Watershed Project,* 1:34.
10. O'Neal, *Muskegon River Watershed Assessment,* 26–27.
11. U'ren, *Muskegon River Watershed Project,* 2:33.
12. O'Neal, *Muskegon River Watershed Assessment,* 26.
13. "Indian Chiefs, Lumber Barons . . . River Has Seen Many Colorful Characters," *Muskegon Chronicle,* September 12, 1999, 5A.
14. Jonathan Eyler, *Muskegon County: Harbor of Promise* (Northridge, Calif.: Windsor, 1986), 22.
15. George Ruddiman, letter, in *Michigan Pioneer and Historical Society,* vol. 21 (Lansing, Mich.: Robert Smith and Co. State Binders and Printers, 1894), 673.
16. "Legendary Muskegon: Historic Romance Surrounds Its Early Days," *Muskegon Chronicle,* October 22, 1903, 5.
17. *Portrait and Biographical Album of Newaygo County, Michigan* (Chicago: Chapman Brothers, 1884), 504.
18. Ruddiman, letter, 673.
19. Ibid.

CHAPTER 2. A WORKING RIVER

1. *Portrait and Biographical Album,* 489.
2. Harry L. Spooner, *Lumbering of Newaygo County* (Newaygo, Mich.: Newaygo County Society of History and Genealogy, n.d.), 1.
3. "Michigan's 83 Counties: Newaygo County," *Michigan History* 72, no. 4 (July–August 1988): 12.
4. Norman Schmaltz, "The Land Nobody Wanted: The Dilemma of Michigan's Cutover Lands," *Michigan History* 67 (January–February 1983): 32–33.
5. "Indian Chiefs, Lumber Barons . . . River Has Seen Many Colorful Characters," *Muskegon Chronicle,* September 12, 1999, 5A.
6. Jeremy W. Kilar, *Michigan's Lumbertowns: Lumbermen and Laborers in Saginaw, Bay City, and Muskegon, 1870–1905* (Detroit: Wayne State University Press, 1990), 101.
7. Bruce Catton, *Michigan: A Bicentennial History* (New York: Norton, 1976), 102.

8. "Legendary Muskegon," 5A.
9. Kilar, *Michigan's Lumbertowns,* 20–21.
10. Joe Eyler, "They Built Muskegon," *Muskegon Chronicle,* March 29, 1978, 21.
11. Kilar, *Michigan's Lumbertowns,* 59–60.
12. Henry H. Holt, "The Centennial History of Michigan," in *Reports of Counties,* 300, available at Hackley Library, Muskegon.
13. Rolland H. Maybee, *Michigan's White Pine Era, 1840–1900* (Lansing: Michigan Historical Commission, 1960), 39–41.
14. Maybee, 37.
15. Alice Prescott Keyes, *Romance of Muskegon* (Muskegon: Muskegon Heritage Association, 1974), 33.
16. *Newaygo Republican,* April 26, 1871.
17. *Portrait and Biographical Album,* 525.
18. Ibid.
19. Ibid., 530.
20. W. M. Harford, ed., *Muskegon and Its Resources* (Muskegon: Harford and Latimer for Muskegon Board of Trade, 1884), 26–27.
21. Stewart H. Holbrook, *Holy Old Mackinaw: A Natural History of the American Lumberjack* (New York: Macmillan, 1938), 108.
22. Spooner, *Lumbering of Newaygo County,* 40–41.
23. *American Lumberman,* August 18, 1900, 1, 24.
24. Robert I. Thompson scrapbook, Fremont Area District Library, Local History Room, Fremont, book 8, p. 75.

CHAPTER 3. THE BERLIN WALL

1. O'Neal, *Muskegon River Watershed Assessment,* 41–43.
2. George Bush, *Future Builders: The Story of Michigan's Consumers Power Company* (New York: McGraw-Hill, 1973), 84–85.
3. Ibid., 85.
4. Ibid.
5. Ibid., 89.
6. "Hydroelectric Dams Kill Thousands of Sport Fish Annually," *Muskegon Chronicle,* September 12, 1999, 1A.
7. Ibid.
8. Thompson scrapbook, book 8, pp. 14–15.

9. "Lake at Hardy Near Top Level," *Newaygo Republican,* April 16, 1931, 1.
10. "Visitors Come from All over the United States," *Muskegon Chronicle,* August 22, 1931, 1.
11. O'Neal, *Muskegon River Watershed Assessment,* 42.
12. Bush, *Future Builders,* 430.
13. Roger Morgenstern, Consumers Energy Company, to author, September 15, 2003.
14. O'Neal, *Muskegon River Watershed Assessment,* 43.
15. Ibid., 92.
16. Vecsei, interview, April 18, 2003.
17. Stephanie M. Carman and Reuben R. Goforth, *An Assessment of the Current Distribution and Status of Freshwater Mussels in the Muskegon River, Michigan,* Michigan Natural Features Inventory, Report 2003-18, Lansing: Michigan Department of Natural Resources, 2003), 38.
18. *Native Clams of the Great Lakes,* Species Restoration Bulletin (Ann Arbor: U.S. Geological Survey Great Lakes Science Center, available at www.glsc.usgs.gov), 1.
19. Carman and Goforth, *Assessment,* 38.
20. Thompson scrapbook, book 8, pp. 12–13.
21. Mark and Jeanette Knoph, interview by author, May 7, 2004.
22. Tom Huggler, *Fish Michigan: Fifty More Rivers* (Davison: Friede, 1996), 56.
23. David N. Cassuto, *Cold Running River* (Ann Arbor: University of Michigan Press, 1994), 2–3.

CHAPTER 4. SMALL WONDERS

1. *Old Growth Forest Foot Trail,* brochure at Hartwick Pines State Park, Grayling, 2003.
2. G. W. Wendel and H. Clay Smith, "Eastern White Pine" in *Silvics of North America,* vol. 1, handbook 654 (Washington, D.C.: U.S. Department of Agriculture, Forest Service, 1990), 972–93, available at www.na.fs.fed.us.
3. O'Neal, *Muskegon River Watershed Assessment,* 38.
4. Jim Lithen, "A River Trip, Part I: In the Beginning," *Marion Mill,* August 2000, 1.
5. O'Neal, *Muskegon River Watershed Assessment,* 45, 155, table 27.
6. U'ren, *Muskegon River Watershed Project,* 1:3.
7. Michigan State Historical Commission sign, Local Site 2054, Marion, 1999.

8. "Breaking up (Dams) Is Hard to Do," *Muskegon Chronicle,* September 13, 1999, 8A.
9. Spooner, *Lumbering of Newaygo County,* 5–6.
10. Logging Museum exhibit, Hartwick Pines State Park, Grayling.
11. "Dams: Disasters Waiting to Happen," *Muskegon Chronicle,* September 13, 1999, 1A.
12. *Crossroads* (quarterly newsletter of the H. John Heinz III Center for Science, Economics, and the Environment) 1, no. 2 (2003): 1.
13. Data provided by Michigan Dam Safety Unit, Michigan Department of Environmental Quality, Lansing, 1999, in possession of author.
14. "Dams and Rivers: Scientists Take a New Look Downstream," U.S. Department of the Interior press release, December 18, 1996.
15. U'ren, *Muskegon River Watershed Project,* 1:65–66.
16. Mike Wiley, interview by author, October 7, 2004, Ann Arbor, Mich.
17. Richard P. O'Neal, *Ecological-Fisheries Evaluation of the Middle Branch River, Osceola County* (Lansing: Michigan Department of Natural Resources, 2002), 7.
18. Thomas F. Waters, *Wildstream: A Natural History of the Free Flowing River* (St. Paul, Minn.: Riparian, 2000), 477.
19. "Hydroelectric Dams Kill Thousands of Sport Fish Annually," 1A.
20. Catherine Riseng, interview, October 7, 2004.
21. Richard P. O'Neal, interview by author, February 26, 2004.
22. Ustipak, *Analysis of Wild Rice,* 28.
23. Donald J. Bonnette, "Ecosystem Management at Houghton Lake, Michigan, with Emphasis on Wild Rice Ecology" (master's thesis, Central Michigan University, 1998), 64.
24. Ustipak, *Analysis of Wild Rice,* 6.

CHAPTER 5. ALIEN INVASION

1. Gwen White, Michael Murray, and Sara E. Jackson, *Ecosystem Shock: The Devastating Impacts of Invasive Species on the Great Lakes Food Web* (Washington, D.C: National Wildlife Federation, 2004), 8.
2. Ibid., 34.
3. Dennis S. Lavis, U.S. Fish and Wildlife Service, Ludington Biological Station, letter to author, September 2003.
4. William H. Becker, *From the Atlantic to the Great Lakes: A History of the U.S. Army Corps of Engineers and the St. Lawrence Seaway* (Washington, D.C.: Historical

Division, Office of Administrative Services, Office of the Chief of Engineers, 1986), 2.

5. Carleton Mabee, *The Seaway Story* (New York: Macmillan, 1961), 17.
6. Ibid., 24.
7. Ibid., 253, 256.
8. "EPA Urged to Act against Lake Invaders," *Muskegon Chronicle,* November 14, 2002, 1B.
9. Cassuto, *Cold Running River,* 104–5.
10. Michigan Department of Natural Resources annual fish stocking reports, available at http://www.michigandnr.com/fishstock/default.asp.
11. O'Neal, *Muskegon River Watershed Assessment,* 27.
12. "Food Fight—Tiny Source of Fish Food Disappearing from Big Lake," *Muskegon Chronicle,* December 4, 1997, 1.
13. Liz Wade, interview by author, September 2003.
14. John Flesher, "One Thing's Certain—Exotic Species Are Here to Stay," *Muskegon Chronicle,* October 12, 2003, 1C.
15. White, Murray, and Jackson, *Ecosystem Shock,* 34–36.
16. "Some Ships Could Lose Lake Access," *Detroit Free Press,* December 30, 2004, 1A.
17. U.S. St. Lawrence Seaway Development Corporation and Martin Associates, *Economic Impact Study of the Great Lakes St. Lawrence Seaway System* (Lancaster, Pa.: Martin Associates, 2001), E-2.
18. John C. Taylor and James L. Roach, "Ocean Shipping in the Great Lakes: Transportation Cost Increases That Would Result From a Cessation of Ocean Vessel Shipping," Allendale, Mich.: Grand Valley State University, December 6, 2005.
19. "GVSU study: Ocean Freighter Ban Not Too Costly," *Muskegon Chronicle,* December 20, 2005.
20. Bonnette, "Ecosystem Management," 2.
21. Dick Pastula, interview by author, October 28, 2003.
22. Mark A. Heilman, *Management of Eurasian Watermilfoil in Houghton Lake, Michigan* (Carmel, Ind.: SePro Corp., 2003), ; Kurt D. Geisinger, U.S. Army Corps of Engineers, Vicksburg, Miss., and Anthony Groves, Progressive AE, Grand Rapids, Mich., in *Michigan Riparian,* 18.
23. Craig Cotterman, interview by author, October 20, 2003.
24. Video of Eurasian water milfoil treatment of Houghton Lake, Mich. (Carmel, Ind.: SePro Corp., 2001).

25. Pastula, interview, October 28, 2003.
26. O'Neal, interview, February 26, 2004.

CHAPTER 6. BOTTLENECK

1. Jess Soltess, "Mackie Opens Key Link," *Muskegon Chronicle,* June 30, 1964, 1A.
2. "Giant structures form dam across Muskegon River," *Muskegon Chronicle,* October 29, 1962, 1A.
3. Emert Lange, interview by author, January 21, 2004.
4. Wiley, interview, October 7, 2004.
5. O'Neal, *Muskegon River Watershed Assessment,* 43.
6. Richard Rediske, *Lower Muskegon River Preliminary Habitat Assessment,* MR-2000-01 (Muskegon: Annis Water Resources Institute, Grand Valley State University, 2000), 54–55, 60.
7. Ibid.
8. Marta Dodd, "Mighty Hardy Dam Performed Well during Deluge," *Muskegon Chronicle,* October 5, 1986, op-ed page.
9. "What Would Happen If the Hardy Dam Failed?" *Muskegon Chronicle,* April 19, 1987, 1B–2B.
10. Sam Nesselroad, interview by author, October 29, 2003.
11. Stewart Montgomery, interview by author, June 7, 2004.
12. "Nature Puts on Fearful Display of Awesome Power," *Muskegon Chronicle,* September 12, 1986, 7A.
13. Stan Peterson, interview by author, May 1, 1999.
14. Wiley, interview, October 7, 2004.
15. Rediske, *Lower Muskegon River Preliminary Habitat Assessment,* 59–60.
16. Wiley, interview, July 26, 2003.
17. O'Neal, *Muskegon River Watershed Assessment,* 26.
18. Gale Nobes, interview by author, May 2, 2004.
19. Lange, interview, January 21, 2004.

CHAPTER 7. PARADISE FOUND

1. O'Neal, *Muskegon River Watershed Assessment,* 42.
2. Matt Supinski, interview by author, September 26, 2004.
3. Carl Richards and John Krause, *Hatches of the Muskegon River II* (Grant:

Antekeier and Krause, 1996), 1.

4. "Fish Flourish Where Dams Don't," *Muskegon Chronicle,* September 13, 1999, 1A.
5. "River Offers Natural Reproduction," *Muskegon Chronicle,* November 10, 2002, 1A.
7. "It'll Be Water over the Dam, Not Walleyes," *Muskegon Chronicle,* March 25, 1967, 1A.
8. Mr. and Mrs. John Scheeres, "An Open Letter to the People of Newaygo," *Newaygo Republican,* November 14, 1968, 2.
9. Janet L. Strahl, "The Removal of the Newaygo Dam," research paper, Western Michigan University, March 1971, 5.
10. "Catching on . . . Muskegon River Gaining Reputation as Trout Fishery," *Muskegon Chronicle,* March 20, 2000, 1A.
11. Matt Supinski, *Steelhead Dreams: The Theory, Method, Science, and Madness of Great Lakes Steelhead Fly Fishing* (Portland, Ore.: Amato, 2001), 111.
12. Nesselroad, interview, October 29, 2003.

CHAPTER 8. POLLUTION REVOLUTION

1. Al Lemke, interview by author, November 27, 2004.
2. O'Neal, interview, February 26, 2004.
3. "Once Ringed with Sawmills . . . Now Being Loaded with Junk," *Muskegon Chronicle,* May 23, 1970, 1B.
4. Eyler, *Muskegon County,* 109–10.
5. Ed Subler, interview by author, November 27, 2004.
6. "Wastewater Plant Gets Fresh Start," *Muskegon Chronicle,* December 13, 1992, 1B.
7. "Sewage Leak Ruins Season Opener for Anglers, Shops," *Muskegon Chronicle,* April 24, 1999, 1A.
8. "Mill Views Aired," *Muskegon Chronicle,* October 30, 1975, 1A.
9. "Steel Mill Hearing: Stand Up and Be Counted," *Muskegon Chronicle,* October 12, 1975, 7A.
10. "Muskegon Loses Mill," *Muskegon Chronicle,* November 8, 1975, 1A.
11. Bob Kingsley, "Catching the Big Cats," *Muskegon Chronicle,* June 2, 2002, 7B.
12. "Killed Mill Left Muskegon a Boat Bonanza," *Muskegon Chronicle,* September 15, 1996, 1A.
13. "Study Finds Tar Balls on Lake Floor," *Muskegon Chronicle,* March 21, 2000, 1A.
14. "Toxic Creek Cleanup Years Away," *Muskegon Chronicle,* October 24, 2000, 1A.

CHAPTER 9. SACRED COWS

1. "DNR Wants to Pull Plugs on Hydroelectric Dams," *Muskegon Chronicle,* August 23, 1989, 1A.
2. Ed Burch, interview by author, October 15, 2004.
3. Ibid.
4. American Society of Civil Engineers Task Force on Dam Removal, *White Paper on Removal of Functioning Dams, EWRI Currents,* 5, no. 2 (2003): 1.
5. *Crossroads* (quarterly newsletter of the H. John Heinz III Center for Science, Economics, and the Environment) 1, no. 2 (2003): 1.
6. David D. Hart, Thomas E. Johnson, Karen L. Bushaw-Newton, Richard J. Horwitz, Angela T. Bednarek, Donald F. Charles, Daniel A. Kreeger, and David J. Velinsky, "Dam Removal: Challenges and Opportunities for Ecological Research and River Restoration," *Bioscience* 52, no. 8 (August 2002): 669.
7. N. Leroy Poff and David D. Hart, "How Dams Vary and Why It Matters for the Emerging Science of Dam Removal," *Bioscience* 52, no. 8 (August 2002): 666.
8. "Stronach Dam Removal Enters Final Phase," *Hydro Reporter* (Consumers Energy newsletter), March 2003, 3.
9. Poff and Hart, "How Dams Vary," 667.
10. American Society of Civil Engineers, "Dams: Issue Brief" (1997), available at http://www.asce.org.
11. *The Cost of Rehabilitating Our Nation's Dams: A Methodology, Estimate, and Proposed Funding Mechanisms* (Washington, D.C.: Association of State Dam Safety Officials, 2002), 3.
12. Jennifer Granholm to George W. Bush, August 20, 2004, in possession of author.
13. Helen Sarakinos and Sara E. Johnson, "Social Perspectives on Dam Removal," in *Proceedings of the Heinz Center's Dam Removal Workshop,* ed. William L. Graf , published by the H. John Heinz III Center for Science, Economics and the Environment, Washington, D.C., 41.
14. Brian Graber, "Potential Economic Benefits of Small Dam Removal," in *Proceedings of the Heinz Center's Dam Removal Workshop,* ed. Graf, 63.
15. Denny Caneff, presentation at the annual meeting of the Michigan River Alliance, October 8, 2004, Big Rapids.
16. Sharon Hanshue, interview by author, October 20, 2004.
17. "Dam Removal," November 17, 2003, available at http://www.michigan.gov/dnr/0,1607,7-153-10364_27415-80303—,00.html.

18. "Breaking up (Dams) Is Hard to Do," 8A.
19. "Dams: Disasters Waiting to Happen," 1A.
20. O'Neal, interview, February 26, 2004.
21. *Water Quality Limits Evaluation for the Hydroelectric Projects Located on the Muskegon River,* report to Michigan Department of Natural Resources Fisheries Division (Lansing, Mich.: Kleinschmidt Energy and Water Resource Consultants, 2003), 5-1, 5-2.
22. Neal A. Godby Jr., Edward S. Rutherford, and Doran M. Mason, *Diet, Consumption, and Production of Juvenile Steelhead in a Lake Michigan Tributary* (Ann Arbor: Michigan Department of Natural Resources, University of Michigan, and National Oceanic and Atmospheric Administration, 1999), 18–22.
23. Judy Chesley, interview with Consumers Energy researchers, in possession of author, 1993.
24. Supinski, interview, September 26, 2004.
25. "Hydroelectric Dams Kill Thousands of Sport Fish Annually," 1A.
26. O'Neal, *Muskegon River Watershed Assessment,* 65.

CHAPTER 10. A TANGLED WEB

1. Ruddiman letter, 673.
2. *Mute Swans in Michigan,* Wildlife Issue Review Paper 12 (Lansing: Michigan Department of Natural Resources, 2003), 1.
3. Nobes, interview, May 2, 2004.
4. Notes with author, May 20, 2004, Muskegon, Mich.
5. Peter M. Wege, interview by author, November 20, 2003, East Grand Rapids, Mich.
6. Terri McCarthy, interview with author, November 20, 2003, East Grand Rapids, Mich.
7. Peter M. Wege, *Economicology: The Eleventh Commandment* (Grand Rapids: Economicology Press, 1998), 144.
8. Wege, interview, November 20, 2003.
9. Interview by author, January 10, 2005, Lansing, Mich.
10. "The Rouge River Project: Bringing the River Back to Life," available at www.rougeriver.com.
11. Michael Grunwald, "An Environmental Reversal of Fortune," *Washington Post,* June 26, 2002, 1A.

12. Ibid.
13. Michael Grunwald, "A Rescue Plan, Bold and Uncertain," *Washington Post,* June 23, 2002, 1A.
14. Peter M. Wege, interview by author, East Grand Rapids, Mich., May 10, 2004.
15. Gary Noble, interview by author, November 7, 2004.
16. Ibid.
17. Alan Steinman, interview by author, January 30, 2004.
18. *Muskegon River Management Plan,* River Management Plan 04-2003 (Lansing: Michigan Department of Natural Resources Fisheries Division, 2003), 17.
19. Steinman, interview, January 30, 2004.
20. Wiley, interview, October 7, 2004.
21. "Study: Reducing Pollution Will Cost Millions, Require Lifestyle Changes," *River View* (newsletter of the Muskegon River Watershed Assembly) 1, no. 6 (January 2006): 6.
22. John Koches, interview by author, May 19, 2003, Muskegon, Mich.
23. Amy Peterson, *Into Every Life a Little Rain Must Fall* (Lansing, Mich.: Michigan Department of Environmental Quality, 1997), 17.
24. Koches, interview, May 19, 2003.

CHAPTER 11. HUNGRY WATER

1. George Trueman, interview by author, May 20, 2004, Newaygo, Mich.
2. Rediske, *Lower Muskegon River Preliminary Habitat Assessment,* 11.
3. O'Neal, *Muskegon River Watershed Assessment,* 34.
4. *Muskegon River Management Plan,* 2.
5. Phil Dakin, "Muskegon River Erosion and Sedimentation Control," *River View* (newsletter of the Muskegon River Watershed Assembly) 1, no. 3 (April 2002): 5.
6. Wiley, interview, October 7, 2004.
7. Stewart Montgomery, interview by author, Newaygo, Mich., August 30, 2004.
8. Wiley, interview, October 7, 2004.
9. Dick Schwikert, "Sand," *Mainstream* (newsletter of the Pere Marquette Watershed Council), summer 2003, 3.
10. Gaylord Alexander and Edward A. Hansen, abstract of *Decline and Recovery of a Brook Trout Stream Following an Experimental Addition of Sand Sediment,* Research Report 1943 (Lansing: Michigan Department of Natural Resources Fisheries Division, 1988).

11. Schwikert, "Sand," 3.
12. Nobes, interview, May 2, 2004.
13. Trueman, interview, May 20, 2004.
14. Ibid.
15. Supinski, interview, September 26, 2004.
16. Vecsei, interview, April 18, 2003.
17. Trueman, interview, May 20, 2004.

CHAPTER 12. FATAL ATTRACTION II

1. Don Bollman, *Run for the Roses: A Fifty-Year Memoir* (Mecosta: Canadian Lakes, 1975), 313.
2. "Canadian Lakes: Creek 'Obliterated' to Create Lakes," *Muskegon Chronicle*, September 14, 1999, 4A.
3. Dave Fongers, "Cedar Creek Hydrologic Modeling" (memo to Tim Hall), Michigan Department of Environmental Quality, Lansing, May 27, 2004, 15, in possession of author.
4. James Muston, interview by author, September 2, 2004.
5. Unpublished data from John Koches, "Sustainable Futures Project," Grand Valley State University, Annis Water Resources Institute, Muskegon, Mich., 2004, in possession of author.
6. Estimates based on U.S. Army Corps of Engineers design standards for wastewater treatment plants, in possession of author.
7. Fongers, "Cedar Creek Hydrologic Modeling," 15.
8. Unpublished data from John Koches, "Sustainable Futures Project."
9. Steve Vallier, interview by author, May 20, 2004.
10. Wiley, interview, October 7, 2004.
11. Ibid.
12. Ibid.
13. Unpublished data from John Koches, "Sustainable Futures Project."
14. Vanessa Lougheed, Michigan State University, letter to author, June 6, 2004, referencing data in V. L. Lougheed, R. J. Stevenson, S. H. Gage, R. A. Hough, D. T. Long, C. A. Parker, B. Pijanowski, J. Qi, C. M. Riseng, M. J. Wiley, *Innovation in Ecological Assessment: The Muskegon River Watershed Assessment Project*, paper presented at the North American Benthological Society Annual Meeting, Pittsburgh, Pennsylvania, 2002.

15. Ibid.
15. Catherine M. Riseng, Mike J. Wiley, Brian Pijanowski, and R. Jan Stevenson, "Effects of Land Use Change on Fish Species Diversity in the Muskegon River Watershed," abstract of paper presented at the annual meeting of the North American Benthological Society conference, Pittsburgh, 2002.
16. Wiley, interview, October 7, 2004.
17. O'Neal, interview, February 26, 2004; Wiley, interview, October 25, 2001.
18. Richard Rediske, *Preliminary Investigation of the Extent of Sediment Contamination in the Lower Grand River,"* Report EPA-9050R-99-010 (Chicago: U.S. Environmental Protection Agency, District V Office, 1999), 2.
19. O'Neal, interview, February 26, 2004.
20. The International Joint Commission designated Muskegon Lake a Great Lakes Area of Concern in 1985. "Muskegon Lake Community Action Plan: 2002 Remedial Action Plan Update," brochure published by the Muskegon Lake Public Advisory Council and Muskegon Conservation District, Muskegon, Mich., 4. For more information on Areas of Concern, visit www.ijc.org.
21. "Combined Sewer Overflow and Sanitary Sewer Overflow, 2004 Annual Report," Michigan Department of Environmental Quality, Lansing, Mich., 2005, 57, 77.
22. "Nonpoint Source Pollution: The Nation's Largest Water Quality Problem," U.S. Environmental Protection Agency, Pointer No. 1, EPA841-F-96-004A, 1996, 1, available at www.epa.gov.
23. Mike Wiley, interview by author, Ann Arbor and Newaygo, Mich., October 25, 2001.
24. "For River . . . Boom Could Be Bust," *Muskegon Chronicle,* September 14, 1999, 1A.
25. Nobes, interview, May 2, 2004.
26. Public Sector Consultants analysis of U.S. Census data reported in *Michigan's Land, Michigan's Future: Final Report of the Michigan Land Use Leadership Council* (Lansing, Mich.: Public Sector Consultants, 2003), 11–13.
27. Ibid.
28. Ibid.
29. John Wallace, *The Future of Muskegon County: A Report on Trends and Directions* (Hudsonville: DPM Group for the Muskegon County Land Use Planning Initiative Task Force, 1998), 5.
30. Michael Gallis and Associates, *The Common Framework: West Michigan, a Region*

in Transition (Grand Rapids: West Michigan Strategic Alliance, 2002), 25.

31. Ibid.
32. Ibid., 13.
33. "The Michigan Land Resource Project," cited in *Michigan's Land, Michigan's Future,* 41.
34. Michigan Society of Planning Officials, "Patterns on the Land: Our Choices—Our Future," *Detroit Free Press,* May 1, 1995, 1.
35. Rod Denning, interview by author, May 14, 2004.
36. Ibid.
37. Ted Houghton, interview by author, June 3, 2004.
38. Trueman, interview, May 20, 2004.
39. Supinski, interview, September 26, 2004.
40. "Danger That Floats: Toxic Algae Floating in Area Lakes," *Muskegon Chronicle,* October 17, 2004, 1A.
41. Steinman, interview, January 30, 2004.

CHAPTER 13. LIQUID GOLD RUSH

1. "GVSU Center Draws Crowd," *Muskegon Chronicle,* June 22, 2001, 1A.
2. "Thompson Says Perrier Project Should Go Elsewhere," *Milwaukee Journal-Sentinel,* November 20, 2000, available at www.jsonline.com.
3. Dennis L. Schornack to John Engler, September 25, 2000, 2–3, in possession of author.
4. Perrier production report, Ice Mountain plant, Stanton, Mich., March 1–31, 2004, in possession of author.
5. "Frequently Asked Questions," from "Your Natural Neighbor," Nestlé North America, p. 1, available at www.michigan4icemountain.com.
6. John Engler to Bob Taft, October 2, 2001, 2, in possession of author.
7. "Bottling the Great Lakes: Whose Water Is It Anyway?" *Lansing City Pulse,* December 10, 2003, 1.
8. Eugene T. Petersen, *Conservation of Michigan's Natural Resources,* Pamphlet 3 (Lansing: Michigan Historical Commission, 1960), 12.
9. Terry Swier, interview by author, October 9, 2004.
10. Mark Kane, interview by author, September 19, 2004.
11. Frances X. Donnelly, "Bottled Water Fight Grows," *Detroit News,* May 20, 2001, available at www.detnews.com.

12. *Ice Mountain Spring Water Project: Summary of Groundwater Studies* (Lansing, Mich.: Public Sector Consultants, 2001), study prepared for public hearing in Mecosta, May 16, 2001.
13. Malcolm Pirnie Inc. to Jennifer Granholm, July 5, 2001, 5, table 6-1, in possession of author.
14. "Ice Mountain Is Ordered to Stop Pumping Water," *Detroit Free Press*, November 26, 2003, 1A.
15. *Water Withdrawals for Agricultural Irrigation in Michigan, 2001* (Lansing: Michigan Department of Environmental Quality, 2003,), 6.
16. *Michigan Citizens for Water Conservation v. Nestlé Waters North America*, Mecosta County Circuit Court ruling, November 25, 2003, 44.
17. Greg Fox and Deborah Muchmore, interviews with author, December 17, 2004, Stanton, Mich.
18. *Michigan Citizens for Water Conservation v. Nestlé Waters North America*, Mecosta County Circuit Court ruling, November 25, 2003, 47.
19. *Water Withdrawals for Major Water Users in Michigan, 2001* (Lansing: Michigan Department of Environmental Quality, 2003), 3.
20. "2001 Water Withdrawals for Major Water Uses in Michigan, by Hydrologic Basin," Michigan Department of Environmental Quality, Lansing, Mich., available at www.michigan.gov/deq, 11, table 2.
21. Robert Glennon, *Water Follies: Groundwater and the Fate of America's Fresh Waters* (Washington, D.C.: Island, 2002), 1.
22. Ibid., 3.
23. "Left Out To Dry: How Michigan Pays the Price for Unregulated Water Use," Public Interest Research Group in Michigan, Ann Arbor, Mich., September 2005, 9–20.
24. *The Importance of Ground Water in the Great Lakes Region*, Water Resources Investigation Report 00-4008 (Lansing, Mich.: U.S. Geological Survey, 2000), 2.
25. Jennifer Granholm to John Engler, September 13, 2001, 2, in possession of author.
26. Engler to Taft, October 2, 2001, 2.
27. Dennis L. Schornack, "Michigan Must Protect the Great Lakes," *Detroit News*, July 10, 2003, available at www.detnews.com.
28. Michigan Public Act 148 of 2003, 92d Legislature, 2–3.
29. "No New Bottled Water Operations for Now, Granholm Says," *Detroit News*, May 28, 2005, available at www.detnews.com.

30. "Annex 2001 Implementing Agreements Approved and Signed," available at www.cglg.org.
31. Tom Henry, "The Future of the Great Lakes: Who Will Control the Water?" *Toledo Blade,* June 10, 2001, 1A.
32. Keith Schneider, "Hitting the Bottle" (2002), *Grist Magazine,* available at www.gristmagazine.com.
33. "Address and Special Messages of Governor William G. Milliken, 1969–1982," cited in Great Spring Waters of America Inc. (a subsidiary of the Perrier Group), "Memorandum to the Attorney General of Michigan," July 9, 2001, 9, in possession of author.
34. Deborah Muchmore, interview by author, December 17, 2004.
35. Kane, interview, September 19, 2004.
36. James M. Olson, *Great Lakes Water: Limitations on Privatization and Diversions,* available at www.savemiwater.org.
37. Stanwood, Michigan Plant—Fast Facts," correspondence from Deborah Muchmore to author, December 16, 2004.
38. "Dispute with Water Bottling Plant Settled—For Now." *Muskegon Chronicle,* January 27, 2006, 2B.
38. Swier, interview, October 9, 2004
39. Swier, interview, October 9, 2004

EPILOGUE: CONNECTING WITH THE RIVER

1. Stewart Montgomery, interview with author, June 7, 2004, Newaygo, Mi.
2. Ibid.
3. Ibid.
4. "Cleanup's Start Ends Long Fight," *Muskegon Chronicle,* August 24, 2005, 1A.
5. Montgomery, interview, June 7, 2004.
6. "Danger That Floats: Toxic Algae Floating in Area Lakes," *Muskegon Chronicle,* October 17, 2004, 1A.
7. Knoph, interview by author, May 7, 2004.

INDEX

C

D

E

N

Y

Michigan State University Press is committed to preserving ancient forests and natural resources. We have elected to print this title on 50# Rolland Enviro, which is 100% recycled (100% post-consumer waste) and processed chlorine free. The photo signature was printed on 70# Reincarnation Matte, which is 100% recycled (50% post-consumer waste, 50% pre-consumer waste) and processed chlorine free. As a result of our paper choice, Michigan State University Press has saved the following natural resources*:

30.4	Trees (40 feet in height)
12,726	Gallons of Water
5,118	Kilowatt-hours of Electricity
2,756	Pounds of Air Pollution
1,403	Pounds of Solid Waste

Both Michigan State University Press and our printer, Thomson-Shore, Inc., are members of the Green Press Initiative—a nonprofit program dedicated to supporting book publishers, authors, and suppliers in maximizing their use of fiber that is not sourced from ancient or endangered forests. For more information about the Green Press Initiative and the use of recycled paper in book publishing, please visit *www.greenpressinitiative.org.*

green press INITIATIVE

*Environmental benefits were calculated based on research provided by Conservatree and Californians Against Waste.